Our Own Agendas

*Autobiographical Essays by Women
Associated
with McGill University*

Edited by
Margaret Gillett and Ann Beer

McGill-Queen's University Press
Montreal & Kingston • London • Buffalo

© McGill-Queen's University Press 1995
ISBN 0-7735-1339-6 (cloth)
ISBN 0-7735-1340-X (paper)

Legal deposit fourth quarter 1995
Bibliothèque nationale du Québec

Printed in Canada on acid-free paper

Canadian Cataloguing in Publication Data

Our own agendas: autobiographical essays
by women associated with McGill University
ISBN 0-7735-1339-6 (bound) –
ISBN 0-7735-1340-X
1. Women – Canada – Biography.
2. McGill University – Biography.
I. Gillett, Margaret, 1930–   II. Beer, Ann
LE3.M21087 1995   920.72'0971
C95-900515-3

This book was typeset by Typo Litho
Composition Inc. in 10/12 Palatino.

For
C.L. and M., K., and M.

Contents

Contents

Foreword

Women have always had their own agendas. What has changed over the years is that women are now devising them explicitly. There may not yet be perfect equality, but we have managed to establish our right to decide our lives for ourselves. Not all of us always take advantage of this new and often hard won freedom. Sometimes it is still easier to do what we think is expected of us. But we know that the choices are ours to make. That knowledge is in itself liberating. It can also be a heavy responsibility.

We know, for instance, that true equality will only come when our personal agendas become part of society's collective thinking. Our lives are not simply our own business. What we do with them is an expression of that "other voice," the one that must articulate and define the values, aspirations, strengths, and perceptions women contribute to society as a whole. Our endeavours to be ourselves speak for us as individuals. But they also have a wider connotation. Gathered together they represent a view of the world that we must see becomes part of the ordering of society. Until womankind can speak and be heard for itself on its own terms, equality will depend on the good will of society, not on the reality of its make-up and the justice of its social relationships.

The autobiographical agendas of the women whose stories you are about to read give eloquent expression to that other voice, although they speak with many. They evoke the authenticity of accepted identity, the courage of commitment, and the compassion of caring. Singly they are all "good reads." Collectively they paint a moving, vibrant, and entertaining panorama of personal aspirations and experience. They cover a wide generational, occupational, sociological, and ideological span. The diversity of their combined perspectives gives breadth and depth to the telling of how women face pain and

Chancellor Gretta Chambers
Photo: James Seelly

pleasure, hope and despair, private and professional commitment, dreams and reality. In the ordering of their individual agendas, in the choices they have made and those that await them in the future, there are lessons to be learned for all of us, men and women. But perhaps the most compelling quality of this anthology is the reflective plea-sure it will bring to those who follow its story line from start to finish.

Gretta Chambers
Chancellor, McGill University

Acknowledgments

Many people have helped in the preparation of this book and we gratefully acknowledge our debt to them. We wish to thank all those who helped us prepare the manuscript and deal with our correspondence with the authors and the publisher. In particular we feel beholden to Fernanda Dias, Lisa Harden, Carole Kleistvul, Mary-Lynne Keenan, Shirley Strohl, Linda Anderson, Winston Emery, Gia Deliveaux, and Kim Lee.

We also deeply appreciate the financial support given this publication by McGill University, the McGill Faculty of Education, the McGill Centre for Research and Teaching on Women, the McGill Institute for the Study of Canada, the Canadian Studies Program of the Department of Canadian Heritage, Ottawa, and generous individual contributors.

M.G. & A.B.

Introduction

A Canadian cabinet minister born in Rome, a doctoral student from Cameroon, a judge, an artist, a composer, a Cree teacher, and a physicist whose doctorate was awarded in 1928 ... what could these people possibly have in common? All are women, all are contributors to this volume, and all have surprising stories to tell. *Our Own Agendas* brings together a wide variety of autobiographical essays, written in response to a request we sent out to women in many places and professions. Each woman has contributed a personal account that in some way makes sense of her particular path through life. Each story is distinct, yet there are many common themes. One of these is the idea of autonomy, an idea reflected in this book's title. "Our Own Agendas" clearly asserts that self-directed paths are possible for women and that we can be our own persons even in contexts where we struggle to be recognized, face unfallen barriers, and remain acutely aware of the interests of those around us. *Our Own Agendas* salutes the fact that contemporary women are freeing themselves from the constraints of custom and are willing to write about their lives.

Virginia Woolf, the inspiration for so much recent writing by women, "understood that telling what you remembered and writing down what had happened to you when you were young were radical acts of personal history that would force the rewriting of social history."[1] We agree that personal stories have a value that goes well beyond the individual. They may explore the significance of key events in a community; confirm the story-teller's place within a culture; and, as well, link past, present, and future so as to create a shared sense of history. Yet in industrialized cultures that have long been dependent on the written word, the status of story-telling, with its origins so firmly in the oral tradition, has been uncertain.

Co-editors at work: Ann Beer (left) and Margaret Gillett (right)

For centuries in Western countries, autobiographies and memoirs existed mainly on the margins of "great literature," and were only taken seriously if justified in certain special ways. For example, they might have been shaped as spiritual conversion texts, or the intro- spective musings of Romantic authors, or the success stories of powerful leaders. Almost all the autobiographies known and widely discussed in print were written by a now noticeable minor- ity: educated and/or privileged white men. More recently, however, the older and broader tradition, of which this collection forms a part, has begun to reassert itself. Personal narratives from many sources, new and rediscovered, oral and written, now seem to abound. These narratives are part of a change in thinking which at last acknowledges that the autobiographies of "ordinary" people can construct new knowledge about society. They can also challenge and reconstruct historical understanding in ways unthinkable even a generation ago.

Women's autobiography is central to this change, a change that is much more than a paradigm shift; it is a kind of Copernican revolu- tion.[2] In recent years there has been an extraordinary burgeoning of attention to the lives of women. Works like Carolyn G. Heilbrun's

Writing a Woman's Life[3] have become best-sellers, biographies and autobiographies have multiplied, and new theoretical perspectives have been applied to the life-writing genres.

Our Own Agendas offers a particular contribution to this changing knowledge. It assembles autobiographical texts by women linked through their connection to one historic Canadian university but diverse in almost every other respect. Interdisciplinary and multi-generational, this collection of essays seeks to recreate some of the traditions of oral autobiography. It signals and explores key life events; it affirms the identity and position of individual women and their relationships with their families and communities; it contributes to a historical understanding of women's changing roles (and hence the changing roles of men) in particular times and places. The book also shares another crucial feature of story-telling: it gives its readers the special pleasures of empathy, with its vivid glimpses of women's lives.

THE POWER OF PERSONAL NARRATIVE FOR WOMEN

In the latter half of the twentieth century, both women and men have gained new understanding of how women live. Women's struggles for a political voice, reproductive freedom, equal pay, and equal rights have had important repercussions. Consciousness-raising groups have helped to confirm that many of women's experiences are culturally and politically shaped. Feminist research has led to a heightened understanding of gender as being socially constructed rather than natural or divinely ordained. Studies in psychology have shown how female experiences of public and private selfhood have been strikingly different from male experiences. Sociological scrutiny has proved that most major institutions, such as the universities, schools of medicine, law courts, and parliaments (until recently almost entirely closed to women), are constructions of patriarchy. Such exclusionary institutions might not have been designed deliberately by individual men but were developed by a systemic and often hidden ideology. They were long held in place not only by laws and the control of financial resources but also by belief-systems. Powerful and persuasive leaders with these beliefs spoke *for* women about their proper place and duties, yet did not listen *to* women or allow them to speak publicly for themselves.

While feminist scholars confronted the old ideologies, many women from all walks adopted the slogan: "The personal is political." This became a rallying cry for those who were interested in achieving greater self-understanding, in making the patriarchy visible, in seeking change, in achieving empowerment. They have been sufficiently successful that the claim has been made that "feminism has redrawn the boundaries of critical enquiry and everyday life."[4]

A crucial tool in this "redrawing of boundaries" was the sharing by women of accounts of their own experiences that challenged the status quo. Personal writing of all kinds – autobiographies, letters, journals – has helped transform women's knowledge from an ephemeral, intimate circle to a more permanent, public level. And part of the excitement of feminist scholarship has been the discovery and rediscovery of the old autobiographical writing that had been left undisturbed in faded manuscripts and dusty volumes in attics and archives.

Writers and scholars studying colonialism and its aftermath are currently showing how cultures in Africa, Asia, and elsewhere, and inheritors of those cultures in the West, have highly developed traditions of oral life-stories and have often produced written autobiographical materials. In many cases, these stories are created and preserved by women. They include letters, journals, and memoirs that have long existed but until recently have received little attention in the West. A memorable example of rediscovered personal writing is given in Shula Marks's account of a black South African girl, "Lily," whose letters record how racism, sexism, and class prejudice drove her to madness.[5] Such stories deserve serious study no less than the autobiographies of the European tradition. They speak vividly of the relation between the self and society, and are often written with great power.

More discoveries of this kind have been made by social historians who have located working-class women's narratives which tell of lives of hardship and struggle. These narratives are surely not part of the traditional autobiographical canon. Their purposes and their chances of wide publication are quite different from those of the educated or middle-class autobiographies that celebrate professional success and individualism. These working-class accounts are reflections of the "ordinary" lives of women but, nonetheless, may be of extraordinary interest.

Both the contemporary autobiographies now being produced and the past texts being rediscovered help to provide women with new cultural maps, maps which can be used to mark previously hidden achievements as well as to identify remaining barriers. Individual autobiographies have also begun to undermine stereotyping and other broad generalizations about women's lives. They show that society can no longer take for granted that women will be willing to take second place, to be confined to domesticity or to be denied advancement.

But, even as the view of a unitary or common female experience has given way to a more accurate and powerful understanding of what it means to be born female, an appreciation has grown of the cultural, racial, and economic differences which are particular to the patterns of life experiences women may expect. Furthermore, there is no longer a single feminist view; white middle-class feminism no longer holds centre stage. Thus, there is now a "feminism of difference," and autobiography has been central to its development.

Women who define themselves primarily in solidarity with a particular class, ethnic group, or race – even women who define themselves in terms of a profession or vocation, who insist on multiple loyalties or refuse any contextual definition – can all, now, speak with greater directness because of the work that has been done. Whether they see themselves as "women of colour" or "women from Westmount," they have a better chance of being heard and of being taken seriously than they could have had in earlier times. Women's recognition and acceptance of pluralism, as well as their awareness of possible power hierarchies within feminism itself, have become central features of current feminist thinking. No one can speak for women as a whole. As *Our Own Agendas* shows, women can disagree with each other's views of life as profoundly as they may agree.

THEMES IN WOMEN'S LIVES

Along with the central belief in the significance of the personal and the acknowledging of difference, women autobiographers tend to deal with certain recurrent themes. Gender inevitably enters into their discussion. The fact that a baby, a child, or a person is female affects her expectations, her aspirations, and her opportunities. "Whether she has accepted the norms or defied them, a woman's life can never be written taking gender for granted."[6] This is in striking contrast to male autobiography, where gender is rarely an issue.

Some contributors to *Our Own Agendas* write of the effects of being judged by race, class, or religion as well as by gender. For Juliana Abbenyi, discriminatory experience was never far away once she came to Canada from Cameroon. She wrote:

I had classmates for whom my Africanness automatically implied an inability to cope academically at McGill. I had a professor who could not understand what an "uncivilized" woman/breeder could be doing at McGill. (p. 260)

Similarly, Annie Neeposh Iserhoff recounts memories of brutal prejudice in the residential schools which Cree children had to attend:

We heard that some of the older girls tried to run away, but got caught. We also saw the older ones get humiliated, until they finally fought back physically. This again would require another strapping. We, the younger ones, were informed that we were not allowed to speak our mother tongue. It was hard to follow such a requirement, since we didn't know the second language. (p. 155)

Freda Paltiel recalls similar aggression in the course of a Montreal childhood:

In grade school I was almost invariably the only Jew in the class. Giving too many correct answers, too early or too eagerly, or memorizing and reciting with feeling too many poems, brought penalties from bullies lurking around corners. (pp. 112–13)

Still other contributors write of the uneasy, yet often instructive, relationships they have had with social institutions. Patricia G. Kirkpatrick vividly recalls an early encounter with one Christian group's view of women:

I attended a meeting organized by a group of Anglicans calling themselves the "Council for the Defence of the Faith." Nothing could have prepared me for what I was about to hear, unless I had had a knowledge of the workings of the Ku Klux Klan ... (p. 128)

Monique Bégin writes of what she learned as a cabinet minister under Pierre Trudeau:

The newcomer must ... assert herself, but must do so within the limits of what is allowable by her new chauvinistic and patriarchal universe, even while remaining true to herself. However, paradoxically, she has entered into the egotistical world of personality cults, where one must have an extreme style and know how to come through the television screen as a virtual exhibitionist! The experience was difficult and uncomfortable ... (p. 16)

On the other hand, our authors write of community and family – usually differing markedly in this respect from the typical male autobiographer, who existed as a lone protagonist pushing through life on an individualistic journey of experience. For many women, definition of self still includes connectedness, an awareness of emotional and day-to-day relationships. Family ties are crucial. For Lise Demers, an account of her life must include a description of the influence of her two sets of grandparents (Algonquin and Québécois) and her mother's Algonquin community.

Women write of their body experiences, of health and sickness (Gibbs, Poulson, Cleather, White, Johnston, McCall); of the bearing and rearing of children (Joron, Abbenyi, Lamontagne, Williams, Beer); of sexuality, safety, and a search for physical freedom (Ghosh, Anonymous, Jones, Iserhoff, Demers). They write of the delights of education, and the struggle for it (Paterson, Archer). They fondly remember mentors of both sexes, who may have been parents, teachers, colleagues, or friends (Bégin, McCall, Johnston, Rowles). They describe successful marriages (Rowles, Williams, Abella, Mappin) and the pain of divorce (Joron, Gibbs). And they write of the psyche – spirituality, creativity, and the psychology of growing up female in particular cultural contexts (Joron, Archer, Ritter, Stewart).

Not surprisingly, since the common link between the authors is a connection with McGill University, a central theme of *Our Own Agendas* is the relationship between women and higher education. This was also true of *A Fair Shake*,[7] the first collection of autobiographical essays by women associated with McGill. While these two volumes have this and other concerns in common, they also differ in ways that affect both tone and subject matter. These differences suggest some of the changes that have taken place in society and in women's lives in the decade since *A Fair Shake* was published. The very title "A Fair Shake" suggests the quest for an equal chance; "Our Own Agendas" implies a stronger, more "in-charge" approach.

The steady increase of women in the paid workforce generally and in academe in particular, their appointment to senior administrative positions, the formal adoption of equity policies, the narrowing of the male/female salary gap, and the fact that women now constitute more than 50 per cent of the undergraduate population are but some of the indices of a "fairer shake" for women. The title of the present book celebrates these advances.

Nevertheless, *Our Own Agendas* takes cognizance of the fact that new constraints and difficulties have appeared, especially in the years of recession and fierce competition for resources. Even the most recent graduates know from experience that the educational milieu has not yet thrown off all its inequities and that, at the very least, overtones of male superiority still haunt the campus. And in society at large, reports continue to appear of increasing stress among women, of their difficulties in balancing the demands of work, personal relationships, and family life, of the tendency of institutions to regress to the old status quo, and of widespread violence against women.

One of the most striking changes produced in the last decade is self-disclosure in discussion of matters that were once taboo. Radio and television talk-shows now flourish on intimate revelations; literature and films portray explicitly sexual scenes as a matter of course; people are outspoken on issues like abortion, rape, and other "unmentionables." There was little or nothing of this in *A Fair Shake*, but *Our Own Agendas* does reflect the increased openness of our society. More than one of the contributors writes candidly about very painful experiences. Some dare to make their anger visible. Others discuss openly their sexual orientation, whether it is heterosexual, bisexual, or lesbian. Even now, personal revelations like these are not easy to make, especially in a context where the authors are known. We recognize that, even in the 1990s, self-disclosure takes courage, and we appreciate the frankness of our contributors' stories.

GENRE AND FORM IN WOMEN'S AUTOBIOGRAPHY

Autobiography is more complex than it might appear at first glance. Carol Shields muses that "Biography, even autobiography, is full of systemic errors, of holes that connect like a tangle of underground streams."[8] And Liz Stanley says, "A concern with auto/biography shows that 'self' is a fabrication, not necessarily a lie but certainly a highly complex truth: a fictive truth reliant on cultural convention concerning what 'a life' consists of and how its story can be told both in speech and, somewhat differently, in writing."[9]

Contemporary theorists of the genre have tried to deal with other difficult questions. How does the autobiographer create what Virginia Woolf called "a mould, transparent enough to reflect the light of our life"?[10] How does autobiography relate to fiction? Does it tell a "true" story of the past? Or is it the reflection of the past in a present consciousness? If language as a shared symbolic system "shapes" what it presents, is all autobiography inherently artificial, changing irrevocably the non-verbal experiences it tries to capture? How does the intended audience for an autobiography influence its shape, meaning, and value? And how is the reader's experience influenced by an autobiography's concealment of its fictional status, or its open confession of unreliability and partiality?

The autobiographies represented here show a wide variety of responses to such questions. Consciously or unconsciously, the authors chose the literary form that suits them. Their approaches include the personal journey (Bégin), the comparative account of two cultures (Demers, Ghosh), the associative linking of formative experiences within reflections on memory (Iserhoff), the topographic analysis of self as seen by others (Donald), the use of letters to reflect on key moments (Johnston), the poem, the work-history, the speech, the public essay, and the private meditation. Some authors, such as Sheldon Collyer, give a strong impression of purpose and unity:

The fabric of the narrative appears seamless, spun of whole cloth. The effect is magical – the self appears organic, the present the sum total of the past, the past an accurate predictor of the future.[11]

This approach to life history is often grounded in a confident sense of authority. Yet others of our contributors, such as our author who chose to remain anonymous, offer a deliberately non-authoritarian narrative. Disjunction, anonymity, the personal voice of poetry, all contribute to an anti-authoritarian stance that is appropriate to this writer's account of resistance to the acts of male aggression in her life.

We, the editors, made no effort to control or influence the form of the contributions to *Our Own Agendas*, but we are delighted with the variety that has emerged spontaneously. We believe that this variety of approaches will be of particular interest to any reader concerned with the nature of autobiography.

WHAT REMAINS UNSAID

In the process of deciding on this project, inviting contributions, working with authors, and bringing the manuscript to publication, we as editors have been acutely aware of our own contextual and historical positions. "Privilege tends to blind the privileged to the mechanisms and effects of its own operations."[12] We have at least tried to identify our own particular kinds of privilege. We are among the lucky ones and, as we worked, we were often reminded of the struggles and inequities that exist for many women, including those who have never had the opportunity to attend universities.

We are two academics, one close to retirement, the other just seeking tenure. One of us was born and educated in Australia, the other in England. Both of us are now Canadian citizens. We have, therefore, been able to provide different perspectives from a generational and international point of view. Like ourselves, however, many (though by no means all) of our contributors are white and/or middle-class. Some women from non-traditional backgrounds whom we invited, among them well-known figures in Canadian society, declined our invitations or withdrew during the process. Others, including some McGill support staff, also decided not to bring their essays to completion. We can only speculate with regret at the loss of their particular voices. Did overwork, a feeling of "not fitting in" with this volume, or simply the pressure of other priorities cause their silence?

One highly successful woman also declined because she believed that a collection of essays by women only is unnecessary – that to single out members of her sex is inappropriate, or amounts to reverse sexism. We do not agree, for all the reasons given above. We make no apologies for presenting the lives of women only, or for using their varied connections with McGill University as a starting point for this publication.

We are well aware of McGill's reputation as a venerable and powerful institution in Canadian life and are proud that the University and McGill-Queen's University Press believed in the value of our work enough to give it their support. While we must take responsibility for any shortcomings of *Our Own Agendas*, its achievements depend on all those who so generously, and in some cases, bravely, wrote their stories. We believe that they have succeeded admirably. They have not shied away from showing complexities and contradictions. They have revealed doubts and struggles that are not always overcome, but they have also shown strength, determination, humour, intelligence, and compassion. These are not necessarily superwomen, but they are women of our times and have written with honesty and grace. We thank them all.

M.G. and A.B.

NOTES

1 Louise DeSalvo, *Virginia Woolf: The Impact of Childhood Sexual Abuse on Her Life and Work* (New York: Ballantine 1989), 15.

2 Gerda Lerner, *The Creation of Patriarchy* (New York: Oxford University Press 1986), 13.

3 Carolyn G. Heilbrun, *Writing a Woman's Life* (New York: Ballantine 1988).

4 Michael Kaufman, ed., *Beyond Patriarchy: Essays by Men on Pleasure, Power, and Change* (Toronto: Oxford University Press 1987), preface.

5 Shula Marks, "The Context of Personal Narrative: Reflections on *'Not Either an Experimental Doll'* – The Separate Worlds of Three South African Women," *Interpreting Women's Lives: Feminist Theory and Personal Narratives,* ed. The Personal Narratives Group (Bloomington: Indiana University Press 1989), 39–58.

6 *Interpreting Women's Lives,* 5.

7 Margaret Gillett and Kay Sibbald, eds., *A Fair Shake: Autobiographical Essays by McGill Women* (Montreal: Eden Press 1984).

8 Carol Shields, *The Stone Diaries* (Toronto: Random House 1993), 196.

9 Liz Stanley, *The Auto/biographical I: The Theory and Practice of Feminist Auto/biography* (Manchester, UK: Manchester University Press 1992), 242–3.

10 Anne Olivier Bell, ed., *The Diaries of Virginia Woolf*, vol. 1: 1915–1919 (London: Hogarth Press 1977), 266.

11 Shari Benstock, "Authorizing the Autobiographical," *The Private Self: Theory and Practice of Women's Autobiographical Writing*, ed. Shari Benstock (Chapel Hill: University of North Carolina Press 1988), 19.

12 Geraldine Finn, ed., *Voices of Women, Voices of Feminism* (Halifax, NS: Fernwood 1993), 3.

Our Own Agendas

And I Shan't Be a Saint

To tell the whole truth, yes, there was a time when I wanted to become a saint! But when my younger sister, Claire, rashly disclosed this to a journalist not long ago, I was speechless. Claire was being interviewed about the bonding and the relationships between us – the four Bégin sisters in a family of seven children – and she said the period of my saintly aspirations was a chance for her at last to play the bossy elder sister. At the time I thought her statement about me quite indecent, but now, I must admit, the idea somehow captures the tone of the Quebec in which I grew up and also reflects our father's ongoing pursuit of perfection.

Events seem to have separated my life into segments that are quite distinct from each other, almost unconnected, although I am living my life as one single, unified, continuous journey into foreign and, at times, exotic new lands full of new people and fresh discoveries. The metaphor of the traveller has helped me through many a rough moment.

But I should begin at the beginning. I was born in Rome, Italy, on March 1, 1936 to a French Canadian father and a Flemish Belgian mother, raised in Paris until we had to escape the war through the roads of France to Spain and Portugal, finally arriving, via New York and Farnham, at a very modest flat in Notre-Dame-de-Grâce, Montreal. There was my father, Lucien, my mother, Marie-Louise, plus Monique, Claire, Catherine, and Paul. Three more children were to follow: Sébastien, Marie, and Thomas d'Aquin.

I often wonder if living in NDG was not the reason why I studied sociology. Those years of my life bring back, even today, almost palpable memories of a tightly knit solid community, well off and deeply bourgeois, full of clichés and prejudices, yet with great characters, a protected island which stood outside of time. "*Le Village de Notre-*

Communion solennelle (1947)

Dame-de-Grâce" as it read in our church crypt. For me, NDG meant the public school from which well-off girls went on to Villa Maria, Marguerite-Bourgeois College, or St Paul's Academy after grade 7; the parish library of Mademoiselle Brunet and Le Manoir where we skated; the company of Girl Guides; the swimming at the Prud'homme Street community hall; the Westmount public parks where the whole family had to spend so many Sunday afternoons; the fights with the boys of Daniel O'Connell or the girls of St Augustine's. All of it pointed to people who were rich and people who were poor, those who lived on the good streets and those who lived below (south of) Sherbrooke Street, to owners and tenants, to those who could afford the classical colleges and those who remained in public schools, and, of course, those who spent their summers in the Laurentians or Maine and "the others." This class consciousness operated in another context: the unspoken but clear opposition between the French and the English, two NDG solitudes living on the same territory, families which never met despite our parents' multilingual competence. A very small world indeed, but one where I belonged.

Our family had been cast in the role of the first immigrants of the parish, original, extremely religious, and so very European. A sound engineer in the movie industry at the time, who had married at forty after an adventurous life in different countries, my father had cast himself in the role of the family patriarch, absolute monarch of this restricted circle, requesting total obedience and compliance from the clan at all times. He had in turn cast me in the role of the eldest, lecturing me on the law of primogeniture; the fact I was a daughter did not disturb him a bit. Loving justice and tolerance, valuing cultural differences, a stranger to nationalisms of all kinds, a man of total integrity, a humanist and a scientific mind with a broad culture, brilliant and funny, Father was also authoritarian, argumentative, and stubborn. And at times, quite violent with words and even with sticks. There were days when I prayed God for him to die, but paradoxically, we would never have wanted to change him for the father of any of our friends.

Mother was quite the opposite. An only child, a reserved and romantic young woman, working in accounting in a movie firm in Brussels (I think it was MGM), she eloped to Italy one day at age twenty-nine to marry her boss (Father) in Rome! To her death, I always knew her as a reasonable, quietly cheerful person with a touch of gentle irony, the epitome of common sense and balance, a bit impatient, disciplined and hard-working. She had to flee two world wars, but in 1950 she could not bring herself to return to Europe with her seven children. (One other baby died at birth on the roads of France, and, exhausted, she also went through one stillbirth in Canada.) She always seemed to me vulnerable, but it must have been more appearance than reality; at the end of her life, fighting cancer, she had managed to find paid employment, working on contract as a translator. She was elegant despite our poverty, and she taught me beautiful textiles and finishings, styles, and the Old World sense of quality. When we got told off by her in Flemish, we knew it was not too serious! People liked her immediately and she always adjusted nicely (for example, the actor colleagues of my sister Catherine loved her), but I do not believe she had close friends with whom to exchange feelings and find support.

At home, besides love and affection and the balanced presence of Mother, we had great principles, great culture, and great food, and not much more. Friends were absolutely forbidden in our apartment. So was the outside world in general. Radio, newspapers, magazines, phonograph, even the telephone, were banned from home. We had lost everything during World War II, and from the very comfortable and elegant property of Taverny (a Paris suburb) where our father had designed our Art Déco furniture, we went to a rented modest five-room flat where the family stayed until mother's death in 1967

(Father had died in 1965), with no furniture other than a table, chairs, two bookcases, and army bunk beds, and lots of orange- or butter-crates turned into whatever else was needed as furniture. Hungry for a spiritual excellence he could not reach, Father was always torn between the good life and an aescetic mission, all of which he tried to impose on his children. Born in 1895 into a rural Quebec family with eighteen children, he was European in spirit, yet remained an ultra-montane Quebecer. "Children," he would declare emphatically, "this will shape your personality!" And here we go, the seven children (I, already age fifteen or sixteen) having to kneel down on the sidewalk of St Catherine Street in front of Eaton's at noon on a Saturday to recite the Angelus. All I remember is being terribly mortified ... Father could not stand conformism for the sake of conformism, but we, the children, longed for some. At home, we had to obey one set of rules; and outside, we tried to act and look like little French Canadians. But we very much felt like dual personalities, not knowing if we were Europeans or North Americans, the latter being for Father the ultimate materialistic society he abhorred. Yet, despite material facts which may suggest a sad and dark childhood, my memory is also one of years of laughter, happiness and great expectations.

Books and Girl Guide camps saved me from madness. Besides the chores and numerous responsibilities of the eldest daughter – I used to think I was the mother of my mother, wanting to protect the poor soul lost in a new country, stuck with that crazy husband and these unmanageable, active and noisy children – I spent every free minute reading everything I could get hold of. I had to be in bed every day by nine until the age of twenty-one, but I always managed to read for a few more hours thanks to the street lamp. Adventures, cartoons, history, the Harlequin romances of the day, biographies, essays, lives of the saints, and much more, I read. I also listened for hours to adults, above all at the parish library where I was always welcome to help as a volunteer.

It was as if time was suspended; something would happen, something still unknown. I went through public elementary school in NDG, then high school in St Henri, at Esther-Blondin's, and on to the Teachers' College at Rigaud, where I boarded for two years, and started teaching, back in St Henri, at age nineteen. Very rapidly, I saw that it was not for me. I wanted to study, and study, and study. What exactly, I did not know; a classical baccalaureate of arts to start with was all I could think of. But life seemed blocked by lack of money and my responsibility to help the family financially. I began to feel quite desperate.

From age eighteen to my mid-twenties, I found life particularly difficult and painful. Projected out of the Middle Ages into the twentieth

Among the Girl Guides

century, thrown out of home by Father at my twenty-first birthday during a grand dramatic scene, I could not find a place in the order of things. I felt rejected and no good. I had more or less finally made up my mind that I would not become a nun, even though the Sisters of Ste Anne had had the Mother General come to Rigaud in person with the contract for me to sign. How I found the courage to put the pen down and say that I would wait one more year, I still do not know. Once in a while I would, in later years, be attracted to the idea of entering the monastery as an enclosed nun or of joining the Little Sisters of Charles de Foucauld. But despite the guilt created in me by the strong ideological pressures emanating from outside sources, never from home, I suspected deep inside that a religious vocation was not for me. (I still recall the nuns at school repeating to me in front of everybody the New Testament parable of the ten talents, adding that, in my case, I had received eleven and would be held responsible for each one.) On the other hand, I did not want to just marry as an end in life, as my schoolmates had started doing, and I rejected without hesitation a first proposal by a young engineer of a good NDG Belgian family, for I did not want a settled life. I still did not know what I wanted to be and to do. I had been given only two points of reference: the importance of the pure intellectual life and the quest for knowledge, and the significance of saints and historical characters who had accomplished outstanding things by pushing themselves to the limits. Neither idea satisfied me; I wanted peace, harmony, and balance, and at the same time I wanted to live passionately for a worthwhile cause and I wanted to change the world to make it a better place. I was torn as my father had been, and had no one to turn to.

This is the period in my life when I developed cynicism and anger against the Catholic church as an institution. I had always been shocked by men preaching one thing and practising another. The wealth of the Vatican, the intolerance and narrow-mindedness of many priests, their sense of "quiet possession" of the one and only truth, the authoritarian hierarchy, the unacceptable power relationship of the Church and the State in Quebec, were characteristics I loathed. It was easier for me to deal with the sentimental and meaningless rites that were the common denominator in Quebec; Father had always denounced them at home, taking us through the history of the Church and its various heresies. It was the abuse of power and the social hypocrisy that I could no longer stand. But I could not tell that to anybody. It was during my second year at l'École Normale of Rigaud that I concluded to myself that there was no point trying to change or accept the status quo. I withdrew silently into myself even more.

After my first four months of teaching, I left the Montreal Catholic School Board, and while studying at night, taught in a private French school, gave private lessons, and finally was hired as a secretary to Father Guillemette, OP, the director of the School of Social Work at the University of Montreal. A friend had suggested I try the first level of "Rhétorique" of the baccalaureate exams from the Université de Caen, France through the Marie-de-France and Stanislas Colleges. This was the only program that did not, at least in theory, request that one be a registered full-time student. I prepared by myself between January and June 1957 while being a secretary. This was quite a challenge, since I had almost no base of classical studies. I chose Latin and Italian. The oral exams were such an ordeal that I could not see myself going on with the philosophy level. I had, however, obtained good to excellent marks in every subject except trigonometry, which I failed miserably. By early July, I had switched to the University of Montreal's adult baccalaureate designed for teachers, and by special arrangement I was allowed to complete it over two summers, plus the year in between, five evenings a week and all day every Saturday. Some courses were eye-openers, and I remember to this day a course in history and philosophy of sciences given by Roland Lamontagne, a scientist in a private-sector firm. Two weeks after having completed my BA in August 1958, I was starting in the master's program in sociology, as a regular student, a dream come true. Life was starting!

I had hesitated a little before choosing sociology; I had considered going into medicine or biology or botany. The financial burden of these longer studies settled the issue for me. The three years of the master's in sociology were stimulating ones, working for a living, studying and discovering more of Quebec society. The courses themselves were a strange mix of Thomist philosophy, the social teachings of the Church, and modern American sociology, and we lived through many ideological differences between our professors and the university administrators. Up to my last year, when Guy Rocher came from Laval, the department director was by tradition a priest appointed by the Church. With hindsight, I can see this reflected the transition from a religious to a lay society nurtured by the Quiet Revolution, with all the related uneasiness of social change. Sociology was also carving for itself an occupational niche in this changing Quebec; sociologists were to replace, as we used to say ironically, priests and psychiatrists. The fact is that while we were nine graduates in my class in 1961, all deeply worried about finding any kind of employment, 150 students graduated the following year with their MA (sociology), thus becoming the new generation of political aides and executive assistants, senior provincial civil servants, and *animateurs sociaux* of the Lesage government.

Marquita Riel, now a professor at the Université du Québec à Montréal (UQAM), and I were the only women in the class. We had a real group conscience and group existence. I organized a series of cultural anthropology films, the "Cinanthrope," where we learned of Margaret Mead, Ruth Benedict, or Oscar Lewis, as well as weekly informal seminars where we discussed controversial authors. The first book I suggested was Simone de Beauvoir's *The Second Sex*, finally available in Montreal in 1959, ten years after its publication in France. Her thesis, and later her novels, came as a revelation, at least to me. The women's movement was to start in another ten years, and I did not belong to any women's associations. I had no idea that just five years later I would co-found with other women, under Thérèse Casgrain's leadership, the Fédération des femmes du Québec. I easily related to *The Second Sex* on the grounds of justice and equality, but did feel uncomfortable with its dogmatic dimension.

For many years, I sincerely believed that I had been brought up in an egalitarian family, in a totally non-sexist fashion. I felt a free spirit as a woman. It was true in terms of domestic roles; both parents were great cooks; Father could iron perfectly; he had taught me carpentry; and the boys had to do their beds and help with the dishes. I naturally always perceived myself as a feminist, and wondered when and how I had internalized the traditional feminine role of which I was quite conscious. Obviously from the school and the nuns, especially at teachers' college, as well as from the whole society. It took me literally decades to understand the most subtle and pernicious sexism Father preached at home in his speeches to us, especially to me. His repeated quotes from the Old Testament, St Paul, St Augustine, St Thomas Aquinas, and other sources, even his dear Léon Bloy, reveal a profound philosophical contempt of women.

On a lighter note, as a graduate student, I kept on observing what was proper female social behaviour, but not with any particular success, thinking all of this mannerism was rather stupid and boring. One thing had become clear to me: before all, a woman had to be dependent on men. Processing the problem in my mind, I discarded various dependencies that I did not want to develop and chose, rationally, that the dependency I would keep would be not to know how to drive a car. We never had a car at home, so the idea came naturally to my mind as one successful way of depending on men. The result is that today I still do not know how to drive a car, having built through the years a mountain of fears which prevented me from learning when I needed to!

The period that followed my MA studies was also, in retrospect, one of more experiences and more preparation towards a still unknown and unfocused future. With a small scholarship, I spent two years, 1961 to 1963, in Paris at the Sorbonne, doing doctoral studies. I lived very poorly in a room in the middle-class neighbourhood of the fourteenth "arrondissement." In sociology, none of our professors in Quebec had connection with their French counterparts, and Quebec students were landing in the unknown and complex academic hierarchy of Paris with no networking and no assistance. Georges Gurvitch and Georges Friedman were still the old masters of the French school of sociology. Michel Crozier, a Friedman protégé, had just developed his book on bureaucracy, bringing an American "scientific" perspective to his colleagues. Friedman, with whom I was to do my thesis work, was also protecting a new group interested in mass communications around l'École Pratique des Hautes Études. Edgar Morin and the late Roland Barthes were our two most illustrious young professors. I confess that academic games seemed to me so disconnected from reality that I had more and more difficulty playing them. But Paris was much more than the Sorbonne, and so was sociology. And I went from discovery to discovery of myself and of others, of ways of life, of places, of other countries (England, Belgium, and Italy), of political issues. The decolonization war in Algeria was at its worst, and the apartment adjacent to mine was blown up in a *"plastiquage."* A student was killed in front of me by the military police the first morning I entered the court of the Sorbonne. Tanks patrolled the city. General strikes followed each other. We all had serious discussions on these major subjects, hearing polarized viewpoints and witnessing violence in a way unknown to most young Canadians. During that time, François Hertel was often at La Maison du Canada, in the Cité universitaire, preaching separatism with passion to young Quebecers.

The fall of the Canadian dollar and my usual financial problems became so serious, despite secretarial work I was able to secure in Paris, that I gave up my doctoral project and came back, without a thesis and without a project. When I returned to Montreal, Guy Rocher offered me a job as a lecturer. As usual, and contrary to the people around me, I had problems with the simplest of things. In this case, I thought it would have been quasi-immoral for me to accept, still knowing so little about society and sociology. I honestly believed that I should teach it only after years of practice, if I may say, of its various institutions. At the time in the social sciences in academic francophone Quebec, not holding a doctorate was not an issue. I realize now that I had no idea what an academic career was all about and I do not recall any discussion about this with my close friends who were to later build distinguished academic careers in sociology, history or other disciplines. Although life has since made me a university professor after years of institutional "practice," holding a doctorate is now an imperative, and I can see how naïve and marginal I was – in fact, a lousy sociologist who had not even understood how to play the game.

The various tasks I undertook when I returned from Paris – a few months with the very beginning of Expo '67, consultant work for Place des Arts, personnel research at Steinberg's, and my work in applied social research – would make no sense without mentioning the name of Fernand Cadieux, an exceptional human being with whom I worked in many innovative projects over some eight or nine years. A true intellectual, sociologist by training, he has been a key figure in the Quiet Revolution in his own right. Pending a full biography of Cadieux, I can only try to summarize his role in our society. From the teaching of new mathematics to the creation with Pierre Juneau of the Montreal International Film Festival, everything interested him and he was *un lanceur d'idées*. If I have to identify my mentors, as women who have played public roles are now often asked, he would be one. (His friend and my former professor of sociology Hubert Guindon would be the other.) This mentoring was not about passing on to me the tricks of the trade, social behaviours or strategies, but preceding me in exploring different paths of the forest, pointing to new important directions, bringing in fresh air from elsewhere. When I was asked by Marc Lalonde, then in Lester B. Pearson's office, if I was interested in the Royal Commission on the Status of Women (RCSW) to be created shortly, it was Fernand who pushed me out of his office, so to speak, and into the national scene. I did not quite know what a royal commissioner had to do, and I explained to Lalonde, who took good note, that what rather attracted me was the full-time, daily operations of the commission. In April 1967, I left Montreal for Ottawa as the executive secretary and director of research of the RCSW for its duration, an enriching experience that I still cherish. The rest, as they say, is history.

Normally, I would have come back to work with Fernand Cadieux in Montreal when the work of the commission was over in the fall of 1970, but I accepted an offer from Pierre Juneau, and became a civil servant, the assistant director of the Research Branch at the new Canadian Radio and Television Commission (CRTC). These were the great days of the CRTC, with the Canadian ownership and the Canadian content policies being developed. Juneau, as chairman, had given a sense of purpose to everyone. But somehow, I was not fulfilled and I did not know why; I kept the whole thing to myself. The team was remarkable and wonderful, with André Martin from France, and John Grierson and Northrop Frye as honorary members, Rodrigue Chiasson, Patrick Gossage, Mary Wilson, Cathy Richards, Liska Bridle, and others. After six months in the job, I received my second phone call from Marc Lalonde, by then in Prime Minister Pierre Trudeau's office, asking me to run for the Liberals in a by-election (which never took place) in St Henri (Montreal). I burst out laughing, thanked him, and turned him down on the spot. I felt like a little girl dressing up and playing house.

Life continued at the CRTC. A year later, in April 1972, Lalonde phoned again, this time asking me to go to the Prime Minister's Office (PMO) for a meeting. (I had never phoned Marc Lalonde myself and knew him only a little through Fernand Cadieux; but his three phone calls were to bring about significant new experiences in my life.) I left the CRTC with my copy of the report of the RCSW, convinced that we would discuss some aspects of its implementation. In the room were men like Jean Marchand, Jean-Pierre Goyer, and others, and the offer to run for the Liberals was repeated. Now it was as a candidate in the impending general election, in Eric Kierans's vacant Duvernay riding! This time I did not laugh; I took five days to think it over and consult quietly; and I accepted after my three conditions (at least three women in Quebec; a "safe" riding; financial help) were agreed upon. I needed a brand new challenge.

Besides wanting to know "what it was like to be a minister under Pierre Trudeau," people often ask the two following questions: How did you enter the world of politics? What was it like for a woman to be in Cabinet? The fact sheet first. I joined the Liberal party of Canada after that meeting at the PMO in April 1972 and, a true political neophyte who, moreover, was rather idealistic, I won four general elections: 1972, 1974, 1979, and 1980, the last two with the biggest majorities ever in Canadian politics. A backbencher for three years, I was first appointed parliamentary secretary to the secretary of state for external affairs (the Honourable Allan MacEachen) (1975–76); then, minister of national revenue (1976–77); and minister of national health and welfare (1977–84), and, for a brief period of nine months (1979–80) within this last mandate, member of the Official Opposition and critic for my last portfolio.

From the age of thirty-six and for the following twelve years of my life, I was as dedicated to politics as one can be dedicated to religion. I loved all those years: I lived them to the fullest, with great satisfaction, being at the heart of a world attained by few men and even fewer women. But throughout that period I had had to resort in my heart of hearts to my metaphor of the solitary traveller in far-away lands, where the natives are strange and the mores incomprehensible. I felt I had landed in a surprising universe. So, while I was at the peak of my popularity in the polls, but after deciding that I wanted to preserve my personal integrity without getting out of my depth, that I did not have enough love for power to want to become the party leader, and that I had made the most of the political experience, I quit politics simply by not running in the 1984 election.

I never heard Napoleon's battles discussed more than in the Liberal caucus of Prime Minister Trudeau, despite my reading of Liddell Hart's work on military strategy through Fernand Cadieux! Certainly, this resulted from the solid political culture of an astonishing prime minister, but while the rules of action originate in military strategy, it is not common for most people to hear them discussed openly. My first observation, then, was that political discussion was a military metaphor. As one of the few women in politics, I felt from the start that I was in forbidden territory where I was a tolerated exception. Not that I suffered from discrimination or was singled out. Nor was I, technically, the only woman in caucus: Jeanne Sauvé and Albanie Morin, both older than I, were declared elected later in the evening of the same 1972 general election. However, one of them became a minister immediately and we did not see her often, and the

The Honourable Monique Bégin (1976)

other, an early victim of cancer, occupied a position related to the Speaker. For all practical purposes, I was the only woman in an eminently male world constantly punctuated by a language that I had never heard before and that was not mine.

The first task asked of a newcomer by the party whip is to stay until the end of the daily sitting to "kill a bill" (of the Opposition, of course). Discussions constantly focus on "the enemy" or "the adversary," "attacks," "traps," "ambushes," electoral "battles" and "victories." "To resort to the use of force," "the strategy" and "the strategists," "reserves," and "tactics" are expressions used in many cases. "To have your back to the wall," "trench warfare," "to go on the offensive" or on the "counter-attack," "covering the rear" are others.

The bipartite system of Canadian parliamentary government, the adversarial design of the House of Commons, the partisanship that results, and the legalistic framework of procedures only accentuate the rhetoric that particularly repels women, and, I believe, a number of men from community environments, small family businesses, or middle management, to name some occupational sectors where the vision of human relationships may still more or less mirror that of the family. Of course, we say that "life is a long battle," but this is meant in a moral sense. Most people in most situations trust one another instead of constantly being on their guard.

In addition to this alienating, combative rhetoric, the ferocious competition that exists among colleagues of the same political party, from MPs to ministers, is another dimension for which women of my generation received no preparation. Furthermore, to this day, I am tempted to disappear, to return to my own territory, when faced with a situation defined by competition. I detest all of this, unless it is a question of defending ideas or values. If it is a case of competition between individuals in the flesh, I feel that I am not in the race. Worse, I tend to condemn it. As the regimental mascot, I was treated in a friendly manner by my colleagues in the Quebec caucus during my very first years. Then, without understanding why, I began to hear nasty and slanderous remarks about myself, which hurt me. It was not until much later that I realized that this change coincided with my first responsibilities: co-presidency of the first national party convention to review the Trudeau leadership, appointment as a permanent delegate to the United Nations, vice-presidency of the national Liberal caucus. I was no longer the charming caucus newcomer; I was a competitor and it was war.

One day when I had won an additional fifty million dollars for medical research "against" an able Cabinet colleague who wanted it for his own department, Judy Erola, who became my friend for life, told me, as I was grumbling and uneasy with my success, "You, like many women, cannot enjoy the taste of victory! A real "Cinderella syndrome"! You should read the book."* I was cut to the quick. (But I ended up reading the book.) She was right. Others writers have noted the same phenomenon. Mariette Sineau, the French political analyst, devotes a complete chapter to patterns of failure and overcompensation in her book *Des femmes en politique*, based on interviews with French women politicians. Sheila Copps's hypothesis is that men benefit by having learned how to win and how to lose in school group sports like hockey, baseball, football, or soccer. We did not learn anything of the kind at Rigaud, where the only sports in which we indulged were some figure skating and croquet!

During my secondary and post-secondary studies, in Girl Guides and in girls' youth camp, I learned that the role of women was above all an unassuming role of support and service to others. You did not ask questions, and nobody asked what happened to those who had "character." As we were only among girls, it was difficult to observe different behaviours or to make comparisons. The true woman, we were taught, is one who listens, approves, seconds, helps, and consoles. She is soft and certainly not aggressive, does not put herself forward, and does not make noise. She labours in the background and knows how to create a happy family atmosphere. She creates harmony and peace in her surroundings, especially in her home. To pursue the military metaphor, she does not go up on the barricades; she is the warrior's rest. She is not the warrior.

Words also express behaviour. The newcomer must therefore assert herself, but must do so within the limits of what is allowable by her new chauvinistic and patriarchal universe, even while remaining true to herself. However, paradoxically, she has entered into the egotistical world of personality cults, where one must have an extreme style and know how to come through the television screen as a virtual exhibitionist! The experience is difficult and uncomfortable, and I had never lived in that way, not at the Fédération des femmes du Québec, nor at the Royal Commission on the Status of Women in Canada. Of all my experiences, the most stupefying was certainly that of the enormous size of the male ego. I remember example upon example of minister, senator, or MP fishing for compliments for an ordinary performance related to his everyday role. The exploitation, pretensions, bragging, and need to save face are all facets of what we used to call at home *"la bella figura."*

In all my years as minister, although I had the good sense never to admit it to anyone, I often thought that I was inadequate as a person

---

* Colette Dowling, *The Cinderella Complex* (New York: Summit Books 1981).

in authority and felt guilty without reason. Shortly after I began my mandate as minister of national health and welfare, in one of those sometimes astounding "psychological profiles" that one occasionally reads about oneself, a journalist wrote that "Marc Lalonde [whom I succeeded] was strong, but Monique Bégin was aggressive." This short sentence bothered me for a long time. I was certainly not succeeding a lamb! Unable to recognize myself as an aggressive woman, I was, however, conscious of the type of personal failure that this image represented. For five years in Parliament, the media had referred to me from time to time as "a refreshing figure in Canadian politics" or "in the ranks of the Liberals." What had happened to make me seem "aggressive"? I knew from experience that I had not changed and that this judgment of "aggressive woman," with all that it implied, was completely unjustified. Certainly, I knew where I was going, but I believed in team work and sought consensus above all. As a good listener – another notable female role – I let others say what they wished and tried to convince rather than impose my views like an authoritarian or bang my fist on the table.

All my visceral feminism was not enough to make me understand that by occupying a position of authority and exercising leadership at the top of a pyramid in a bastion of male power and in the eye of the cameras, I had simply deviated from the traditional roles expected of men and women. As I mentioned years later to Simone Veil, former minister of health in France and former president of the European Parliament and a woman whom I admire and like very much, I was extremely happy to read in another of these famous "profiles" that she sometimes got angry! There were at least two of us!

All of this can seem to be of little importance, if not ridiculous at first glance, but a politician lives in a never-ending hall of mirrors that cannot be ignored. The image portrayed by the media is the preferred vehicle of social clichés about women who occupy non-traditional roles. A disproportionate part of girls' education is spent on appearances. If, in addition to the psychological image, a physical image enters into play, the situation can be hard to manage! I speak from experience, having unfortunately gained some weight during the first six months of ministerial life. Journalists asked me who the father was, when my due date was, and so on. Moreover, the debates in the House of Commons had begun to be televised, and I had difficulty living with my image as it was projected. I did not recognize myself and felt diminished. Although this hogwash did not come from my home life, I had learned the importance of appearance to define a "real" woman. There again, I felt abnormal and insecure when I needed my intellect to be in control and at ease.

More than once, I heard my male colleagues vulgarly mocking the appearance of female MPs in a way that I do not remember hearing them speak about one another among themselves. When Pat Carney quit politics in the fall of 1988, *Maclean's* magazine could not find anything better to write than the following:

A Vote for Weight Loss

Treasury Board President Patricia Carney shocked her Conservative colleagues recently when she announced that, because of health problems, she might not run in the next federal election.

"Mrs. Moneybags," as she calls herself, frequently complains about chronic back pain. But both her doctor and Prime Minister Brian Mulroney have suggested that a strict diet might be the solution to the problem.

When I had announced my own departure from the political scene, the daily *Globe and Mail* remembered me to readers as "a tubby lady in need of a couturier she did not have." This is the making of history.

As a woman in politics, I always had the somewhat palpable feeling that I was exceptional, special, and extraordinary, a feeling reinforced by the inevitable "My wife likes you very much!" and the high visibility of such a small number of women. In fact, although I had always resisted the idea, we were token women. (Feminist theory has it that "tokenism" in large corporations is 15 per cent or less of minorities in the dominating group.) Consequently, we did not have the right to diversify among ourselves and had to obey, symbolically, models of excellence in the name of all women. In the rare instances where the subject lent itself, we were to give "the women's point of view." I also felt that I was existing to others – that is, to male colleagues – as a woman rather than as an individual or a person.

To summarize, it seemed to me that men and party strategists thought, without ever saying so, that there had to be a few women in a modern democracy. However, this was for balance and not for equality. From that, to have felt tolerated! Therefore, I had to know my place, to be both an innovator and a go-getter while respecting the limits of established order and acceptable behaviour (for a woman). This image of women's place in politics became clear to me very early in my political career, on a summer day in 1976 when I was walking along Rideau Street to get to my office in the Confederation Building. Rumours of a major Cabinet shuffle were building, but, according to the rules of the game, nobody knew until the event actually happened. I met Jean Chrétien, then President of the Treasury Board. Always sympathetic to mere MPs, he confided to me, without my asking, that I was ready to be a minister but should not be disappointed if I did not become one, "because we already have one woman in Cabinet and it is unthinkable that there would be two." I was scandalized and very discouraged by such an attitude. I remember how deeply I felt about the intrinsic injustice in the established order. A few weeks later, in true Trudeau fashion, there were three female ministers!

I have often felt that men, even remarkable men, did not understand the marked abnormality of women's absence in their work world. They did not understand what we had to contribute, nor the increasing subtlety of injustices and barriers that we had to conquer. The presence of some women in the ranks was understandable, even important, they thought. Obviously, they did not realize that these were always overqualified women who were generally twice as competent as their male colleagues. But, they believed, simply wanting as many women as men in politics (or in business, senior university administration, or elsewhere) was exaggerated, even extremist. In fact, it was uncalled for. They were really convinced of this. However, my greatest shock came one night in my constituency in July 1984, shortly after my press conference announcing that I would not run in the election just called by John Turner. My political organizers, all men, and I had met at the home of my association president in Saint-Léonard. They were French Canadians and Italian Canadians who had worked together with me for twelve years. I had decided to do my best to give the opportunity to a candidate of Italian origin to succeed me. It happened that a young Italian lawyer who was trilingual, bright, sociable, and a mother had told me that she wished to be a Liberal nominee. I had very much liked both my constituency and my political organizers, to whom I felt very close and from whom I had always received warm and unfailing support. However, their reaction was spontaneous and undisguised: "Not another woman!" they exclaimed, deeply and openly worried. It was as if the gulfs of the unspoken and the tolerated had opened before me. I felt yet again as if I had been an exception admitted to a forbidden world where I could absolutely not cross the boundaries. If I must state the obvious, a man succeeded me. Such balance!

Power is a scary word for most. It is even dirty, if not criminal and dangerous. This is what many people, especially women, believe. It is not enough to receive the assets needed to exert power – a title, legal authority, a budget, a department – or to become minister of national health and welfare, despite that department's some $23 billion, at the time almost a quarter of the federal budget. One must occupy power in exercising it; one must take power. Nobody gives it to us on a silver platter.

As in all upper levels of decision-making, politicians win some and lose some. It is not that easy to understand why. We can therefore not stop ourselves from wondering whether we count and how, particularly if we feel set aside from others, which is the case of women. I often told myself how unfavoured I was in the beginning because I was not a part of the Canadian elite. I saw nevertheless that some of my interventions "counted" and that "the boss," as we nicknamed Trudeau, seemed to listen to my observations. In my opinion, the fact is that the majority of federal and provincial ministers who have or seem to have power owe it to the elites of our society. They are chosen and protected by a very small number. They can fast become part of a closed circle. This power is gained quickly, but can be lost as quickly as a sand castle. In contrast, rare people, and I believe that I was one, derive their power from the popular grassroots. As much by inclination as by being pushed by Monique Coupal (my then-Chief of Staff) and Roméo Leblanc, a friend who was Minister before me, I saw my role as that of a privileged spokesperson for the clients for whom I worked: children, women, senior citizens, Native people, ill people, health and social services professionals, and medical researchers, to name a few. I represented them, which is not to say that I did not try to exercise leadership or that I did not show solidarity with the government or that I belonged to lobby groups. Links, first tenuous, then stronger and stronger, developed from meetings, briefs and recommendations that were received and discussed, conferences, and tested ideas. The *Canada Health Act* (1984), for example, would never have passed without this extraordinary power base. My other great luck, certainly, was to have remained in the same department for more than seven years, contrary to the "in vogue" concept where male colleagues liked to change portfolios to expand their contact networks for their eventual leadership candidacy.

We were so few women at the time that it was impossible to create a female power base. We came close to it on a few occasions, however, when we, the two or three women in Cabinet, closed ranks on questions of criminal law (rape, prostitution, sexual harassment), the loss of status for Native women who married Whites, and social policies. I worked with similar networks of women in other levels of government, and also within my own department. The greatest advantage, in as much as these women had more or less made a feminist analysis, was that we did not have to explain the mysteries of life before each hot issue! My former colleagues would probably cringe upon learning that certain feats were successful only because of the help of two, three, or four relatively unknown women and that the power, on that day, was female.

One day, quite suddenly and to the general surprise, I announced my departure from politics. I left my ministerial office just after the September 4, 1984, election. The day after, I arrived in South Bend, Indiana, lost in a drab rented furnished apartment, about to change career once more. I now was a professor at Notre Dame University.

As it happened, the day after the news announcing my decision to retire from politics was released, Dr Sam Freedman, then vice-principal (academic), had invited me to be a visiting professor at McGill. This invitation, from an outstanding medical researcher, a humanist, and the former dean of medicine, touched me deeply. It was like the thread of continuity in my life. It was also a job. So, after a year at Notre Dame, I came back home to Montreal, where I imagined that I would stay for the rest of my life. I was pinching myself when crossing the grass of McGill for the first time: I could not believe it. Although I had travelled the country trying to explain us to each other – francophones, anglophones, and old- or newcomers – it was quite an experience for me to enter anglophone Montreal through one of its most prestigious institutions. My current employer will not be jealous if I add that I always felt a particular attachment to McGill, where I later served on the Board of Governors and on the university press, and from whom I received in 1991 a honorary doctorate in science. I suppose the links started developing through McGill's network of students, professors, and deans of medicine and nursing, privileged links to this day to which I owe great friendships.

After my time at McGill, I was for four years the first holder of the Joint Chair in Women's Studies at the Universities of Ottawa and Carleton, commuting again (for twenty-two years altogether!) between Montreal and Ottawa. After that I found myself back again in the field of health when I was appointed dean of health sciences at University of Ottawa on August 1, 1990.

Except for my childhood, I have not yet told the reader of my private life. I am still a captive of my former public life, when I kept the two worlds completely separate. In fact, from age fifteen I chose to keep my private life very private. Suffice it to say here that, although I always remained close to my sisters and brothers and to my nieces and nephews, our paths somehow parted ways. However, an elective family made up of friends of all ages and kinds, including a few very "significant others," has slowly settled in. I never had children of my own, but I have always been surrounded by some youngsters – tots, teenagers, or young adults – with whom I have a special bonding: my three godsons, the daughter of very close friends, a niece, and others. I think I share myself in *la vertu d'enfance*, as we say in French. I consider myself very lucky and I find myself still astonished at the gift of friendship and affection.

Reflecting on my life, I am tempted to conclude that, so often, I was the right person at the right place at the right time. So much for hard work! But I also often felt like shouting that there was a mistake about the person. I was not exactly who they thought I was. A bit of a misfit, a little marginal, a little different. Just enough to feel uncomfortable and to cultivate doubt about the world around. Then I would remember home, where my patriarchal but totally anti-conformist father had enacted, for my mother and their seven children, some improbable, nightmarish, and crazy situations to, as he put it, "build your character and to overcome your fear of the judgment of others." I realized that after all, a patriarchal, far from normal, and anti-conformist education might have been the best possible preparation for a woman of my generation to survive, even to enjoy, the male worlds of power.

JANE POULSON

A Journey Within

I began living differently in my body in 1980. This was not the result of any premeditated plan to embark upon a journey of self-discovery or any other altruistic task we often set for ourselves following a period of non-productive activity. Rather, it was something which I resented bitterly and resisted for many years. In the earliest days, I was not at all grateful for the challenge thrust upon me. Although I dearly wish that the stimulus to my journeying into self knowledge had been initiated by almost any other event than that which precipitated my reflections, I am now able to stand back enough to recognize that refusing to acknowledge reality serves only to isolate me from circumstances which are a rich part of who I am. The content of this essay would have been much different had I been asked to write it only several years ago. The journey which has allowed me to reach the point where I can speak of the richness of my experience, rather than simply the anger or pain, has been rocky, almost straight uphill, and at times tortuous and convoluted. I was accompanied on this journey by three friends, each unknown to the others, whose insistence that I confront my issues was compelling but whose faithfulness to being there with me was compassionate and sustaining. I fully expect to be journeying in this way for the rest of my life, but hope that the initial steep path behind me now will give way to a more gently undulating terrain with plateaus and points of refreshing respite.

DENYING THE UNTHINKABLE

I was well practised in denying the reality of my existence. As a fledgling adolescent, I developed diabetes mellitus, a disease which was to affect and distort my life in the worst ways imaginable. Like many diabetic teenagers, I spent tremendous amounts of energy trying to carry on with my life, pretending that my world had not been turned upside down. It was critical to me that no one knew the albatross I was carrying around with me. Rather than succumb to severe limitations and restrictions upon my activities, I endeavoured to do more than I might otherwise have striven for. I was determined that I was going to have the upper hand over the beast which haunted me every minute of every day. I played every sport I could and pursued a number of extracurricular activities in high school and university. From the outset of high school, I had entertained the notion of wanting to attend medical school. I completed a bachelor's degree in science at Queen's University, Kingston and went on to do a master's degree in pharmacology before enrolling in medical school at McGill. For the first time, I felt as if my life was finally taking on some sense of direction. I was enthusiastic about what I was doing and, for once, started to feel that the energy being spent was resulting in worthwhile outcomes. Having direction in my life changed my perspective on everything. It felt as if my battle against myself was usurping less of my talent.

It was absolutely unthinkable then for me to learn in my penultimate year of med school that the diabetes was threatening my eyesight and that treatments needed to be started immediately to prevent any loss of sight. Treatments were, in fact, embarked upon with haste, but ultimately to no avail. I lost the vision in one eye suddenly in late third year. This precipitated an intensification of concern about the remaining eye. It was much less affected than the first but was causing some concern to the team of specialists involved in my care. Expert opinion was unanimous that I should undergo surgery to prevent any impairment of vision in the remaining eye. The rest is history. I underwent the surgery in fourth year med school, six weeks before graduation. The surgery was fraught with difficulty and upon awakening, I found that the disaster we had been trying to prevent had been precipitated by the surgical intervention itself. I was blind.

After three short years of feeling as if I was working in unison with my body, I found myself back in the position of expending tremendous amounts of energy to convince myself, if not the rest of the world, that nothing much had happened and that no doubt the universe was unfolding exactly as I thought it should. I returned to med school two weeks after the surgery to complete classes and did my exams orally. I graduated with the rest of my class and began a series of battles with the medical authorities to allow me to take various qualifying exams orally. The answer was always the same: "There is no precedent for persons writing these exams without being able to read or write." My answer was always the same: "I am the precedent." Although it took considerable time and consternation, the various regulating boards agreed, one at a time, to allow me to write qualifying exams. The first was the Medical Council of Canada. These exams take several days for sighted persons to complete. I did these exams with the assistance of a reader from McGill who read me each of the multiple choice questions and marked down my answer. I was allowed twice as much time as the other candidates, but each exam had to be completed within the same day as the other students. This meant an exhausting twelve or fourteen hours of exam writing each of two days in succession, but it was successfully accomplished, and I completed my qualifying papers to practise medicine in Canada.

The summer of 1980 was a time of great soul searching for me. I had been ready to start my internship at the Montreal General Hospital on July 1. By a particularly cruel twist of fate, this was instead the first day of my rehabilitation at the Montreal Association for the Blind. My med school friends phoned me each evening to report on the traumas they had experienced during the day learning to deliver babies or assisting in surgery. For my part the only new tasks I could report upon were learning how to go down stairs without breaking my neck or how to keep walking in a relatively straight line in a long corridor. Each day was a voyage of discovery of a myriad of tasks, things that once could be accomplished without thought, but which were now major hurdles to overcome. The prospect of leaving behind a career that had been so important to me seemed unbearable. My distress was so great that my friends began arranging to meet me at the door of the hospital to take me to various rounds to keep up my interest in academic medicine. At about this time, an article appeared in the *New England Journal of Medicine* reporting that a doctor in the United States had recently completed his fellowship exams in internal medicine despite having lost his eyesight in his second year of residency training. I contacted the *Journal* and asked that they forward a letter to this physician. It was a revelation for both of us that there should be someone else in the world feeling so miserable and in such an untenable position. We became fast friends. I travelled to Pennsylvania to meet him and to spend several days with him in his hospital.

I returned to Montreal convinced that I, too, could continue my medical career. I approached the authorities at McGill and the Montreal General Hospital and, with a surprising minimum of discussion, they agreed to allow me to attempt to pursue my residency training in medicine. Neither the hospital nor I knew whether our proposed plan would succeed, but we proceeded on the understanding that, if either party felt that the experiment was not succeeding, we would discontinue it without penalty or malice on either part. In April 1981,

I embarked upon a four-year residency training program in medicine that, although ultimately successful, nearly did me in at many times. Once again, I was the precedent-setting case for the Royal College of Physicians and Surgeons of Canada, the regulating body for specialists in Canada. Following the third year of training, physicians are required to write gruelling exams testing factual knowledge. The reward for passing these exams is permission to do even more gruelling clinical exams at the end of the fourth year of training. Once again, I had to do the written exams with the aid of an amanuensis from McGill who read me multiple choice questions for two entire days. I was successful and in 1985 became the first blind physician to qualify to practise as a specialist in internal medicine. I was offered a position in the Faculty of Medicine at McGill and in September 1985 took a position as an attending staff doctor in the Department of Medicine at the Montreal General Hospital and assistant professor of medicine at McGill University. In October 1987, I was awarded the Order of Canada for my accomplishments.

REPEATING PATTERNS

What is striking, as I look back on those years, is how similar were my approaches to the early years after losing my sight and the early years of dealing with the diagnosis of diabetes. I learned early on that no one else was interested in one's problems, particularly if they were insoluble, and the best way to deal with them was to simply keep quiet and get on with the job at hand. As I had single-mindedly made it through high school, undergraduate work, and ultimately medical school, so I set my attention to getting through a four-year medical residency training program. My major reader was my mother, who tirelessly read for hundreds of hours, transferring thousand-page textbooks into cassette tapes. I designed a filing system, which although aggravating to the ultimate degree, still served the purpose of allowing me to retrieve information from these tapes. I also recruited medical students, fellow residents, and almost anyone who showed any interest, to read to me and help me to acquire the massive amount of information to be mastered during that four-year period. Years of practice whistling in the dark have given me a capacity to perform calmly, and without a hint of the massive self-doubt and panic felt deep inside. During those years, I learned not to stop and reflect upon how I was feeling as I approached presenting material at rounds or conferences without the benefit of notes, or before stepping inside the room of a new patient. Rather, I simply carried on about my business deferring the associated emotions until some time in the future. This

Receiving the Order of Canada from the Right Honourable Her Excellency Jeanne Sauvé

behaviour was extremely adaptive, as it allowed me to accomplish what I believe would otherwise have been impossible for me to do.

My apparent peace with myself and my cool, calm, and confident manner were important for my professional colleagues and patients. My calmness helped others not to be concerned about my blindness if I conveyed to them that I was not unduly concerned by it. After a period of about a year, most of the other physicians and nurses in the hospital were quite comfortable with the notion of an unsighted medical resident. To my delight, my visual impairment was not an impediment to my patient relationships. I taught my patients how to read the numbers on the blood pressure machine and most of them took great delight in being able to help me out with the readings. In a paradoxical way, I found that my handicap very often facilitated patient relationships. Most people upon entering the hospital find themselves in a terrifying and foreign environment. There is a total imbalance of power between doctors and patients. The doctor is clothed, armed with knowledge, assured and comfortable in the technological environment. The patient is naked, lying in bed, scared, and feeling totally incompetent no matter how competent he or she might be in the outside world. It redressed considerably this imbalance of power when I presented myself as less than omnipotent and asked of the patient help in proceeding with business. I think it often made me feel more approachable than some of my other colleagues. With rare exceptions, my lack of vision did not seem to be perturbing for patients or families. Sublimation of bothersome feelings and affect was certainly productive as far as accomplishing certain tasks was concerned. It would have been impossible to earn a place among fellow health professionals had I demonstrated how I was often feeling. Acquisition of information was much slower for me than my comrades and it was far easier to study and work if I was not focused on the sadness and pain I had to be feeling. For a considerable period of time then, I deferred thinking much about what had happened and the pain and grief for all that I had lost. I was not consciously suppressing these emotions, it just seemed to be a habit that I adopted. The downside for me, of course, was that I did not feel much of anything during those years. It was too much to ask of oneself to feel simply those emotions which were socially acceptable or personally desirable. Thus, I was mildly surprised at my own lack of enthusiasm or excitement during the ceremony when I received the Order of Canada. It was a glittery event such as one is not likely to experience often during a lifetime. I was once again very calm and almost nonchalant about the whole thing. Much of me was feeling that I would far rather have simply done the residency under normal circumstances than have won an award for doing it under adverse conditions. While this unflappable emotional state was productive during that period of my life, it impaired me from being in touch with my real person.

NEW DIRECTIONS

I was unexpectedly challenged to enter a new phase of living by a comment made by a dear friend one day during a luncheon date. Although we only met several times a year, we were always open with each other. To my surprise and without much warning, my friend commented that he felt I had never accepted my blindness. I was shocked by his comment and even outraged. As is often the case with comments which hit us at vulnerable points, his stuck with me for years. In my outrage, I responded in my own musings, "What more could anyone expect?" "I have far exceeded anyone's expectations." "I have given countless interviews about my work." "What more could I do to show that I am continuing on with my life?"

Still, his comment continued to irritate me like a piece of sand in an oyster. I was never quite the same after that luncheon date. It took me about five years to really be able to look at his comment. I had chosen to ignore the chronic fatigue and internal hollowness that come from suppressing vital aspects of our person, regardless of how strong the impetus for that suppression might be. Years of ignoring their existence had failed to eliminate the many aspects of me that I had not been expressing. My friend's comment fell upon fertile soil. What gradually became clear to me was that I had confused dogged persistence to carry on against the odds with acceptance of what had happened to me. I had interpreted my success in the professional realm and my ability to continue working and teaching with coming to grips with what had happened in my life. While it was true that I had been able to accomplish far more than most would ever have expected, this was in no way synonymous with accepting and processing all that had happened.

I spent the next five years of my life in a frame of mind where often I felt as if I was losing all that I had ever accomplished. My old ability to simply write off sadness and dysphoric feelings seemed to leave me. While I could still perform my professional duties as before, it was never as certain to me that I could pull off a flawless performance. I never did let myself down in this period but I was increasingly aware of the sad, disappointed, angry, frustrated, or tired person within my body where before there had been an absolute rock. I wondered, when this new somewhat tentative being was emerging from within me, if this was the beginning of the end. I was unaccustomed to such feelings of uncertainty and darkness. Those who were party to my musings and fears of what was happening were enthusiastic and supportive, encouraging me to allow these new voices within me the chance to express themselves.

My worst fears were never realized. I initially felt that to allow expression of dark feelings would mean that I was no longer able to work or teach or accomplish the tasks I had valued so highly all this time. What I learned was that perhaps there would be times when my output was not quite as great as I would have liked. This, however, was not the end of the world either. Coming more into touch with my whole being allowed me to be softer and gentler with myself. New and different items are beginning to appear on my agenda. Previously, I was more likely to do what I felt ought to be done in order to show that I was not expecting any concessions because of my health. I no doubt expected more of myself than anyone else expected of me. Gradually, I am apportioning more energy to activities which are simply pleasant. When sighted, I got much pleasure from playing the piano. That was all thrown out when I could no longer read the music. With some trepidation, I began taking music lessons again. I was afraid that the snail's pace of learning new music would prevent me from enjoying the experience of playing once again. There are times when the frustration drives me to tears. That is not the time to be playing. I have set no standards for myself other than that I enjoy the playing. A colleague recently was trying to sell his baby grand piano and it was a mutually satisfying arrangement that I should buy it. The return to making music has been a rich and pleasurable experience. I remain focused upon the music I can produce and do not allow myself to be sidetracked by thoughts of what I might be playing if I could still see the notes.

Acknowledging all of who I am continues to be a voyage of discovery. Sometimes when I feel lost in a morass of conflicted feelings and emotions, I think how much easier it was when I simply got on with the project at hand and gave it little thought. I have turned onto a new path from which there is no return. There continue to be sidetracks, ventures down dead ends, and long convoluted detours. At first these annoyed and concerned me. Five or six years into this new *modus operandi*, however, I can usually take these detours in my stride and know that minor setbacks or diversions into scary or bothersome emotions will subside, and I am the richer for being the kaleidoscope of personalities that I am. Decisions about all aspects of my life now reflect this breadth of potential. Not since I was diagnosed with diabetes have I lived as the person I am, rather than expending huge amounts of energy trying to convince myself that I am totally unaffected by the sad but undeniable events of my life.

A NEW SPACE

Perhaps in reaction to having been told as a young teenager that I would have to do most things differently from most of my peers, I always felt it was important that I do everything the same as everyone else. On the surface, there has been nothing wrong with this policy. The consequence for me, however, has been that I could ignore the fact that many things are grossly different for me than they are for most people. Failure to acknowledge these differences has on the one hand prevented me from dealing with the pain associated with that knowledge, but on the other hand has prevented me from examining the full breadth of who I am. Nothing that happens to us is ever all bad. Failure to acknowledge to myself, if not to any other single person, that something of enormous magnitude had befallen me and was to haunt me every moment of my life meant that I was also not able to acknowledge the strengths, talents, and energy which I possess, and which had allowed me to overcome tremendous adversity. I was able to expend enormous amounts of compassion, empathy, care, and concern for my patients, friends, or colleagues who found themselves in difficult circumstances. Accompanying others during times of trouble or despair was one of my strong suits. How sad then that I was almost totally lacking in compassion when it came to myself.

What I have learned is that the giving and receiving of help is all relative. Where once I saw myself only as a recipient of help, I now know that everyone needs help from someone else. Although I continue to receive help with tasks easily accomplished by others, I am able to help many people with problems burdensome to them. I for my part am very pleased to be able to help other people with their burdens and have therefore learned to ask for and receive help with a sense of grace rather than shame.

I become angry when people, trying to find something good to say about being blind, quote such trite lines as "You see so much more than those of us who can see." Although I am loath to admit that there might be some truth in such statements, I do think that I am learning to be able to look at qualities and characteristics which I never spent much time thinking about. In my sighted days, I valued my abilities to play squash and other racquet sports, accomplish long lists of tasks in a single afternoon, and do any number of things which, in fact, are not all that important in the overall scheme of things. I was a much more superficial person when I could see and was in fact blinded by my sight. Forced by circumstances, I am now much more attuned to the person with patience, forbearance, and an abiding capacity to see the humour in any situation. There is much more to a person than what we see reflected back to us in a mirror. On bad days, this seems little comfort, but learning that there is more to me than meets my eye has made me much more diligent in the search for these characteristics in people I meet during a day.

WE STILL MAKE CHOICES

In some respects, I feel that I have been describing someone who is destined for beatification. If that is so, I have failed in my intent to share with you part of my journey. I have risked sounding like a "Pollyanna" – finding the good in every situation and failing to see any downside. If that is so, I must set the record straight. I do not wish to imply that it is all right with me that I cannot see. It is not. It is a source of ongoing pain, frustration, and sorrow for me. At the same time, however, I have had to learn that I am blind. I must live as someone who cannot see and never again will see.

We do not get a say in what fate holds out for us. We do, however, have control over the choices we make in how we deal with it. My options have been either to deny the impact of my blindness and live in an unreal world or, painful as it has been, to try to meet and embrace my whole self. Encountering my entire person has been intolerably painful at times, but has lead me onto a path of discovery which was barred until I chose to acknowledge my reality. Some days I long for the times when I lived in a world where I chose to insulate myself from the truth, but that is no longer possible. The rewards of knowing who I really am will be much more valuable in the end and provide a sounder soil for rooting.

I am grateful for the love and support of my friends who have insisted that I confront my whole self, and have supported and encouraged me to continue on this journey no matter how bleak it sometimes seems. I might not have persisted had they not assured me that they loved the whole Jane much more than the carefully manicured version they had once known. Along with more than my fair share of troubles, I have been very richly blessed.

Long Experience and a Happy Existence

When asked to contribute to a collection of McGill women's autobiographies I was most hesitant. I am neither a great achiever nor even one of the generation of women with interesting experiences in fitting together family and work. But I admit to a long experience and a very happy existence in the McGill community, so shall try to give a picture of life as I have seen it.

I was born in 1904 at the home of my maternal grandfather and grandmother, Edwin and Inez Howe, in the delightful small village of Hatley, originally called Charleston, in the Eastern Townships of Quebec. The original Howe settler in Canada was Squire Howe, who registered his first land claim in 1804 near Barnston in Stanstead County, where he and his wife, four girls, and one son, Jonas, farmed. Jonas married Prudence Hollister and had nine children. One of them was my grandfather Edwin, who spent most of his married life as an auctioneer selling farms and acted as town secretary-treasurer for many years. In 1912, when the village became the municipality of the village of Hatley, he was one of the first councillors. My mother, Nina, was the youngest of Edwin and Inez's three children.

My father, Walter Chalk, came from a very different background. His father was William Henry Chalk, a businessman in London, England. Walter was very much a Londoner, having been born in a house on a street in front of St Paul's Cathedral. At the age of five I was taken to see the "house where Daddy was born," but by then it had become a novelty shop, and the whole area was completely demolished by bombs during the Second World War.

My father attended Dulwich School and then got various teaching positions at boys' private schools while he studied for an extramural London University BA degree. He qualified in 1888 at the age of twenty-seven – not bad when one considers that in those days one

Laura Chalk, second from the right (circa 1906)

wrote the examinations and passed or failed without even knowing which subjects of the classics, English, history, and mathematics were satisfactory.

By this time a colleague from one of the schools where he had taught, Dr Charles Moyse, had gone to Canada to teach English at McGill University. Through him my father got a teaching position at Williamson's School – a private boys' school in Montreal. He arrived after a very rough passage of nineteen days to Boston and by train to Montreal. At that time he recalled that the horse-drawn cars went "as far west as Greene Avenue." After a short time he went to Quebec City to teach at the old Quebec High School for boys, and a few years later to Westmount to the old Westmount Academy – a brick building on Stanton Street which housed all primary and high school grades. There he made friends with Ralph Howe, who invited him to visit for a week in Hatley before school opened in the fall. He met Ralph's sister, Nina, and, despite his forty-one years, apparently fell in love at first sight and asked her to marry him at the end of that week.

My mother at twenty-six had gone home planning to help her mother, who had been ill, and "be an old maid," despite the fact that she had not only got her teaching diploma from the old Normal School on Belmont Street in Montreal, but had taught several years in Point St Charles. She admitted being taken aback, but reconsidered;

they become engaged and were married at the old St James' Church in Hatley in June 1903. She had local friends stand up with her while my father's best man was Percival Molson, one of the family of the well-established Molson Breweries, who, sadly, was killed in World War I, but left the bequest which built the Percival Molson Stadium.

When I was born, in 1904, along with a twin sister, Lilian, we lived in a rented building on Ste Catherine Street near the old Montreal Athletics Association – a strange bit of architecture of four storeys. The top two storeys were one house, lived in by my uncle and his family, and the lower two another, where we lived. Behind the house was a large shed for coal storage, whence the necessary coal for the furnace was carried in, scuttleful by scuttleful. Light was by gas mantle lamps, with one open flame in the bathroom. It sounds almost unbearable, but we were very comfortable. Mother had a maid who lived in and not only helped with washing, ironing, and housework but also relieved her in looking after the babies.

So life progressed, and when I was five plans were made to book passage for England, where we were to spend the summer holidays. Sadly, my sister Lilian was ill all the way across the ocean, got weaker and more listless daily, and died from cerebral meningitis in a Liverpool hospital the day we landed. All the family was devastated but tried to make up to me for the sister I had lost. I must have been a terrible drag on my poor mother, for I seemed to "go into a decline" and, even up to Christmas of that year, had no incentive to play or do anything else alone. I even cried myself to sleep on Christmas Eve because I didn't want Santa to come without Lilian. When the new toys appeared, however, I began to live again.

At age six I was sent to Queen's School on Oliver Avenue. By this time my father was not only principal of the Westmount Academy but also superintendent of the four Westmount schools – King's, Queen's, Roslyn, and the Westmount Academy. The first time he appeared in our classroom I called out "Hello Daddy," but, after being admonished when I got home, I remember merely catching his eye on subsequent visits and surreptitiously waving at him across the room.

The following year we moved to Western Avenue (now de Maisonneuve Boulevard) and I transferred to King's School, graduated from there with the silver medal for highest standing, and went on to the new High School on the park, where my uncle was made principal. Because of my interest in mathematics I chose to take the higher mathematics (trigonometry and more advanced algebra) instead of drawing in my last two years. As I had been doing well in art, my uncle felt that the standing of the school in the matriculation examinations would be better if I kept on in that, but I was finally permitted to have my own

way. On graduation in 1921 I again took top standing and earned a
gold medal this time round, and also a Macdonald Entrance Scholarship to McGill University.

McGill was the natural choice, for I could live at home. Many of my
earliest memories were visiting at the Moyse home on Sherbrooke
Street where the galleries ran right round the house and made a nice
place to play. I think the last time I was there was when, in 1918, we
were invited to use those same galleries to watch what was intended
to be the Victory Loan Parade to launch the newest Victory Bond issue. It turned out instead to be the Victory Parade celebrating the
signing of the Armistice at the end of World War 1. With no radio in
those days the news spread gradually across the city and then everyone celebrated, though many were still grieving over their dear ones
lost in the tragedies of war.

By the time I went to McGill there were quite a number of returned
veterans on campus who lent an air of mature stability among the
students, which was probably good for us, as we established ourselves in our new surroundings. We were no longer schoolchildren
but adults who had to stand on our own.

The first year, nearly all the courses were compulsory. For an arts
degree this meant six full courses in English, French, Latin, mathematics, history, and either biology, chemistry, or physics. Part way
through the first term it so happened that the Men's Society at
St Matthias Church, to which my father belonged, had a lecture on
their fall program to be given on radioactivity by Dr A.S. Eve, whose
first-year lectures I was attending. My father thought I would be interested and, even though I was not a man, he took me along. After
the meeting I met Dr Eve and told him I was in his first-year class. He
immediately showed some interest in me, asked if I had done physics
as one of my entrance examinations, and also how well I had done.
When I told him he asked what I was doing in his class. There was no
alternative given by the person who had registered me, so Dr Eve
asked me to come to his office, suggesting that I should be in the second-year engineering course in heat, light, and sound. Subsequently I
followed his advice, was lost for several weeks while I tried to catch
up on the work I had missed, and finally passed, but with fairly poor
marks, at the end of the year.

Then came second-year registration. This time my own family, my
uncle (the high school principal) and my high school mathematics
teacher all urged me to take a general course rather than the possible
mathematics and physics honours course. Though I agreed to follow
their advice, I still felt it would be a good idea to complete a second
level in electricity and magnetism statics and dynamics to go along

with what I had already done in heat, light, and sound in my first year. But I ran into an objection when trying to register for one of the mechanics courses because it was only given to science students and I would have to get special permission. So back I went to Dr Eve and explained my problem. He just leaned back in his chair and said, "Why don't you do it all and do it properly?" That was all I needed. I checked with the family over lunch time, went back downtown and registered for the honours course in mathematics and physics.

When classes got started I found three other women who had also registered in the honours mathematics and physics course and one man! This was a rather surprising ratio but, by the end of that year, the other three women were recommended to change into a general course, and one man was added from engineering physics. So we remained until graduation. Most classes were augmented by chemists, engineers, and graduate students, so we were never a threesome, as I recall.

Scholarships for students entering second, third, and fourth year were only available to those who won them on the basis of special examinations in the autumn. I wrote these examinations on entry to second year for physics and French, and third year, for mathematics and physics. I was a scholarship recipient on both occasions – the latter being for two years. Most of my contemporaries were taking summer jobs of one kind or another, but my family always spent the summers at our cottage on Lake Massawippi and wouldn't leave me alone in the house in Westmount, so I studied for scholarships instead. In this way I didn't disrupt the family holiday or the enjoyment of my two younger brothers, and was at least earning enough to cover my fees, and very probably more than I could have cleared in the summer job market.

On graduation I won the Anne Molson Medal, obtained a National Research Council Bursary (about $700 for the year), and made plans to stay on at home and do research at McGill. The various professors in the physics department provided prospective students with lists of suggested projects in their respective fields. Dr John Stuart Foster, who had just joined the staff following his work at Yale University, presented what seemed the most interesting programs, and I elected to work with him. Bill Rowles, who had come from the University of Saskatchewan with an honours physics degree and an NRC bursary, also joined Dr Foster's group at this time.

So to the Stark laboratory in the sub-basement of the old physics building. It was dark and partially filled with the brick pillars of the so-called vibration-free tables of laboratories higher up in the building and a large unused machine in the middle of the room. It was also so radioactive that we had to be careful always to use fresh photo-graphic plates because old ones would get badly fogged just lying in the drawer in the darkroom. Amongst these and along the walls there were long slate work-benches, a few stools, and a closed-in portion, with sink, to be used as a darkroom. On one table was a Hilger "E" two-quartz spectrograph, and on a shop-made stand a large six-prism glass spectrograph which had to be adjusted by hand – prism by prism – to operate in the desired region of the spectrum. Since this adjustment was never twice the same, new focus plates had to be taken each time it was moved.

We graduate students were expected to build our own vacuum sys-tems, McLeod gauges, and charcoal traps and to make basic changes in our Stark effect tubes, so that early on we spent a lot of time in these activities and even in rushing down to Montreal East to get our own liquid air when the regular errand lad was not available. When beginning our graduate "training" period, all our glass blowing had to be done with soft glass because pyrex was too expensive for us to practise on. What a lot of hours were wasted! This necessitated mak-ing our own ground glass joints with expensive pyrex, which we ground by hand, to make connections from soft glass vacuum systems to the pyrex Stark effect tubes which were designed by Dr Foster. Working with J.S. Foster proved an inspiration to us all, and I believe to all who followed, both in the Stark effect days and later during the years of designing, building, and operating the McGill cyclotron. With-out his drive and confidence this would never have been accom-plished.

In due course the necessary vacuum equipment got made and, us-ing the six-prism glass spectrograph, photographs were achieved, but not before dozens of repeated attempts. At the end of one year I pro-duced a thesis on "Potential Distributions in the Crookes Dark Space" and got my M Sc. The following year was largely taken up with passing French and German language requirements and preparing for the dreaded general Ph D exams in physics and in mathematics. These could be based on any material from courses we had taken both as graduates and in undergraduate years as well as subjects discussed in colloquia which we had attended. Despite choices among the questions given, there were five papers set in separate fields of physics, all of which had to be passed separately, so the whole performance was quite an ordeal. Moreover, that year Dr Foster was on leave doing quantum analysis in Bohr's laboratory in Copenhagen, setting up his calcula-tions for the Stark effect of helium. When he returned, we got involved in doing bits of the calculations with hand-operated calculating ma-chines.

Having survived all this, we applied our efforts in our third year to getting data for our Ph D theses. William Rowles and I were Dr Foster's first two Ph D students. His thesis was "The Stark Effect in Complex Spectra" and mine was "Observed Relative Intensities of Stark Components in Hydrogen." We both graduated at the spring convocation in 1928 and our research results were published in the *Proceedings of the Royal Society of London*. My results were the first published data to check the validity of the new Schrödinger's wave mechanics calculations.

Prior to graduation I had applied for one of the Moyse Travelling Scholarships. The awards committee was in favour of me up to the last minute when one of the members announced that I was engaged to be married, whereupon the decision was made in favour of a psychologist. As a matter of fact, I was not engaged at that time, nor did I become engaged until after my appointment to teach on the Macdonald Campus two years later. I must admit disappointment at the time, but Dr Foster offered me a position as research assistant, working on the effect of parallel electric and magnetic fields on the helium spectrum. I did this for one year, reapplied for the Moyse Scholarship and received it for the year 1929–30 to go to London, England, to work with the then-recent recipient of the Nobel Prize, Professor O.W. Richardson, FRS at King's College in the Strand.

Soon after my arrival in London, Dr Richardson gave me his most recent calculations on the band spectrum of molecular hydrogen and suggested that I should continue his search and get any further information I could come up with. This proved to be an uninspiring project, but since I had been accepted by him to do research, all I could do was comply. As the months rolled by I discovered a few more bands to add to Richardson's earlier research results and wrote a paper which he presented at a meeting of the Royal Society in London. I was fortunately allowed to attend, along with Rutherford, Sir Oliver Lodge, Aston, Dirac, and others.

That summer I joined my parents in Paris for a bus trip, going to Geneva, the Passion Play in Oberammergau, back through Germany, and then to England for a family visit. While in Dresden I got confirmation of my appointment to join the physics staff of McGill's Macdonald College. On my return to Montreal I was informed that the half-time position I had been given had become a full-time possibility. Dr William Rowles, who upon graduation had immediately joined the Macdonald College physics staff, was already head of his department, and it seemed ordained that we were to be together again. I went to be interviewed by Dr Barton, then dean of agriculture and home economics, and despite my lack of teaching experience, he gave me the full-time position. My duties consisted of teaching one course of

Laura Rowles as her students knew her

grade 10 high school physics, an introductory physics course to the women taking a two-year household administration diploma, and also first- and second-year mathematics to agriculture degree students. This kept me busy but not strained intellectually. That year, I commuted by train from Westmount Station, but I gave up the full-time job and did half-time from then on because I got married in June 1931 to William Rowles.

After I had spent about five years in this position, McGill decreed that, because of the state of the economy, no wives could hold positions in their husbands' departments. So I lost my job and thereafter was employed only intermittently "as needed." Occasionally I demonstrated in an advanced laboratory class when help from suitable postgraduate students was not available. Once when a staff member died suddenly just as term started, another woman who also had a physics PhD was available, so she and I shared the required teaching which the deceased professor had been doing. Another year, when a staff member left unexpectedly, I filled in again. During the Second World War, when McGill had to teach a crash course in electricity theory to five hundred Canadian Air Force men prior to their going to the Royal Air Force to be trained as radar officers, I again found myself on the staff, this time on the downtown campus. It was a *very* hectic time, with everyone busy lecturing, demonstrating, and devising laboratory experiments suitable for their future requirements. Radar was still not understood by the public, or by us, but the required knowledge was fed to the organizers of the course by the RAF. I did a second round of this, with smaller numbers, the following winter when of course the two Macdonald men went back on their regular teaching program.

After the war came the big Department of Veterans' Affairs grant classes, so again I was called on to help out. This time, my most strenuous year was one when I demonstrated to the engineers who were being taught at the improvised overflow campus at what had been an Air Force training centre at St Jean. One day a week I went by train from Ste Anne's to Montreal to St Jean and then by bus to "Dawson College," arriving there at 9 a.m. The demonstrators marked lab books for two hours, entering marks in a record book, demonstrated to first-year engineering students for two hours, and lunched in the cafeteria (a one-time aircraft hanger). I then demonstrated in a three-hour fourth-year engineering electrical measurements laboratory class where all pairs worked on different experiments. Afterwards I returned by the reverse route, augmented by about an hour's wait at Montreal West for my train to Ste Anne's, and walked home. On Thursday of each week the reports from this electrical measurements laboratory arrived by express from St Jean and I spent most of the weekends marking and recording the marks, always a slow job because of the diversity of experiments.

Clearly I was never a famous scientist, but I kept busy in my field a lot of the time and was glad to be needed. I never felt discriminated against in any way except, perhaps, when turned down for a scholarship because I was reported to be engaged to be married; but I might well have voted with the committee, had I been a member. I still am sympathetic towards their decision. I always felt myself to be just one of the boys. Whether or not I received the same pay as the men for the positions I had, I don't know, but believe I did. I never thought about it. All I know is that I never got much, but nor did the men! There were no regular increments and apparently no policy except in the days of the depression when everyone took cuts, many of which were not restored until the recipient received a promotion. I recall after the war my husband received a letter from the principal, Dr James, in which he acknowledged appreciation of his continued loyalty and support over the hard times, and was pleased to inform him of a salary increase of $100 a year! We both sat down and laughed.

I now turn to our campus life from the time of our marriage. My husband William (Bill) and I became a team in every way, so in writing about this side of our interests I can only write "we" as I refer to our activities.

We lived in an apartment on the Macdonald College campus, and never had any children, so that we were free to take part in many of the students' activities, and we made friends with many of them. The agriculture and home economics staff were mostly in college houses or in nearby Ste Anne de Bellevue and, with cars still scarce commodities in the early days, we were a close-knit community. There was staff volleyball for the men and mixed badminton in term time, and in summer a nine-hole golf course for academic staff and secretaries. Other employees had a very good bowling green situated in the space behind the chemistry-physics building.

The students carried out an extensive athletics program and we attended many hockey, basketball, and football games. Bill was regularly busy on the annual field day with stop watch in hand. But we were mainly involved in Literary and Debating Society activities, judging plays and debates in interclass competitions, often acting as directors as well as judges. We were both honorary officers of the Students' Society, and my husband many times honorary president of the Literary and Debating Society, and Gold Key Society. We spent countless nights at student formal dances, both as patrons and also as paying participants because we both liked to dance. The "formals"

Drs Laura and William Rowles

were elaborately staged four or five times a year. In the early years dress was formal – white tie and tails and long dresses – but it became "semi-formal" as time went on: men wore business suits and women dressed up. The last time we were invited as patrons, I recall asking one of the staff wives what was meant by "semi-formal" these days, and she replied, "No jeans, I guess."

After the war, huts for married McGill students were put up where the Centennial Centre now stands, spoiling our golf forever. Later the exodus of the Faculty of Education to the McGill Montreal campus, the arrival of John Abbott College and erection of the Macdonald-Stewart Agriculture Building – to say nothing of the numerous student-owned automobiles – changed the picture beyond recognition. We were most fortunate through all this because Bill's last year of lecturing coincided with the final year that the old college first-year classes were given. His successor had the job of overseeing the move from the old chemistry-physics building to the new agriculture–home economics Building.

Just before that we had bought a house of our own in Baie d'Urfé. Gardening displaced boating on the river, and we began to lose touch with the newer students. However, we have not been wholly forgotten. Not only was a bursary endowed in Bill's name at the time of his official retirement as chairman, he was also named Professor Emeritus. After this, he continued to teach for five more years and voluntarily conducted a laboratory course he had designed. When the college celebrated its seventy-fifth anniversary, he was given the first Mastery for Service Award for "contributions to the Macdonald Community."

At the 1989 reunion of the class of 1944 – the class that adopted us as honorary members years ago – members began to collect for a graduate bursary "in recognition of the friendship of Drs William and Laura Rowles." We could not ask for more! But by the time of the class reunion banquet Bill had had an accident and was losing ground. Still, this news was one of the bright spots in his last days. And now I am told that the college is planning to name one of the buildings after us, to be known as the Rowles Building.

In addition to scholastic interests and our close relationship with our students we both had numerous other activities. While at school and college I played basketball, including one year when I was on the intercollegiate girls' team play-offs in Toronto. As soon as skiing was introduced into the Montreal area, I gave up my regular Saturday afternoon skating to bands at the MAAA and joined the skiers on Mount Royal and some years later joined a group of students in London for a memorable nine days skiing in the Engadine Valley in Switzerland, all without benefit of ski lifts. We did use climbing skins, but basically all my skiing was done the hard way.

By 1930 Bill was well established as a curler at Ste Anne de Bellevue Curling Club and I joined the ladies' branch. After forty active years I was given an honorary life membership. Meanwhile Bill had followed up his apprenticeship as a choir singer in Saskatoon and Westmount, and over fifty years in Ste Anne de Bellevue, and we both sang with the McGill Choral Society in *Pinafore* and *Iolanthe* in our student days. Bill also sang in *Tom Jones* and participated in the McGill Drama Club, and his final contribution as a singer was to join me as a Volunteer at the Ste Anne's Veterans' Hospital for Sunday church services and Tuesday singsongs. He felt he could still make a contribution until he was over ninety. I had been on the Red Cross Hospital visiting committee since February 1942 – mostly as chairman, handing out smokes and chocolate bars, until the service was discontinued in 1982. I received a citation from the Montreal branch. After that I continued with the volunteers on Sundays and Tuesdays, and last year was honoured at their annual meeting for fifty years of service.

I realize that one important aspect of living has been neglected in what I have written. Boy friends? Of course. I lived a large part of my early life mostly with males, including my two younger brothers, and true friendship with men was just a part of living. I was taken out and entertained by quite a number – several over a period of years – but never concentrated on any particular one until I got engaged to Bill after my year in England. Moreover, though seven of them got to the point of proposing marriage, I never had any one ask for any sexual favours, and none were given. I somehow mentioned this as I prepared a cup of coffee for the young man who had been raking garden leaves for me, and he – married and father of an infant daughter – said nostalgically, "That must have been nice, but it sure isn't like that now."

For me it was the right century in which to live and to see all the technical progress and changing social behaviour – from crystal radio sets to satellites, sleigh bells to multiple-car families. I have watched with interest the agitation of women as they have gradually been relieved of many of the duties of their forebears by modern inventions. Naturally, as time and the advantages of extended academic education became available, women have broadened their interests and their horizons, and have had to face the fact that the odds are against them when their aspirations involve displacing men in fields which had "belonged" to them.

In my day, and I think it is still true, the majority of women were more concerned with social problems in the world than with mathematics and abstract science. This being the case, so-called "equity" is fundamentally incompatible with logic when it comes to choosing people for specific positions. It might be applicable at the lower end of the scale in the work force in a few cases, but adaptability, physical strength, and even physical size and appearance come into consideration when the position involves relationship with the public and with other workers, and in a free society we must be allowed to discriminate in all sorts of situations – after all, we still choose our own spouses without having the government interfere.

I agree with the feminists in our ranks who have achieved some useful ends for women at large, but picayune fussing about the words "chairman" and "chair," and similar activities, I feel, can only lower the level at which we are seen by men and also by those of us who just use our own abilities to prove how and where we can fit into the work force. True, I lost my regular teaching position when McGill made the law during the worst of the great depression disallowing women in their husbands' departments. It was not that I was a woman, but because I was drawing a second salary which was earned in my husband's department. The wife of my contemporary Dr Terroux, who happily was a physiologist and not in a position in any way related to her husband, kept her position right up to retirement.

Since I have experienced life for nearly a century it may be of interest to know how my philosophy has changed. Having been brought up to attend church and Sunday school regularly, my interest in religion led me, when I was quite young, to believe I should plan to be a missionary in Japan, the country of my choice – influenced, I think, by a very nice postcard picture of Fuji Yama. While at university I taught Sunday school, took part in discussion groups of the Student Christian Movement, and was even persuaded to attend an Anglican Summer School Session at Knowlton, Quebec, to teach Sunday school teachers how to teach. By this time I was considerably less assured of my own convictions with respect to theology and quite sure that I was out of my depth in this role.

As the years rolled along, I became more and more exposed to science and found that the more I learned, the less I seemed to know; and what I "believed" became more and more cloudy – e.g. quantum theory and wave theory of light were each true in describing certain phenomena, but never both applicable for any specific case. More and more, I have given up trying to tie faith in God to any form of religion. All religions offer their followers some hope for the future, and as such should be supported and preserved. Certainly the world is a better place because of the Judaeo-Christian outlook, if the only things we experience are its contributions to architecture, music, and ethics which we see all around us. The same, of course, is true of the religions of India and China.

Beyond this, the very meaning of the word "believe" becomes meaningless, though something we call faith seems to persist in an intangible way as we gradually watch the unfolding of the mysteries of the birth of stars in super nova, the seeming disappearance of matter into black holes, the unbelievable variety in living matter and its adaptability to change through evolution, and even our own private experiences of almost miraculous intervention in seeing us through times of stress.

We do, however, also see the effect individuals have wherever we look. Our little ripples, good and bad, spread out and influence others forever, and as we see this, we know we live on. I recently was looking up a reference in Bartlett's *Familiar Quotations* and came across the well-known words of Longfellow, written out on a sheet of paper in my husband's handwriting. These lines, I believe, express our joint beliefs and what we have lived by, always hoping to lead in the right direction:

Lives of great men all remind us
We can make our lives sublime,
And, departing, leave behind us
Footprints in the sands of time.

Fighting for My Own Agenda:
A Life in Science

One afternoon early in 1974, I was sitting at my desk in my basement office, the pale January light filtering in through the skylight, when the telephone rang.

"This is President Bok's office calling." The caller identified neither herself nor the university, but I vaguely recalled that Derek Bok was the new president of Harvard. The female voice asked me if I would be willing to sit on an *ad hoc* committee to appoint a professor of biology at Harvard University.

I was so astonished I blurted out, "You must be asking me because I am a woman."

"Well, yes," she agreed, "Health and Welfare has requested that we send them the composition of every selection committee by race and sex."

The committee, it turned out, consisted of President Bok, Dean Rosovsky, three Harvard professors (one a Nobel Laureate) in departments other than biology, and three outside experts, all world-renowned plant physiologists, all male, and me. Harvard's rules call for three outside experts on each selection committee. Either I was a last-minute addition, or they wanted to dilute out a woman's vote. The outside guests were housed the night before the meeting in Harvard's historic Dana-Palmer House. I dined that evening with one of the committee members, one of America's most eminent plant scientists. He said to me, "I don't see how you've done it."

I've often thought about his comment. At that time, I was forty-three years old, had just been recommended for promotion to professor of biology at McGill University, and had a small research group and a modest international reputation for high-quality research in a minor field of biology. But I suspect he was most impressed that I was a member of that illustrious committee. Second in glory only to a call

Sally at the helm of the "Blue Heron" (1934)

to become a professor at Harvard is a call to sit on the committee that names that professor.

How have I done it? I certainly did not plan to do it. It was definitely not part of my mother's agenda for me, or part of the prescribed agenda for most American women born in the Depression to middle-class, educated parents. My mother's agenda for me was to be pretty and popular, have lots of friends, go to college, marry well, have lots of children, and devote myself to them. Mother's goals for my sister and me were ordinary ones, but my mother was far from ordinary. She was highly intelligent, a college graduate, imaginative, always on the go with energy to burn. Everyone said she was a remarkable woman. Those who knew her best added that my father was a saint to put up with her. A psychiatrist has told me she was unipolar manic. One minute she would be in a state of feverish excitement, the next moment she would flash into a terrible rage. My earliest memory is of her rage. I was two and a half and I had lifted my sister out of her playpen. Ann had crawled almost to the top of the stairs when mother discovered her and started yelling at me. I was bad, bad, bad. She screamed at us daily and beat us often. My father escaped – to work, to the church, to the boat, to the car – but Ann and I could not escape. She managed every detail of our lives. My friends thought she was marvellous, she gave such elaborate birthday and Hallowe'en parties. I felt like a small bit player in my mother's productions. I was frightened and wanted to hide, but inevitably I was drawn back to the noise and excitement. To this day, I feel that the lights and action are where Mother is, or as she declines into senility, where my sister and her noisy tribe are.

By the time I was thirteen, I had discovered two ways to escape my mother's constant criticism. One was to go to my room and study.

"Mother, I can't, I have homework to do," was one excuse she accepted.

More important, I became an ardent birdwatcher, a passion that has persisted to this day. A gentle, kindly woman, Mrs Devereux, taught me enough about birds for me to qualify for my Girl Scout badge in bird lore, but I soon graduated to the Brookline Bird Club. It was wartime and gasoline was rationed, but, every Saturday I could, I went by bus and trolley from Lexington to Boston's North Station where I joined the Brookline birders. We took the train to Newburyport or Ipswich, and then we walked all day along the coast. It was late in the evening when I got home, exhausted, but exhilarated. Mother did not approve. Looking at birds was harmless enough, but she considered the Brookline Bird Club members a scruffy bunch of misfits, old maids, scraggly boys, a few couples, and older men, not at all the type of company she wanted for her teenage daughter. Most of all, mother wanted for her daughters the goal that had eluded her, to be popular with the boys. For each Saturday bird trip she let me go on, I had to go to a dreary dance accompanied by a boy of her choice, the principal's son. Poor Richard, I considered him such a drip, but when we met again a few years ago at my fortieth high school reunion, I found him the most accomplished and charming of men.

It was not that I was uninterested in boys, but the boys I liked, I admired in secret. They were either brilliant or eccentric, usually both, and I knew that they would never pass muster with mother.

By the time I was sixteen, the war had ended and gasoline was once again available. That winter Fred Burrill drove me and my young neighbour, Winty Harrington, on all the bird trips and on many shorter excursions as well. Fred was curator of birds at the Peabody Museum in Salem, and he knew more about birds than anyone I had ever met. I liked him a lot – the smile in my yearbook picture was for him. I went

Sally and her mother (1950)

around singing to myself the line from the popular song, "They're either too young or too old." Winty was thirteen; Fred was thirty-three. The three of us had such wonderful times on our trips that I have seldom been happier, but one evening some old biddy from the Brookline Bird Club telephoned my mother and told her that Fred's attentions to me were quite inappropriate. The next day, Mother telephoned Fred and told him to come see her. When he arrived at the house, she did not dare invite him in, so she drove with him in his car and sat with him in some country lane. I do not know what she said to him there; it was probably appalling, and, certainly, completely unjustified, but my wonderful trips with Fred and Winty abruptly ceased, and I never heard from Fred again.

My passion for birding gave me the first item on *my* agenda. Often during my high school years, I proudly announced that I was going to be an ornithologist and go study birds in Mexico. But the rest of mother's agenda was still firmly entrenched. I did not intend to go alone. I planned to marry an ornithologist, travel with him and help him write his books. And that is pretty much how my life unfolded during the next ten years.

At my birth, Mother had enrolled me in Smith College, her alma mater. I did apply to Smith, but only to please her. My only serious choice was to go to Cornell University, which was strong in ornithology, as well as in all vertebrate zoology. Mother even drove me to Ithaca in April of my senior year of high school, and I had an interview with a young admission officer, Robert Storandt. Or rather, my mother and I had an interview with Mr Storandt. I am sure mother did most of the talking. Whatever transpired, it was sufficient to win me a four-year Cornell National Scholarship, $1200 a year, an enormous sum in those days, for it paid both tuition and room and board. It did not give me independence from my parents, though, for all the money was sent to them. My daughter has recently been reading my college letters home (Mother had saved them all), and she says their constant refrain was "Please send money."

By the end of my sophomore year, I was engaged to Bob Gibbs, my lab partner in comparative anatomy. Bob was tall and handsome, very intelligent, and as avid a birdwatcher as I was, an ideal husband for me in every way, or so it seemed. We married at the end of my junior year, and Bob started his Ph D studies in ichthyology the next fall. Money was short, so I, like many of my friends, started on my Ph T, "putting hubby through." In the summers, I taught birds and insects at the Children's School of Science at Woods Hole. After I finished my senior year, I decided to do a master's degree in zoology with a minor in education, so that when I finished, I could support Bob by teaching high school.

They were busy, hectic, happy years. I had discovered to my surprise that the dullest-looking zoology course, histology, the study of tissues and cells, was the most fascinating of all my courses. So, for my master's degree, I looked at the development throughout the secretory cycle of a small gland in the sea lamprey, the buccal gland, which secretes an anticoagulant that allows the lamprey to feed on the blood of other fishes. My studies were fascinating, involving everything from wading in the streams and picking up breeding lampreys by hand to studying the secretory cells of the buccal gland under the light microscope. The six education courses I had to take were dreadful, but the six weeks of practice teaching in Ithaca High were wonderful. But when I graduated with a master's degree two years later, newly qualified to teach in New York state, there were no teaching jobs available within a sixty-mile radius of Ithaca, so I settled for a technician's job in the zoology department staining a dog's brain.

I had now been married for three years, and I confess it was as much pressure from my mother and my relatives as my own desires which made me decide that now was the time to have a baby. Had it not been the next step in my mother's agenda for me, I might not have decided to become pregnant. For that I am eternally grateful to her, for my daughter, Elizabeth Dorothea Gibbs, born July 4, 1955, has been the greatest joy of my life.

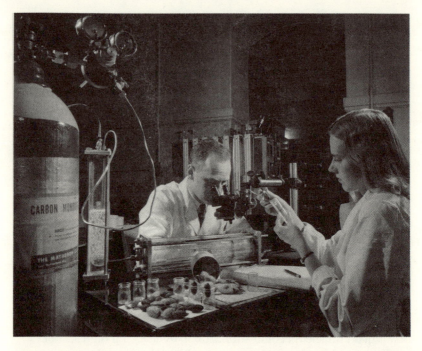

In the lab at Cornell

Six weeks later, Bob had finished his PhD, and the three of us headed off for Plattsburgh, New York, where he had an assistant professorship at what was then Plattsburgh State Teachers' College. The less said about our year there the better; the college had deplorable standards, the town was dreary, and I was stuck at home all day with a new baby. To keep my sanity, I took calculus and analytical geometry three hours a week at the college. By Christmas, Bob had landed a temporary job at Woods Hole Oceanographic Institution, which he accepted with alacrity, and we settled in Woods Hole in June. I promptly went looking for a technician's job and within two days had found one with Ralph Lewin, an eminent phycologist working at the Marine Biological Laboratory.

This job was the turning point of my life. Ralph had hired me on the spot as soon as I walked into his office simply because I was pretty, but he soon discovered I was also intelligent, and he treated me as one would a graduate student. Monday afternoons I had to transfer cultures, and Fridays I had to wash dishes, but Tuesdays through Thursdays I was free to pursue any research project I chose. Electron microscopes were just becoming commercially available, and MBL had one run by an excellent microscopist, Del Philpott. I was fascinated by the wealth of new discoveries being made about cell structure with this new instrument, so I chose a problem which would require working with the electron microscope. I chose to study the flagella of paralysed mutants of the alga *Chlamydomonas*. Every night I could, I was back at the lab in the library reading the new EM literature. Many a Saturday morning, Ralph would telephone me.

"Hello, Sally, this is your technician. I am going into the lab today. Can I do anything for your experiments while I'm there?"

My own agenda was rapidly taking shape. Thanks to Ralph, I was essentially doing independent research at the forefront of biology, and I loved it. My teenage dreams of writing books with my husband had lost their luster. I had written several papers with Bob and had proofread another fourteen for him. But now my marriage was coming apart. It had never been a real marriage (I was still a virgin a year and a half after the wedding), but my friendless year in Plattsburgh had shown me how unhappy I really was. I also realized I was as smart as my husband, possibly even smarter, and that it was much more fun to do my own research and write my own papers than proofread his. Divorce was such a shameful thing then that I did not dare even think of it, but after working two years with Ralph and writing my first paper with him, I secretly decided to apply to Harvard to do a PhD, even though it would involve a long commute. Luckily, out of the blue, Bob was offered an assistant professorship at Boston University, which he took up in January of 1958, the same month I entered Harvard's biology department as a graduate student.

I started my graduate studies under the direction of a very distinguished plant physiologist, Professor K.V. Thimann. I was told, as were most other Harvard students, that my Cornell courses were worthless, and I would have to start again and take at least ten courses at Harvard. My professors were correct about this; Cornell then was an old-fashioned school with emphasis on anatomy and taxonomy, and by the time I graduated in 1952, the revolution in biology had not yet reached Cornell. On the other hand, Harvard was definitely the leading U.S. school in cell and molecular biology in 1958, and my many courses there gave me an excellent foundation in the subject without which I would not have been able to do first-rate research. Professor Thimann set me on a problem to determine if the plant hormone auxin had an effect on the growth of the alga *Acetabularia*. I took a full course load and started to grow *Acetabularia*. I was dismayed at how slowly it grew, and that summer I spoke to some German *Acetabularia* experts at Woods Hole who convinced me that growth in *Acetabularia* was too variable to ever see an auxin effect, even if there were one. When Professor Thimann returned in September from a term in India,

he called me in for a research conference. I told him of my discouragement with *Acetabularia*'s slow growth.

"I could have a baby between each experiment."

I asked if instead I could do electron microscopy and look at the ul-
trastructure of the chloroplasts of algae. He asked me, "Where do you
want to be in ten years?"

"Just where you are, Professor Thimann."

He was appalled by my flippancy and my absurd aspiration to be a
professor at Harvard. That night, I went home and wrote him a detailed
research proposal, asking for his permission to work on *my* problem for
six months. If I made no progress, I would return to the *Acetabularia*
problem. By noon, there was a brief note in my mailbox kicking me
out. "This decision," he said, "arises not just from the nature of the research problem, but from the realization that our attitudes towards
graduate studies have nothing in common."

I promptly walked down the corridor to the office of George Chapman, the young electron microscopist whose course in EM techniques
I had taken in the spring, and said, "George, can I be your graduate
student? Dr Thimann has kicked me out."

"It's high time, Sally, you saw the light. Wait a minute, I'll have to call
Dr Thimann." And, after the phone call: "He says you are in a hurry to
be through." And with that, I became George's graduate student.

George Chapman had been the only doctoral student of James Hillier, the man who succeeded in building an electron microscope at the
University of Toronto in the late thirties. I was one of the first of
George Chapman's many students, and I liked to think that I had
come full circle when I came to Canada in 1965 to become the electron
microscopist in McGill's new Stewart Biology Building.

In the late fifties, electron microscopy was a very difficult technique. George had many students who worked for other professors,
but who came to him to learn electron microscopy. Without him, none
of us would have succeeded. He and Hillier had built the ultramicro-
tome we all used to cut thin sections, and he made all the scope's mi-
nuscule apertures by hand. He taught each of us how to align the
microscope and how to correct astigmatism, a day's work in those
days, but much of the time only George was able to get the scope
working well. I was different from the other students, in that I was
working on my own problem, neither George's nor one supervised
by another professor, although I often went back to Ralph Lewin at
Woods Hole for advice. When I finished, I had six ground-breaking
papers, which I wrote under my name alone. I know now that I
should have put George's name on at least some of them, in gratitude
for all the hours of help he gave me. I still feel guilty that I didn't.

When I was a graduate student at Harvard, virtually no one took a female student seriously. Top-notch research universities did not hire women then, so none of my professors expected me to go on and have an independent career in research. Instead, they offered me all sorts of other jobs. Don Griffin suggested I give up my degree and work instead preparing the new biology curriculum for u.s. high schools. I declined. Then George Wald called me in. He had just won a big National Science Foundation (NSF) grant to devise a modern freshman biology course. He said he had just hired the "four brightest young men in the country" (as assistant professors) to prepare and teach the course. He asked me if I would write the lab manual for them.

I said, "But Professor Wald, I want to finish my PhD." He couldn't understand why.

Somehow, once I started doing my own research under the tutelage of Ralph Lewin, I knew instinctively that the only thing that mattered was this research and what I discovered. Stubbornly, I refused to be sidetracked, or do any of the other jobs men offered me along the way. Looking back, I think it was because I had had to fight so hard with my mother to have any independent life of my own that I just kept on fighting. It means I have never been a cooperative team player. But it is "how I've done it."

Of course, in those early days, I worked all the time and never took holidays. I seldom saw my husband. He went back to his office every evening and contrived to arrive home only after he knew I would be safely asleep. Betsy went with me everywhere I went. I took her to nursery school in the mornings, picked her up at noon and took her to the apartment of the wife of a Harvard graduate student in physics who had a little girl exactly Betsy's age. Weekends, she came into the lab with me. She remembers how proud she was putting my prints through the big rotary drier. All the other students were dismayed that a five-year-old could easily do one of their most time-consuming jobs. I had a lot of friends at Harvard and, over the years, a few lovers, one in particular, who has remained a close friend to this day. But he made it clear to me, as did the others, that he certainly wouldn't want to marry me if I were free.

I got my PhD in November 1961, and immediately started a National Institutes of Health (NIH) postdoctoral fellowship with Bill Sistrom, a professor in the same building. That winter I was in terrible conflict. Bill insisted I start my experiments, but I knew it was absolutely essential I finish writing the remaining five papers on my thesis. These I did at night, but my personal life began to unravel. My father's kidney cancer reoccurred in April, and we knew he was dying. And I was plagued by a numb and very painful leg and foot. Eventually, I saw an orthopaedic surgeon, who put my leg in a cast. When that didn't help, he put me in Massachusetts General Hospital to do an exploratory operation on my foot.

The morning of the surgery (I was all prepped), he sent Dr Marian Ropes to see me. She was a world authority on rheumatoid arthritis and by chance a college classmate and friend of my mother's. Within minutes, Dr Ropes had found out the dismal state of my marriage and cancelled the surgery. She said I probably had rheumatoid arthritis (I didn't, but it may have been my first attack of multiple sclerosis), and she put me to bed for three months. Whenever I saw her, she said, "I don't want to hear about your foot, I want to hear about your marriage." She gave me the courage to tell Bob that I would not go to Europe with him that summer and that I wanted a divorce when he came back. At first Bob sent me begging letters to reconsider, then there was a long silence, and then a long letter arrived saying that he had met the most wonderful woman, that he had loved me but that there had never been anything at all like this in his life before, that he was bringing her back with him, and that now he wanted a divorce as quickly as possible. I was existing, but I was barely managing to go to work each day. Every evening, I left Betsy at my sister's and went to sit with my father (we had to keep Betsy away from my folks lest she tell them about the divorce). My father was in unbelievable pain, yet he lived on and on. The doctor told me how much morphine to give him to kill him, but I could not do it. He died at the end of October. I was shell-shocked. At the same time, Bob had gone off to Alabama to divorce me so he could marry the wonderful woman he had met in Germany. Dr Ropes sent me to a psychoanalyst at McLean's Hospital, but I did not like her and left after one visit. All I remember of that visit was her question, "Don't you think it strange that your mother still beats you?"

"Not at all," I said.

I should have entered psychoanalysis then, but I had no money, no job after my post-doc ran out, and no husband. I had never even lived on my own before. What I did was immediately get married again, and I found myself in a marriage only marginally better then my first one.

But my marriage to Ronald Poole did do two very important things for me. It gave me a second much-wanted child, and it took me away from Harvard and from Mother to the enchanting city of Edinburgh. I took my NIH postdoctoral fellowship with me to Edinburgh and continued my project in the medical school there. Then one day I saw an ad in *Nature* advertising four independent research positions in the new Epigenetics Research Group being started by Professor Waddington of Edinburgh's famous Institute of Animal Genetics. Not knowing that Waddington had already selected the four young men he wanted to hire, I hastily put in an application. A few weeks later, Professor Waddington called me in for an interview. One of the young men he hoped to hire would not be available for a few years, so he would like to offer me the job. But there was one small problem. The salary he was paying the three young men was that advertised in *Nature*, £1500 a year. However, he was afraid he could not offer me the same salary, for he had a senior woman in the department who had worked there for many years and she was making only £1000 a year. Thus, he could only offer me a £1000 a year.

I said, "That's fine with me, Professor Waddington, I'll take the job. I am hoping to become pregnant, and I'll take four months off when I do."

I got the job, and a year later, on April 13, 1964, my son, Christopher Harold Poole, was born. Wad wrote me a delightful note sending me his warmest congratulations.

My husband's lectureship in the biophysics department at the University of Edinburgh was only a temporary one, to last until a new chairman for the department was found, so by the summer of 1964 Ron and I were job hunting. In the end, Ron got two job offers, one from the Department of Botany at McGill and one from the botany department at the University of Toronto. At Toronto, there was a promise of a job for me in a year or two at the new campus being built at Scarborough. At McGill, there was a similar promise of a job for me in a year as an electron microscopist, for the new Stewart Biology Building had been built with a spacious suite in the basement for an electron microscope. Ron was interviewed at the Botanical Congress in Edinburgh by Charles Wilson, chairman of botany at McGill, and Gordon Maclachlan. We were both interviewed by the chairman of botany of the University of Toronto. Ron immediately liked Charles Wilson and Gordon Maclachlan, and we both took an instant dislike to the chairman of botany at Toronto. So that decided it. We agreed to come to McGill. Besides, Montreal was virtually next door to my beloved New England. I was coming home.

When I arrived at McGill, Charles Wilson had managed to find me a half-time salary, $3000, out of technician funds. Since all three biology departments, botany, genetics, and zoology, wanted the new electron microscopist and the lovely suite of rooms to be in their department, I was appointed a part-time technician in all three departments. However, I was called an assistant professor and given all the privileges of an assistant professor, and was promised that a tenure slot would be created for me by the next September. It was. Charles had said I would appreciate working only half-time my first year, so I could get my house settled and my curtains hung. But, of course, I got promptly to work on my research (Skip Sheldon in the pathology department kindly let me use his electron microscope). I also hastily wrote several grant proposals, and the following April, I received the largest equipment grant the National Research Council had yet awarded, the magnificent sum of $60,000, sufficient to buy the best electron microscope and all the accessory equipment needed to equip the EM unit. The fact that I, before I even had a real appointment, received this astonishing grant was due entirely, I'm sure, to the behind-the-scenes efforts of the dean of medicine. In the funds for the Stewart Biology Building, there had originally been money for an electron microscope, which had been diverted to the dean of medicine's budget. He subsequently promised to repay it, if I should fail to get a grant for a new electron microscope.

So when I was appointed an assistant professor on tenure track by McGill's Board of Governors in September of 1966, I was already busily ordering and installing equipment; I had hired a young man as a technician, and had a bright young woman about to start her PhD with me. It would be another ten years before my house was furnished and the curtains hung.

The stories of women's lives usually end at marriage, and they are assumed to live happily ever after. In this story of one woman's life in science, the story ends here. I had finally, at thirty-six years old, been appointed an assistant professor on tenure track at a major research university. The rest would follow automatically, given perseverance, hard work, and a normal amount of luck: grants, graduate students, discoveries, promotions, prizes, the presidency of the Canadian Society for Cell Biology, a term on the Cell Biology and Genetics Grant Panel of the Natural Sciences and Engineering Research Council (NSERC), and two years ago, election to the Royal Society of Canada.

My years at McGill have been good ones. I love the city and the university and the wonderful mix of talented, interesting, and caring people who make up the university. It has been good for me to be in Canada, where grants may not be lavish but are quite sufficient to have a student or two and a postdoctoral fellow. And as long as one produces one or two good papers a year, one never has to worry about losing one's grant, for NSERC, unlike any other granting agency I know, funds people, not projects.

A more important question is how much of life I have missed out on by devoting all of my energies to science. I missed out on a good marriage (I've been on my own since 1976), and I deeply regret this, but given my parents and their marriage, it was probably not to be. Also, I regret that I did not have time to be with my son in his early years. Unfortunately, by the time he was born, I was so immersed in my research career that it was not possible to take three or four years off to give him a better start in life. I hired full-time baby sitters who came to my house every day. But even in the evenings when I was home, I can remember being stretched out in my green chair immersed in thought, and Chris would be pounding on my arm, "Mommy, mommy, you are not listening." I have also missed many things that made up my mother's life and that I once assumed would be part of mine: volunteer work, college reunions, neighbourhood friends, long lazy summers at the beach, and giving lots and lots of parties. But my life has been rich in innumerable ways my mother's wasn't, so I have no complaints.

And I have been lucky. Had my multiple sclerosis developed in my thirties, as it does in so many young women, I probably would have had to put most of my agenda on hold. Although I started having unexplained falls and bladder problems from my mid-forties on, it has only been in the last five or six years that my life has become significantly limited by MS. An hour's grocery shopping now puts me to bed for an afternoon, and walking even two or three blocks is painful and difficult. So now I am busy planning a new agenda for the day in the future when I am in a wheelchair. I will sit at my computer and write short stories and send long e-mail letters to my friends. My daughter is already teaching me how to knit. "Mom, can't there be *anything* I am good at that you don't know how to do?" And I've already been initiated as a fledgling author. My first short story was promptly rejected by the CBC Literary Competition.

Letters to an Editor

Sept.'92

Dear Margaret,

I have set aside a beautiful autumn morning to write to you. I am writing from my bedroom which overlooks Lac Tremblant. The view is spectacular. View is important to me, particularly from my bedroom. I can remember quite vividly the view from my childhood bedroom, which looked down on the St Mary's River from what in a little girl's perspective seemed like a very great height. My parents were separated when I was five. But I still had my view. It is hard to believe that a single divorced mother of two little girls could provide such a happy growing up – but that's exactly what my mother did. I think the Bush administration would have difficulty thinking we were a "real" family. Certainly we did not resemble the Waltons.

Security and love seemed to be the driving forces behind my mother's parenting. Security was easily defined. We stayed on the same street, had the same friends, went to the same school, and the bills were paid. All this was done on a social worker's salary. Love was best characterized by her expression "my two beautiful daughters." This was true of my sister, who was pretty enough to be in a toothpaste ad. However, I was short and stocky and sported a female version of the brushcut. In fact, I had a beautiful disposition, so her comment wasn't entirely false.

There's no question I've moved on from those early days in Sault Ste Marie. I'm now a smart dresser, ambitious, well travelled, and living life in the fast track. The view from my bedroom is even more important now. I use the view, particularly in the early morning or evening, to remind myself of those happy childhood years. Love is a powerful force. I consider myself very lucky.

Sharon at the window

There is an evolutionary aspect to my life. This might seem obvious, having gone from a brush cut to a smart dresser. But there is more to this evolution than physical dress. My thinking changed. In the beginning it was enough to be happy or to bring happiness to others. I consider this my home-bound phase. I was having and raising children. I did this so well I ended up with five small daughters in the short space of seven years. I made the fast-track reproduction cycle somewhat more interesting by having these babies in several different cities or countries. My first order of business in each new home was to find a paediatrician and obstetrician. The order of the search depended on whether I was nursing or having a baby. This phase was also a time of helping my husband in his career. I especially enjoyed entertaining because it put me in touch with such interesting people – intelligent people. By now it was obvious that my life would be attached to a university – not as it had been as a student, smoking cigarettes, playing bridge, and generally getting low grades, but as the wife of a dean or a principal. These were happy years, but something was missing.

With the birth of my fifth daughter, now known as Sam, I found myself exhausted and physically debilitated. Three Caesarean sections in the space of three years in two different countries left me feeling unable to cope with my life. This was a difficult time in my marriage because my husband, David, was preoccupied with his career and I was preoccupied with myself. These were heady years for a man of his talents. He was the youngest appointed dean of a law school and seemed to be destined to be the youngest in whatever he did. His life was expanding and mine was becoming increasingly narrow. It was at this time that I learned something about physical fitness. A small story will illustrate. I had a small chest pain, probably associated with anxiety, and an elderly but wonderfully warm cardiologist recommended that I rest for six weeks and then come back for testing. The cardiologist, upon testing me, found that I was quite fit for my age – middle thirties. He asked what I did. I recounted entertaining for my husband three times a week, raising five small children, and completing a B Sc at the University of Western Ontario. He gave me one of the most salient bits of advice I can remember. He recalled that a professional athlete never goes into his season untrained and that I must think of myself as a professional athlete training for my season.

I never looked back. I started a systematic routine of exercise, which culminated in such fitness that I used to run seven and a half miles each day. I started to look at life from my bedroom window again. Indeed, I became the neighbourhood Pied Piper, gathering up mothers in the neighbourhood who felt similarly overwhelmed by their responsibilities and taking them running in the nearby park. This was the beginning of getting control of our lives – feeling fit and ready for anything. My home-bound phase was thus terminated as I started my selfish phase, which centred around my need to feel physically well and intelligent. I would like to think that I was no less fit or intelligent than other women of my age and circumstances. However, going back to do a B Sc and training my body took time – time away from the family. My selfish phase resulted in a very high degree of selflessness on the part of my family.

Sharon

Oct. '92

Dear Margaret,

Almost three weeks have passed since I first wrote to you. It is early morning and I am watching the mist rise off Lac Tremblant amidst all the splendour of autumn colours. My last letter ended with a rather lofty image of a selfless family. To get mother back to school in a serious way required some accommodation. My husband was in charge of the laundry – something he did with a fair degree of expertise.

David had supported himself at university, in part, by maintaining the coin-operated student laundry machines. (Not every woman has the privilege of a Harvard/Cambridge educated laundry service.) My two older daughters, Debbie (now a McGill law student) and Alex (now studying in China), learned to organize birthdays, Easter egg hunts, and Christmas stockings for the "Littlies," as their younger sisters were affectionately named. Later, Debbie and Alex served as the not so "Littlies" disc jockey and/or bouncer. One of those "Littlies" is now an undersized hockey player at Harvard, following in her father's footsteps a quarter-century later. The "older sister" mothering did not hurt her very much. She is a truly happy person. I think the mutual affection my daughters have for each other today stems from the high degree of interaction they experienced in their early years. Certainly they helped me complete my B Sc degree. Although my daughters were and still are my friends, I have never relinquished my parental role – a role which naturally includes discipline. It is hard to discipline your children when you depend on them for support. The one good thing is that I never had favourites and they usually got punished as a group. I hope they think I was fair.

Family selflessness, which really meant "pitching in," was accompanied by the notion of incorporation. Incorporation meant assembling friends to help in the overall enterprise. As I moved from a B Sc to a M Sc to a Ph D it became clear that I needed more than the selflessness of a very busy husband and five active daughters. I needed both paid help and friends. Indeed, it was often difficult to distinguish between the two. One cleaning woman became a godmother, which is a position of very high esteem in our family. Friends, I'm sure, often thought they were hired help. One consequence of doing too much is that I was often sick with bronchitis. My friends were always willing to pitch in while I lay coughing away in a steamed room.

Incorporation did, however, have its humorous side. When the McGill search committee for a new principal decided it would visit the Johnston family in their home in London, Ontario, our household was in an unusual state of turmoil. I was in the midst of exams, my help had quit, the children were fighting, the dog was misbehaving, and there was no food in the house. We were not talking about one or two visitors but a whole (or almost whole) committee. The theory of incorporation was to be put to the test. Neighbours took charge of the dog, the children, and the wine to be served at lunch. Two best friends, sporting maids' uniforms, flew in from Toronto to prepare a gourmet luncheon. The first sign of imperfection came when I offered Archie Malloch a glass of wine and then proceeded to drink it myself. The real dénouement came, however, when my "kitchen help," who had

Sharon, David, and the girls

been liberally sampling the rather good wine in the kitchen, came out in tennis outfits to serve the last course. It was quite clear in that moment that McGill had to take a leap of faith and take us for what we really were – a family blessed with friendship who could never take themselves too seriously. The committee still asks me about my friends – the maids. Just last week I celebrated one of their fiftieth birthdays. I did not come out in a tennis outfit to serve dessert.

Sharon

Jan. '93

Dear Margaret,

I tried to write to you from Alexandria, Egypt, but the hectic pace of the Egyptians was not as conducive to writing as the peaceful scenery of Lac Tremblant. I did manage to watch our entire referendum on the international French network. If Egyptians thought Western women were strange, they were confirmed in this view by the frequency of "middle of the night" room orders made in the course of this eventful evening. I had predicted a strong NO for both Quebec and the majority of other Canadians. I am unabashedly a supporter of the vision of one Canada that was part of the Trudeau era. At forty-nine years, I am fairly typical of that era of Canadian nationalism, called Trudeaumania, for the more exuberant of our crowd. We enrolled our children in French schools, took French courses ourselves, engaged tutors so our children could keep up in class, and so on. The wonderful thing is that the response to official bilingualism was largely positive and voluntary. A reflection of this effort can be seen in the basic choices our daughters have made with respect to education.

They attended French schools, including Collège Jean de Brébeuf, where they had the distinction of not being bad at hockey if not so good in French. Brébeuf is a very tough school indeed. French Quebec had a much greater influence than just motivating them to learn the language. From a social point of view, their friends were largely francophone. From an intellectual point of view, they became stimulated by the power of language learning. The two eldest obtained scholarships to study Mandarin in China, having spent two summers there, including the summer of the youthful tragedy of Tiananmen Square. The three eldest sisters spent a part of last summer in Czechoslovakia learning about the changes in Eastern Europe with democracy. The two youngest spent two weeks with a young family in Paris, using their French to explore the museums and probably some less mentionable spots of Paris. All this was done around the schedule of summer jobs so they could earn the money to take these trips. Two of the sisters spent the better part of the summer learning Spanish. I tell you these things, Margaret, not to boast about our daughters, but to say how much Quebec has been a wellspring of learning for our entire family. It is no wonder that Pierre Trudeau had a vision of one Canada in which Quebec had the respect and sense of partnership it richly deserved.

I can sum up my own short life in Quebec in a single sentence. This is where I feel at home. I am like a duck in water with the two cultures, having grown up in the Soo where if you didn't marry an anglophone you would most likely marry an Italian. In his book A *Nice*

Place to Come From, Morley Torgov explains that there was no anti-Semitism in the Soo because people were too busy being prejudiced towards the Italians. While there was some truth in this post–World War II humour, prejudice was kept very much in check by the fact that the Italians were great athletes and a good part of the professional class. Whether you were looking for a teammate or a lawyer, or both, you could not exclude one third of the population. The Soo was a great leveller and so is Quebec.

Quebec has meant more to me than just a cultural experience. I have developed my interest both as the wife of McGill's principal and as a student at McGill. The really nifty thing about being "Mrs Principal" is that I am called upon to entertain. That this is not onerous and indeed comes very naturally to me can best be illustrated by an historical anecdote. Once my mother returned from boarding school to Lethbridge, Alberta, for holidays, when her mother was giving a party. Upon waking and looking under her bed, she found a rather elderly gentleman. Being a trusting young girl, she inquired, with a minimum of alarm, as to his purpose. He responded with a quick and urgent "Shhh, I'm hiding, can't you see?" As nearly as my mother can remember, the year was 1928, the game, Run Sheep Run, and the hiding gentleman, Chief Justice Tweedie of the Supreme Court of Alberta. My grandmother had, and indeed continues to have long after her death, a remarkable influence on my life, although I have not yet played Run Sheep Run at our parties!

Being a student is much tougher than being a university principal's wife. To get from my bridge-playing youth to publishing scientific manuscripts has been a very long climb. Perhaps this is where I should say "Thank you" to my family.

Sharon

Feb.'93

Dear Margaret,

It is unusual to have only daughters and five of them. We often argue heatedly which kind of feminism is best. Like my daughters', my views on women are quite passionate. Perhaps you will understand the genesis of this passion if I explain a little more about my mother's activities. I remember those dark mornings when my mother left our house with two provincial policemen escorting her through the snow banks and blistering cold. I didn't miss much from that window with a view. It took some convincing that she wasn't being hauled off to jail. I often accompanied my mother, who was a welfare officer, on her rounds – particularly when she went to the reservations. I learned at an early age from these "home visits" what misery men and women can inflict on each other and their children. These social ills are no longer being hidden but are being publicly addressed. I believe my mother was a precursor to this movement.

My grandmother, who lived nearby, was a great support to my mother. She had experienced similar challenges. World War I saw the death of my grandfather, a talented engineer, gassed in the trenches, and of his tiny son, from influenza. My grandmother found herself penniless. But with all debts paid, she set sail for Canada from her beloved England. She began her new life in Lethbridge, Alberta, with one small daughter, a good education for her time, a limited set of finances, and helpful connections. She had been offered the position of director of nurses and later superintendent of the Galt Hospital, Lethbridge. I'm sure, when the hospital board hired this young matron, they didn't know that Run Sheep Run would be part of the hospital policy! Only after my grandmother had long since died did I learn from her best friend how courageous had been her decision to turn her back on her sorrow and start a new life in Canada.

Turning the negative into the positive has always been an objective of my family. So my mother set out to do just that. Being a single parent herself, she was determined not to have this happen to her daughters. By the time I was thirteen I knew I had to marry David Johnston – boy wonder of Sault Ste Marie. The fact that he was a bit of a stuffed shirt and slow to kiss the girls seemed to be an asset. Not, of course, if one considers stored passion a source of kinetic energy. In retrospect I would say, never trust a slow kisser. The saving grace to my husband's passion was his idealism – this helped to balance things out. Our generation preceded the sixties and passion had to be kept in check. One way to do this was to write about your feelings. A letter written by David while he was studying at Cambridge will show the depth of his passion and feeling for the young woman that he wished to marry. What is most special about this letter is the idealism. But the generational differences are quite clear, for manhood in our day was associated with values and womanhood was associated with love. I believe we are now coming closer to the view that women impart both values and love to their children.

Two of my favourite songs at this time were "A Hundred and One Pounds of Fun" and "I'm Gonna Wash That Man Right Out of My Hair" from Rodgers and Hammerstein's *South Pacific*. There was an innocence to our generation that protected us from some of the more hurtful ills of sexism or chauvinism. Many of these protections were removed with the freedom of the sixties and early seventies. Sexual behaviour was much more restrained in our day and the consequences of a lack of constraint occurred less often. I have a tolerance

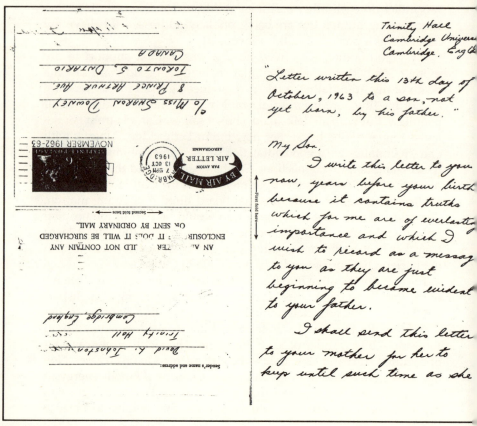

David's letter

Trinity Hall
Cambridge University
Cambridge, England

"Letter written this 13th day of
October, 1963 to a son, not
yet born, by his father."

My Son,

I write this letter to you
now, years before your birth
because it contains truths
which for me are of everlasting
importance and which I
wish to record as a message
to you as they are just
beginning to become evident
to your father.

I shall send this letter
to your mother for her to
keep until such time as she

to determine or to measure this ability to love. It depends on a realization that this person to whom you have given your love is the object of a complete giving of yourself, that with her you share everything that is yours, and in this sharing of your innermost feelings and aspirations, they became most meaningful and one.

My son, your father will attempt to teach you to acquire the tools of manhood — of honesty, of clean living, of integrity in your every act and thought, although his own struggle for these is an insufficient one. But even more important than these is the ability to love in complete trust. This is for your mother to teach you. I know she will. For this she has taught your father.

wishes to give it to you. I hope that she delivers to you its message early in life, for to me, the ability to love of which I speak, is as important as life itself.

It is this quality, the quality of love, which above all others I hope you shall have and learn to use as your mother does in her every moment of life. For it is this, above anything else, that will make you a man, enhance you as a child of God, and enable you, through giving of yourself to another completely, to receive that complete love of the other and know it in the fullest trust.

There are no real tests

which is not shared by my daughters for a certain level of sexism. However, I have limits, and when they are surpassed, I stand up to be counted.

Sharon

August, 1993

Dear Margaret:

It will not surprise you that I am writing my last letter from the north end of Lac Tremblant. A cold, wet, windy day has induced me to write. I think you and Kate Williams are right in suggesting that my story is not complete without some mention of how I balance my PhD with the many things I am expected to do as the principal's wife. Perhaps the best indication that it is not always easy is that I consider it a minor miracle that my first scientific article towards my PhD will be published in the *Journal of Applied Physiology* this month. The fact that I am now analysing data on a computer hooked up to a generator in order to spend time with David during his holidays is simple testimony to the balancing act I must achieve.

I have found, with only a few exceptions, the community of McGill to be highly supportive of my own personal agenda, which includes both family and professional elements. There were many ways I attempted to harmonize what might otherwise have been conflicting demands on my time. For example, in order to balance the time I wished to spend with my children, particularly when we first came to McGill, I often brought them to McGill functions. I also entertained in our home so that our daughters could be part of the fun. Just as my friends enjoyed being maids for the search committee, so did our children enjoy the many McGill functions we held in our home. Universities are filled with interesting people and it didn't take our daughters long to apprise themselves of this fact!

It has not been easy to do my PhD. But if there have been difficult people and awkward obstacles, there have also been helpful people and kind facilitators. I think the helpful people know who they are. I have made some of the most meaningful friendships in the course of my graduate work. Being a graduate student at McGill has permitted me to understand some aspects of McGill that would otherwise have remained incomprehensible, particularly in the area of research funding.

Recently, I spoke to Gretta Chambers about the role of the spouse of a university principal. If I have personally contributed something to McGill, it is to maintain a warm and stable base from which David could face the many pressures inherent in his job. I have personally not found "homemaking" demeaning or uncreative. I have also made sure that I was not the only worker in the house. I consider myself a bright, successful person. But even bright, successful people have homes to care for and people to love. If there is one overriding principle which has guided the pursuit of my own intellectual or professional plans it is to make sure that in doing so I didn't sacrifice my own personal agenda. If I can finish my PhD then I will have achieved the balance.

Margaret, I have not looked out my many windows all these years without developing a view of just how important family life is to society. We need to invest in this. Not by keeping women down but by enhancing their opportunities to work, run homes, and contribute to the community. I hope my daughters take their family values with them into their own independent lives. But more than that, I hope they do not have to compromise these values because the community in which they aspire to make their mark is ill equipped to enhance their opportunities. My daughters are three generations away from their professionally trained great-grandmother, who I think, would be deeply proud of the women who have followed her.

Sharon

An Exuberant Rebuke to History*

I have written several drafts of this speech. A parade of incredible acts of generosity by many people marched through my head, moving me, despite deep happiness, beyond laughter and, in some earlier drafts, beyond words. A remarkable minister of justice, determined to make women judges a three-digit and growing reality, donating me the historic privilege of being one hundredth in the accelerating series; a gracious chief justice whose professionalism and brilliance have been such an inspiration, welcoming me into his warmly collegial court; an attorney-general who endorsed and encouraged Ontario's Law Reform Commission in general and law reform in particular; outstanding law reform commissioners who similarly endorsed and encouraged their chair; a Labour Board and Family Court whose members offered patient support; lawyers and particularly their treasurer, whose patience and credulity I may have tested; organizations like the Women's Law Association who believed in our credibility; and law students who made it all feel worthwhile.

I have had the friendships of people I love, so many of whom are here today – some even from my other homes in Ottawa and Montreal – people who transform millstones into milestones, and milestones into magic. These friends are people who take their work and their friendships very seriously, but not themselves. They are very wise.

Most important, I have been nourished by my family. In 1976, a courageous Roy McMurtry, then attorney-general, in what was to be the first of his several acts of professional chutzpah on my behalf, appointed a twenty-nine-year-old, seven-months pregnant woman to the Ontario Family Court Bench. The child she was pregnant with,

---

* This essay is the text of Madame Justice Abella's speech of May 13, 1992 when she was sworn into the Ontario Court of Appeal as Canada's hundredth woman judge.

Madame Justice Rosalie Abella (1992)

Zachary, is now fifteen, claims to remember nothing of the event, and remains unimpressed even when reminded. His older brother, Jacob, who was three at the time and is now eighteen, does remember and wishes he didn't, because what he remembers is how he broke the quiet solemnity of Chief Judge Andrew's speech with his loud response to his father's whispered bribe to keep him from crying. No parent in the room had to be told what Irving's bribe was when a three-year-old J.J. demanded, "What *kind* of a toy?" And now here sit these two wonderful young men, no longer believing as they once did that only girls grow up to be judges, and no longer bribable with toys, but still the greatest source of joy in their mother's life. I cannot think of or imagine anything that could give me as much pride and happiness as the honour I have felt to be able to say that they are my sons.

As for my collaborator, the kids' *other* mother, the one with the beard, this is his appointment too. In the twenty years since I was called to the bar and have played in the fields of the law, Itch always made it so easy. There wasn't a struggle he didn't know about and help assuage; a job change – and there were a few – he didn't encourage and help facilitate; or a happy moment he didn't seem to revel in. He always urged principle over expedience, patience over despair, flair over fear, and vision overall. He never tried to slow me down because he never made me feel I was going too fast. Above all, he desperately loved his sons and spent the time to prove it.

As you can tell, this is a decidedly personal speech. It is not about the justice system or profession, or human rights, or feminism, or public policy, or national identity, or any of the other public issues I care about. But in its own inexplicable way, the rest of this very personal speech is implicitly about all of those public things.

I was raised with a strong sense of history, took history at university, and married a historian. I believe history is a tutor, and I feel like its awestruck student. Of all the things history has taught me, nothing is more instructive than that nothing and no one is inevitable. I have taken many risks in my life and profession, but the one risk I have never taken is smugness. I believe in opportunities, not entitlements. I presume nothing and take no one for granted.

So when the Honourable Kim Campbell called and said that mine marked the hundredth of many hundreds more future appointments of women in Canada's federal judiciary, I was overcome, I was noisy, I was grateful, and I cried.

There are even more coincidental anniversaries. The month I was appointed marked twenty years to the month since I was called to the Bar, a generation of indescribably intellectual feasts in the legal profession. The country that embraced my family and me in 1950 as Jewish refugees turns 125 on my birthday, July 1, Canada Day. My mother, whose life is the most humbling example a daughter could have, turned seventy-five a couple of weeks ago. What makes these converging anniversaries so emotional for me on a day like today is how law, Canada, and my mother have been my guiding script, stage, and producer.

My choice of law, as many of you know, was made in innocence in very early childhood, an unabashed imitation of my father, who was a lawyer. I had no idea what it meant to be a lawyer, but since he had been one, I wanted to be one too.

This was an aspiration that my parents encouraged without reservation. It never occurred to either of them that I could not – or should not – one day, with hard work, become a lawyer. The journey through childhood en route to a chosen profession felt seamless and joyful.

What is remarkable to me, as I look back with history's eyes, is how I was made to feel such unrestricted enthusiasm in the possibility that the future was within grasp by parents who, from their own experience, knew otherwise. The father who was a lawyer never practised in Canada because, when we all came to Canada in 1950 from Germany, you had to be a citizen to practise law. The mother who wove safety nets for her family found the factories her family owned in Poland nationalized after the war. The parents who so unhesitatingly encouraged the hope that everything was possible spent four years in a concentration camp, lost their two-and-a-half-year-old son and most of the rest of their families, moved to Germany after the war to reconstruct the future they told me was possible, produced me and my younger sister Toni in Stuttgart, and never once let us forget how lucky we were. These people, who had lost everything and practically everyone, never lost hope.

This is the resource they brought to Canada and invested here. I am the product of that investment. From their shared history I have learned the importance of tolerance, of open-mindedness, of optimism, of civility, of commitment, of integrity, and of justice. And from their shared history I have learned to fear only indifference and irrelevance. I have felt ready to earn friends and detractors and to be proud of both.

None of this I understood as I was growing up. Only how happy I was. I kissed a lot – not only because in our house it was like breathing, but because I felt like it. People were wonderful and we were never told there was anything wrong in showing it.

Now I look back and see that my whole life was constructed in an environment designed as an exuberant rebuke to history, where being true to who you were was the operative principle, no matter what anyone else thought or was doing. There is no such thing as a planned, traditional career for an immigrant like me who is the child of Holocaust survivors. Ambition for me is a competition with time, not people, and an urgent attempt to vindicate the heroic lives of two parents and the pain they never showed.

The lawyer father I tried to imitate died two months before I graduated from law school. But the wise, brave, selfless, and lovingly indomitable tower of strength he married two days after Hitler invaded Poland is sitting in this courtroom, seventy-five years old, thinking no doubt with awe about her history and how it brought her to this moment in Canada, as she watches her daughter sworn in as the one hundredth woman on the federal bench. Thinking no doubt about who is not here, and thinking, I hope, that her love and their history have been vindicated. Fanny, this is for you.

Making Music

It was the year 1912 and a special one for my parents, Beatrice and Cesare Balestreri, who were Italians living in Como on Lake Como in the north of Italy. Our family name was translated to "Archer" in 1940 because those who heard our Italian name found it difficult to say. My father had apprenticed to become a chef and was gifted in that specialty. Colleagues of his who had migrated to Canada and settled in Montreal wrote that it was a good place to live and that there was an open field in their line of work. They encouraged him to come. My father, who enjoyed travel and seeing new places, talked the matter over with my mother and they decided to go to Montreal. Montreal was in a new country with a climate very different from the one they knew. But there was a better future in the New World. My father found work, and they decided to remain in Canada.

When they had left Como, they had left my two brothers, aged four and five, with my mother's parents because it would be easier to explore new territory without small children. Then on April 24th, 1913, I was born. This delayed the plan to fetch my brothers to Montreal. In July 1914, my father arranged for my mother and me to go to Como and return to Montreal with my brothers, who were then six and seven years old. However, in August of that year, World War 1 began, blocking all normal travel and making it impossible for my mother, my brothers, and me to leave Italy. We remained in Como until the end of the war. It was a time of anguish for my mother and father because his monthly financial support during those difficult years was often greatly delayed. In July 1919, when I was six years old, we were finally able to travel on a warship to New York from Genoa, Italy. Then from New York, we went by train to Montreal. The autumn of 1919 I began going to school, where I started to learn to read, write, and speak English; I had only spoken Italian until then. I do not recall

Violet Archer early in her career (1945)

having difficulty with English, or with French. In fact, at the age of seven, I was fluent in Italian, English, and French, and could speak, read, and write in those languages.

My mother said that when, as an infant, I heard the sound of a piano, I seemed to become spellbound, but the sound of a violin made me weep. At the age of six I so much wanted a piano that I would go to the home of one of my classmates because she had a piano and was taking piano lessons. I would beg her to play. The pieces she played made me feel ecstatic. They were simple pieces but to me they were terrific.

Then in January 1922, almost four months before my ninth birthday, a new piano arrived at our home. A miracle had occurred. My parents arranged for me to have lessons from a piano teacher who lived in our neighbourhood. Her name was Madame Cadieux-Abran. I recall going early to my piano lessons because the student who was there before me was advanced, compared to me: as she was learning *big* pieces, which, much later, I found out were Chopin Polonaises. It gave me a thrill to hear her perform.

I still have my first piano book. In fact, I have a library of piano music as well as a wide selection of music and books and music textbooks to which I continue to add, as well as my memorabilia. I still remember the pieces in my first piano book and how each new one was special. I know that, since then, to me, *making music was living*.

Less than a month after that ninth birthday, my sister Carolyn was born. The difference in age between us when she was growing up did not seem to matter. She was greatly interested in what I was doing in music.

During my time at the Montreal High School for Girls, I greatly enjoyed participating in stage productions produced by Miss Mabel Brittain, who taught elocution to students in elementary classes leading to high school. My participation was performing piano background music. Among the productions were *Snow White and the Seven Dwarfs* and *Peter Pan*. My next piano teacher, Madame Gagnon, introduced me to *solfège* and also music theory, as well as piano music of French composers along with J.S. Bach, Haydn, Mozart, and Beethoven. Mr James Speirs, the music master at the Montreal High School for Girls, gave me much encouragement and featured me as solo pianist on the program of the school's annual concerts. For me it was a matter of course that when I graduated from high school, I would become involved in music full time and earn my living as a professional musician.

When I graduated, I was seventeen and at that time the Great Depression had started in Canada. Thousands – no, millions – were out of work. My father was among them. The only way I could proceed with my innate drive to continue my music studies was to find myself a position so that I could pay for my courses and piano lessons at the McGill Conservatory of Music. With the assistance of Mr Speirs, I was able to obtain the position of accompanist at the studio of the outstanding singer and voice teacher Merlin Davies. This was a wonderful opportunity to learn the extensive vocal literature – art songs, oratorio, and operatic repertoire. It was a delight. Mr Davies had a full teaching load. Nevertheless, he arranged his schedule so that I could skip out to my classes at the Conservatory and come right back to my accompanying. It was less than fifteen minutes' walk back to his studio.

Since I could only take a few courses and my weekly piano lesson owing to lack of time, I completed the requirements for the teachers' licentiate in piano in 1934, then my bachelor of music in composition in 1936.

In the meantime, at the end of my second year with Mr Davies, I had so little time to study that I decided to turn to teaching piano and theory privately. I had already begun to build a class of piano and theory students, both children (even pre-schoolers) and adults. I found it easy to teach because I loved it, and it is a vocation which I still practise and enjoy. It is exciting to discover the potential in each student.

I began to improvise on the piano when I was sixteen, but I did not think much of the music that I made. However, two years later I became aware of orchestral music. The dean of music at McGill, Douglas Clarke, expected music students to attend both rehearsals and concerts of the Montreal Orchestra. He was its founder and conductor, and a splendid conductor he was. He was also a gifted pianist and organist and a fine musician. The sound of the orchestra mesmerized me. I immediately knew that I wanted to compose, and to compose for orchestra. In fact, in 1936, I composed my first orchestral piece – "Intermezzo." It was my graduation piece, a requirement for the bachelor of music degree at McGill University, as was a work for unaccompanied choir. I composed a Mass. The two works were to be submitted to the dean at the end of the third year of bachelor of music studies, accompanied by a sworn, written statement that the two works were composed without any assistance. These requirements were a challenge which I felt to be stimulating. I never missed a concert by the Montreal Orchestra, or any rehearsal, no matter if there were a winter blizzard. My dream was that the Montreal Orchestra would perform my music and, in fact, in February 1940, Douglas Clarke, after reading the score of my "Scherzo Sinfonico," expressed approval and stated that it would be performed during that month. I was in seventh heaven. That performance was my debut as a composer. I felt then, as now, that composing is necessary to my existence. It is an exciting and wonderful pursuit. It still is not easy for women to be considered equal to male composers. However, the degree of acceptance has greatly improved in recent times.

From 1936 to 1940, I had scholarships to study composition with Douglas Clarke. It was a great advantage which spurred me on. He would suggest some project such as an overture. I would then study scores of traditional and contemporary composers. The arrangement was that I should submit to him my completed score, which he perused and made comments on regarding good and not so good qualities. I waited with bated breath for his comments. One such project was my "Britannia – A Joyful Overture." It was accepted by Sir Adrian Boult and broadcast by the BBC to the armed forces during World War II. Subsequently it was performed on the Scottish BBC, conducted by Ian Whyte. It was given its Canadian première by the Toronto Symphony Orchestra, directed by Percy Grainger, in Toronto in the mid-1940s.

At this point, I began to play in the Montreal Women's Symphony Orchestra, whose conductor was Ethel Stark, a first-class musician and violinist and an inspiring leader. She was a Montrealer who had studied with a celebrated violinist and the great conductor, Fritz Reiner, in the United States. I was in the percussion section of the Montreal Women's Symphony Orchestra from 1940 to 1948. Being in that orchestra was a great learning experience in the "inside" of orchestral sound, and it also made me conscious of the importance of the dynamic value of percussion instruments in the orchestral fabric. I thought it was wonderful when Miss Stark twice chose to include my music on the program of orchestral concerts. The first of my pieces on the program of the orchestra's inaugural concert in the fall of 1940 was "Come Said the Muse" from my work "Leaves of Grass," for women's chorus and orchestra. The second, a couple of years later, was "Seadrift." The texts of these were by the American poet Walt Whitman.

In 1942 I was accepted as a composition student by Béla Bartók, who was living in New York. I studied with him that summer. I became aware of his marvellous music and that I needed to broaden my musical horizon. In retrospect, I feel most fortunate to have been one of three composition students who studied with him. I have a vivid remembrance of what I learned from those lessons.

During the next few years, I became once more aware of the need to deepen my knowledge and understanding of all music and to further refine my compositional technique as well as my self-evaluation. I learned a great deal from my teaching of bachelor of music courses at McGill University from 1943 to 1947.

In 1947 I applied to the Yale School of Music to study with Paul Hindemith and was awarded the Bradley Keeler Memorial Scholarship towards my studies. I was also awarded a scholarship by the provincial government of Quebec that year, as well as in 1948. These assisted me with my living expenses. That same year I was awarded, by the Yale School of Music, the Charles Ditson Fellowship, and in 1949 I was awarded the Master of Music in Composition with Distinction, and the Woods Chandler Prize in Composition.

Paul Hindemith, who was a superb teacher, composer, and performer, encouraged us to try to attain the stature of the "compleat musician." Since then, I have never stopped pursuing that goal.

One of Canada's most distinguished composers (1989)

My music has progressed through early, middle, and now late periods. The first was influenced by the modality of British composers such as Holst, Vaughan Williams, and Delius. During my middle period, I was influenced by the theories of Paul Hindemith and by the expressionistic school headed by Arnold Schoenberg. I have learned much from studying the music of that school, but I have not become atonal. I can say that, at present, I am free-tonal with some tendency to chromaticism. At times I want my music to be crystal clear and not overloaded by too many motifs because I believe in making use of a germ idea which can be developed in countless ways.

I still feel drawn to write for orchestra but equally enjoy composing chamber music, music for solo instruments, and music for percussion instruments in particular in orchestral works. So far, I have composed well above three hundred works. Some works that stand out in my mind are "Britannia, A Joyful Overture for Orchestra," "Leaves of Grass" for women's choir and orchestra, "The Bell" for choir and orchestra, "Fanfare and Passacaglia" for orchestra (preceded by brass choir), "Concerto for Piano and Orchestra," "Apocalypse" for so-

prano, choir, six brass instruments, and tympani, "Concerto for Violin
and Orchestra," "Sonata for Alto Saxophone and Piano," "Psalmody"
for choir, baritone voice, and orchestra, "Piano Sonata No. 2," "Sga-
narelle" and "The Meal" (two operas). Recent works are my "String
Quartet No. 3," "Evocations" for two pianos and orchestra, and "If the
Stars Are Burning" for mezzo-soprano, clarinet, and piano.

Of my solo piano works, which are many, I single out my two piano sonatas and my "Six Preludes for Piano"; of my organ works,
"Festive Fantasy on Pange Lingua." However, I must say that I feel
close to all of my works.

I have gained very much by my teaching at several distinguished
American universities, including the University of North Texas and
the University of Oklahoma, as well as at Canadian universities, including McGill University and the University of Alberta, where I
have been professor of music emeritus since 1978.

A continuing pursuit of mine is to introduce to our schoolchildren
the sounds of the classical music of our century so that they may
grow into an audience which appreciates and enjoys the music of
composers of our own era. This does not mean neglecting the music
of the past, because the music of the present evolves from the past. I
make special room in my composing schedule for creating music for
our younger population. This is an important and continuous pursuit
which will bring about greater and greater appreciation of the music
of Canadian composers in Canada and abroad. In our present time,
our composers have advantages which did not exist before the late
1950s, such as commissioning, of which the Canada Council is a most
important source, and funding for copying of commissioned music –
scores and parts. Composers are deeply grateful for the latter, because
copying of one's music (or any music), even with the aid of comput-
ers, takes countless hours of the time which one needs for composing.

In our time, the image of the musician has improved, be it that of
the composer, that of the performer in orchestral, chamber, and solo
works, or that of the music teacher; be it at universities or in private
music teaching. We look forward to an ideal place for all musicians in
the rapidly approaching twenty-first century.

In Pursuit of Visions

"On your marks, get set, GO!" These were among the first words I re-member hearing as a small child, for growing up in my family was a non-stop, action-packed experience. From being the last one to jump into the lake and named "a rotten egg" to being the last one out onto the tennis court and not finding a spot available to play, it was simply a race from beginning to end – and it was fun. But there was a deeper side as well. Our parents helped us appreciate the arts, especially lit-erature. They also gave us a strong religious background in the Ro-man Catholic faith, and a sense of the importance of other people's needs.

The only girl among four brothers in a family which thrived on sport, physical strength, speed, and winning, I lived my childhood in a highly male-oriented family. Both my parents loved sports of all kinds and still do, to this day, and they encouraged us to take part in everything. We always had our ski clothes laid out meticulously the night before so as to be "up and at 'em" first thing.

It was hard to keep up. The "boys" were faster, tougher, and, it seemed, cleverer than I was. There was a lot of teasing also. I was of-ten an easy target for them and remember feeling rather defenceless. But in a curious way my position in the family, right in the middle with a pair of brothers on either side, gave me a freedom to develop my own independence. I quietly went about my own business with-out ever feeling I had to measure up to them. It's true I felt different just because I was a girl, but it didn't have a negative effect.

From a very long way back I remember yearning for something of my own. My mother was sensitive to that and helped me to look for it. It is not that I wished to reject the family or to alienate myself from it, but I desperately wanted "my own thing." The first and most meaning-ful thing of my own came very much from within the family. That was

Ann in her studio

a special relationship with my father. He had a way of making me feel quite superior to "the boys" just because I *was* a girl. My poor mother, with whom I developed a wonderful and close relationship later in life, had to endure endless giggles, private conversations, and shared jokes between me and my father. But Dad, with his capacity for intimacy and huge sense of humour, was, and still is, simply irresistible.

My father had many passions. He put great energy and interest into his investment banking career, which took him to various parts of the world, but when he returned home he always threw himself into the things he loved. My mother shared many of these interests, which is one of the reasons their life together has been so full and companionable.

My parents' love for the English language and for literature caused us to suffer some unusual punishments. When we were bad we would be assigned a poem or a piece of prose to memorize and recite before the family. If it was not perfectly recited, we would be obliged to go back and learn it again. Although by today's standards you might say my father was a disciplinarian, punishments or the enforcement of rules were usually followed by a joke and hoots of laughter. Not all my brothers would agree, but I personally have no memory of humiliation. We all went on to study English at university, which leads me to suppose that none of these punishments were as bad as they sound. I gained something very valuable from them: I am disciplined enough to do the things I set out to do and I don't ever remember not finishing something I wanted to do.

One of my father's interests which I shared was ballet. He was the first president of the National Ballet of Canada in Toronto, and so there were limitless opportunities to attend performances and rehearsals. We even had dancers staying with us periodically because the underfunded company was unable to pay them enough to live on at times. I am still an ardent balletomane and rarely miss a performance by any company performing in Montreal. There was singing too. Our voices, all untrained but with natural pitch and rhythm, joined together every weekend as we went through my father's extensive repertoire. In the summers at the family cottage, numerous cousins would sing with us.

These gentler though highly intense interests became a counterbalance to the ongoing battles on the ski hill, in the sailing race, or in any of the other sports or games that were a regular feature of family life. For that I am grateful because it gave me a foundation on which to develop my life as an artist. If we had been a family of athletes and nothing more, the creative life might have been quite difficult to find.

As a child there were some things which were mine alone, such as years and years of playing the piano. I practised regularly, passed the Toronto Conservatory examinations, played in recitals and festivals, and even went on to study for a year in Paris. For some time I thought piano would always be an important part of my life, but it turned out that in the area of music, choral singing became a greater interest and continues to be so.

When it came time to choose a university I had the first sense of what independence could mean. Because I had had an interest in French all through high school, my plan was to leave Toronto and to go to McGill. But first a year in Paris, hearing and speaking nothing but French, seemed a good preparation. In that year, away from the influences of family life, I immersed myself in French, the history of art, and piano. Racing down the ski hill in a crouch position seemed far away. In fact I reacted against sport and all forms of physical activity in favour of art and music. For the next ten years I did practically nothing in the way of sport and called myself a non-competitive person. This seemed to be necessary to the process of "finding myself." It was a way of casting off the family ties.

I had some wonderful classes at McGill, notably in modern poetry with Professor Louis Dudek, who would regularly ask Leonard Cohen to come up to the front of the class to interpret *The Waste Land* for

Ann McCall and family in East Africa

us because he felt Cohen could do a better job! Then, getting closer to the path I was eventually to pursue, there were fine arts classes taught by the lively character, "Jud," or Professor W.O. Judkins. He gave a few very subjective courses on art interpretation and made us aware of the existence of artists' intent, expression, and ways in which human emotions can be transferred to the viewer through paint or stone. Professor George Galavaris, still at McGill now, had a more intellectual or historical approach. He made the great medieval period wonderfully alive through his lectures on its architecture, frescoes, mosaics, and manuscripts.

The one course at McGill I was less enthralled with and did rather poorly in was introductory philosophy. However, there were other features which made the course attractive. The conference leader, Storrs McCall, was an intriguing man – much more intriguing in fact than Descartes or Hume. I married him a month after graduating from McGill. This turned out to be one of the very wise decisions in my life.

As soon as we were married we set off for eleven years in Pittsburgh, Pennsylvania, followed by Uganda, East Africa, both teaching posts for Storrs in philosophy. Many changes occured in my life during this period. First there was the adventure of living on another continent and in a completely different culture. East Africa is visually spectacular and we went on many memorable safaris. There were interesting people to meet and new experiences of all kinds.

As well, it was time to start developing in a direction that would be meaningful to me. I wanted to continue with my interest in history of art, and considered working towards an MFA. However, I wanted to do some studio art too, primarily as a way of better understanding aspects of history of art, but I hadn't even been to art school, and besides, wouldn't I be more useful helping the Ugandan people in some way? I settled on teaching art to children at the Uganda School for the Deaf, and also an introductory course in the history of Western art to students at the art school at Makerere University. How glad I was that I had listened attentively during those lively lectures by Professors Galavaris and Judkins in my McGill days. Now I had something to give back to others, with the help of a quite adequate art section in the Makerere library and a collection of some two thousand slides in the art school. I was excited as I went off each day to one of my two teaching occupations. There was still energy and a bit of time to paint at home as well. Being self-taught, I had little awareness of the formal problems to work out in painting or of the range of techniques. But when I submitted a painting to the annual exhibition of the Art Association of Uganda and won a prize I was hooked! I began whirling from the deaf school to the lecture room at the art school to my studio. I don't remember having a clear idea in my head as to how to go about planning a work. I simply painted what and how I felt and hoped the technique would express those feelings. I felt limited but knew that one day I would go to art school to learn techniques and to broaden my vision.

Very soon after our first performance of the "Messiah," as members of the Kampala Singers, an amateur choral group, we had our first child, Mengo, named after Mengo Hospital, the Church of Uganda Mission Hospital. It was a happy time, but there seemed to be too much to do, and I realized that something would have to be cut out. I stopped lecturing at Makerere and continued teaching the deaf children because the need there was greater and also I could take Mengo with me. But easiest of all was the painting at home, which was quite feasible with a child around. After the births of Kai, another son, and Sophie, a daughter, I rented a studio in a friend's house where I painted three to four hours every day.

I was beginning to feel a rapid development going on as a person and in my sense of direction as an artist. Motherhood seemed to be a maturing process. I had the memory of an excellent model for motherhood in my own mother, who dedicated herself to our upbringing, but the difference between us was that I absolutely wanted to have a career as well.

For a while I had thought it would be teaching, but the more time I gave to painting the stronger became the pull to delve deeper. But for years I felt tortured by a sense that I should be doing something useful to others. I was able to offer something to those deaf children in Uganda; by working alone in my studio I wasn't offering anything to anybody but myself. This was the biggest problem I had in becoming an artist. The will was there, the drive to work, the interest, but a heavy sense of guilt about taking the easy route plagued me for a long time. I soon realized, of course, that it wasn't an easy route at all, but even so I felt I was being indulgent. Finally I was able to recognize that not everybody in the world can be doing good works; it became justifiable to work towards my own interest rather than towards what I "ought" to do. Besides, I could develop as an artist without sacrificing the attention and consideration the family needed. It would be a matter of working out the balance.

In 1970, when my youngest was eight months old, I had my first solo exhibition in the Uganda Museum. For the *vernissage* the place was packed, there was press coverage and a television interview, and everything sold. I thought being an artist was not bad – pretty easy too. I didn't realize at that time how many artists there were back home and how competitive the art world is.

After five wonderful years, leaving Uganda was a wrench and moving back to Pittsburgh was a huge adjustment. But I enrolled at the University of Pittsburgh in studio art and found it stimulating, especially because I had been painting alone in a tiny room for five years. From the moment I got there I knew how much I wanted to learn and to work. I thought nothing of staying up late to finish projects and then getting up early with the children. I had a drawing teacher, Susan Hauptman, who had a big influence on me. She was obsessive about her drawing to the point of being manic and I found that strangely appealing. From her I derived the sense that I cannot help doing the work I do because it is as vital to life as breathing.

The art department there was headed by an old-fashioned macho fellow who was dead against allowing "re-treads," as he called older women, into the department as students. There were three of us over thirty who pushed our way into the BFA program despite his resistance. All three won prizes at the end of the academic year.

It was at Pitt that I developed an interest in graphic art, and soon discovered that my style was beginning to be based on a linear rather than a painterly approach. I felt more at home first in drawing, and later in print-making, than in painting and sculpture. I enjoyed the control and detail in drawing, and the step-by-step process of print-making.

When Storrs and I and the children eventually moved back to Montreal, I enrolled at Concordia University to finish the BFA I had started at Pitt. Those were hectic years because the children, as they grew a little older, became more involved in all kinds of activities requiring a parent to drive, or to attend hockey and soccer games or gymnastics practices and meets. A new craze for fitness was one more thing to work in and that was a daily aerobics class at the Y. I remain to this day a faithful participant of the 6:45 a.m. sessions.

In art I was finishing up a series of pen-and-ink drawings begun in Pittsburgh, in addition to the courses I was taking at Concordia. These were detailed renderings of rope hanging in different ways or coiled in a heap, or being stretched taut – all variable expressions using the single image of rope. Jan Menses, who taught me drawing at Concordia, encouraged me to continue working with this narrow and even strange idea. I spent two years with it and then in 1976 submitted the slides to a jury for a solo exhibition in old Montreal. After the jurying of the slides there was an interview, and when I received word that I had been selected for an exhibition, I was excited and lacked no incentive to keep working on the show right up to the end. My work was well received and even got a favourable review in the *Montreal Star*. I couldn't wait for the next exhibition.

Once I had completed the BFA at Concordia, I was anxious to find a place to continue print-making in the medium of silk-screen, which I had learned from Yves Gaucher. What was more important than learning the medium was picking up on his sensitivity to greys and all the subtleties between one grey and another. I had much more to find out about those greys and I was able to do so in a wonderful studio called Graphia which has been my home away from home ever since. It is a loft on Boulevard St Laurent where members share space and equipment. Over the years there has been a fair turnover of artists, but Graphia has never lost its unique qualities, the most important of which is the coming together of kindred spirits. We are able to exchange ideas there, offer one another suggestions and critiques, and plan joint projects in an atmosphere of mutual support.

In silk-screen I used a natural imagery in a rediscovered landscape I had been away from for many years. By mixing colour with a lot of transparency, and by being more at home using soft quiet greys, I was able to come up with an expression of landscape that was reasonably distinctive. I had no interest in high colour, or in heavy texture. The look was almost Oriental, inspired at first by the distant mountain at Oka which I looked at from an upper field at our farm in Lachute. It seemed to hover there on the horizon, its base invisible from where I stood. I entered the first rendering of that gentle mountain in an exhibition, the Ontario Society of Artists in Toronto. It won a prize and the edition sold out. I felt I was on to something.

Continuing in the same vein, I had soon produced seven editions of prints which I felt I could show to galleries in the hopes that one would be willing to represent me as an artist. I started off in Toronto with portfolio in hand, working my way from the least desirable place to the most desirable. The top one in my view was Pascal Gallery, founded by Doris Pascal, who was largely responsible for bringing recognition to Canadian print-making. At the end of our meeting she agreed to take on a few prints, but I said no: she would have to book me for a solo exhibition six months hence or I would take my prints elsewhere. Although I felt certain this was the best way to start, I now realize that it was brash. She decided to take the chance and put me down for a solo in 1977.

The timing for that first print show was good. It was boom time for original prints in all media. Not only were the banks and corporations wanting to include them in their collections but the general public also was becoming interested and informed. In addition there were many opportunities for submitting to print competitions all over North America and Europe. My work seemed to fit into what most jurors were looking for at the time. It was a heady start to an early career. After the first successful show in Toronto, I had others in Montreal, Ottawa, Winnipeg, Vancouver, Calgary, and Pittsburgh. This meant I was always madly printing editions at the studio in order to fill the demand. Eventually, due to the stress of it all, the physicality of every day, and possibly the exposure to the toxic chemicals required in the silk-screen process, I developed an auto-immune disease. A year passed before I started to feel at all well, but during that time I did a bit of reflecting. My head told me to slow down, but my inclination was to speed up to make up for lost time.

While recuperating, I continued sending prints all over the world to be entered in competitions. I didn't want to miss a single one. Although inspired by a zealous enthusism for printing, I also knew I had to spend less time in the studio where I was being exposed to the toxic chemicals. I made two changes in my weekly routine to that end. The first, in 1980, was to take a small studio for painting. This opened up many doors in terms of vision and expression in my work. Painting is more reflective. It is not as physically demanding as print-making. I was working alone rather than with a group as I do at Graphia Studio. It felt entirely peaceful. It was a wonderful revelation that I could find something deeply interesting without having to go at it so intensively. I could actually sit whilst painting, even doze off for a minute or two if I felt like it.

This was a refreshing contrast to the public aspect of being an artist. It is a myth that by definition artists are reclusive or eccentric. In fact, they and the galleries that represent them play a large role in meeting the public half-way by promoting their work. They must communicate with the public at *vernissages*, be interviewed and write about their processes, their ideas, and the meaning of their work. There is also a great deal of mechanical record keeping that must be done and deadlines to be met for submission to juries. Steadfastness and energy are required to sustain the *balance* between care of the internal, creative self and the external work in the world.

The early paintings were reasonably acceptable to me, although I had not yet explored or developed much in the way of ideas or techniques. The graphic style asserted itself straight off with a pointillist application of paint and the same controlled geometric division of space I had been using in the silk-screen prints. But the painting seemed to flow, and with a lot less cost to the body which was still regaining its strength. Around that time I was pleased to be invited as a candidate for membership in the Royal Canadian Academy of Arts and in 1981 was subsequently elected. This was a happy confirmation that my work was acceptable to my peers who vote on the admissions.

Surprisingly, the first exhibitions of paintings went well, and I was encouraged to carry on. But I guess I became more ambitious, and pretty soon the old crazy drive to do more and quickly, as well as to continue producing editions of prints, made me start to feel pressed again. Instead of cutting down I decided to add another activity to my life. My daughter Sophie had a show pony and was training in St Lazare at Pépinière Stables. A group of mothers started taking riding lessons. I watched hungrily, remembering how much I had liked my two years in Pony Club back in Toronto when I was a teenager. It seemed like forbidden fruit even to dream of taking one morning a week off to ride, so I didn't. But eventually, after a year of longing I finally allowed myself one lesson a week. It wasn't too long before I was taking two lessons a week; soon after I bought a horse and got myself on the show circuit.

How curious that riding has become such a big part of my life when the worlds of art and the horse would seem to be miles apart. Somehow for me, they share a common sense of purpose. These are two areas of life that I came to myself. In both I am looking for that elusive perfect *balance* between eye and hand in art and between horse and rider in riding. In art one must first feel and then express that feeling through a process. In riding, one must feel the horse, the pace and rhythm; then once a connection is made through a process, deliver a perfect performance. Both are very difficult. To maintain a perfect harmony between what I want and what I get in a painting

Ann in the ring

from start to finish does not happen very often. Similarly when my horse steps into the ring in competition it is rare to be able to keep a perfectly regular balance between what I want over a course of jumps and what I get. Many things can go wrong to disturb that harmony during the process in art and in riding. Both require discipline to try and fix whatever goes wrong so that harmony can be restored. When the results are good I experience a wonderful feeling of elation. Yet, this can often be followed by poor results. For instance, there was a two-year period when I had simultaneous disasters in the areas of both art and riding.

I had worked on a series of paintings for about a year and a half. Each one was taking three times longer to do than any others had ever taken. There was no flow; the brush couldn't do what the heart was feeling. The eye couldn't seem to fix it. Finally after months of frustration I poured gesso over all the canvases. That, sadly, was the end of those works. At the same time, in riding, I had acquired the horse of my dreams. "Grafix," a flashy seventeen-hand thoroughbred gelding, had great potential and always caught the judges' eye the minute I entered the ring. At first it was wonderful. We won ribbons – good ones too. I thought nothing could go wrong. But the combination proved basically to be a bad one. The harmony was not there and the horse began to lose confidence. I got anxious and made mistakes, and those mistakes paralysed him with fear. It all started falling apart. He became afraid to jump and I kept flying off him when he stopped at the last minute in front of a jump. There was no communication left and we had to part company. It was a dreary time for me, to say the least. But although I was very discouraged I was certain that with a bit of determination I would find a new way to express what I wanted in art. And I knew that eventually I would rediscover the joy of putting in a good performance with a different horse and that we would work together as a team.

I had that same faith when I was sick. It never crossed my mind that I wasn't going to get on top of the disease and find the old energy again. But it seems that everybody must go through periods where things do not go the way one would like and there is a loss of confidence and self-esteem. The crucial thing is to recognize that it is not worth being self-destructively miserable because better times will always come back. Where do we get that faith in ourselves?

Faith in oneself is probably the single most precious thing I hope my husband and I have been able to give our children. It can carry a person through almost anything. I am sure in my case it came primarily from the childhood I had, which was secure and happy. A solid marriage where there is love as well as mutual support for each other's pursuits and goals can help anyone to bounce back during difficult times, just as friends have a role to play in providing comfort and encouragement. But to work hard at what one wants to achieve professionally without disturbing the balance of home life can be tricky. It takes careful consideration and quite a bit of organization. Self-discipline is important as well, so that the less interesting but necessary tasks are dealt with regularly and efficiently without too much loss of precious time.

Now the children are grown up, I can only wish that they be blessed with the same kind of lifelong freedom to develop themselves and their dreams that I have had. It is the pursuing of their goals, even more than achieving them, that will make their lives full and rewarding.

Having reached the half-century mark, I am finding there are always duties or activities which try to push their way in front of what I really want to do. One can't be rigid about not allowing this to happen because many of these activities involve serving on committees or boards where one's experience can be useful to others. But there is a level of activity I would like to ease up on both in my way of life and also in the expression of the painting and silk-screen prints. I want to look at my work and feel a lot of air and space. It must become simpler, less detailed. I would like it to go more that way but without becoming empty looking. The current series both in prints and paintings deals with reflections on water. The water is still and mirrors simple forms. I am striving for that perfect equilibrium between image and mirror image with scarcely a ripple to disturb the harmony. However, I want there to be in those works an element of possible threat in the form of ominous cloud or dark sky which I know has to come eventually to disturb those peaceful reflections because nothing stays the same. But the calm will always be restored and the balance regained. This is what I wish to express at the moment. With a good thirty productive years ahead of me, however, there are all kinds of intriguing possibilities for working which I look forward to pursuing.

I Only Laugh When It Hurts:
That Can't Be Right*

If you, like so many, passed even some of your childhood in that pressboard-panelled penal colony that was middle-class North America in the fifties, then I'm sure you too have reminiscences similar to a particularly potent memory of mine: sitting, as a small child, under the kitchen table in some neighbour woman's house, listening to the mums at their morning *kaffeeklatsch*. The kitchen was, of course, pungent with coffee steaming in mug upon mug of Maxwell House Perk, slightly lipstick-stained on the rim. Because our mums, in those days, put lipstick on for all occasions, even when dropping in down the street.

There would also be the starchy smell of clean but unsorted laundry. Because as well in those days, along with their lipsticks, mums brought ironing or mending with them, and their tag-along-age kids, whenever they made the neighbourhood rounds. And cigarettes, also lipstick-stained. Because mums in those days were big smokers, too, in an era when tar did not exist, and nicotine apparently didn't hurt you one bit.

But more than the various aromas of coffee, clean cotton, and cigarettes, the atmosphere was ripe with the sardonic tone of its conversation. Young mothers (shocking to calculate, much younger than many of their offspring are now) sipping their Maxwell House, inhaling deeply on their cork-tipped Black Cats – and cracking wise about the men in their lives.

"If those sissies had the babies," either your mother or my mother might essay, "you can bet they'd have only one!" A ripple of knowing laughter at that and – presumably nods of assent all around the *klatsch*.

---

* Copyright (1990) by Erika Ritter. Reprinted from *Language in Her Eye* (Toronto: Coach House Press).

From under the table – where the view was only of table legs and women's calves, bare and muscular in pedal-pushers – the visual element of the world above had to be assumed.

When the laughter died, a brief silence would ensue, broken at last by another mother remarking, in a subdued tone of voice, "Well, I guess I best take the kids and be getting on. *He* expects dinner, hot on the table, at noon sharp."

Sober murmurs of assent, then the scrape of chair legs, the gathering up of laundry and children – and the *kaffeeklatsch* was adjourned for another day.

Well, so what, you ask. What does this ironic scene of our mothers' politically repressed past have to do with the topic of feminism and writing anyhow? Just this: as a writer whose principal literary device is comedy, I am often asked (well, not *that* often, but far more frequently, let's say, than for my autograph) if the kind of humour I employ in my writing could be called feminist.

To which I would answer (indeed *am* answering now) with a qualified Yes. The qualification being that my humour is feminist roughly to the extent that the fifties coffee-clusters of mothers I just described could be regarded as pre-feminist collectives. The comedy practised by these wives was the survival humour of the clever slaves in the old Roman plays. Slaves who rolled their eyes at their masters' foibles, and who plotted busily behind the scenes. But who still cringed when the master's whip came down, and tried to ingratiate themselves out of punishment.

The comedy employed by women generally, it seems to me, does contain something of that element of personal on-top-of-it-ness that is supposed to be a component of humour. But it is the mitigated confidence of the Roman slaves, who assumed themselves *morally* superior to the families they served, but lacked political clout. Back in the fifties, it was one thing to joke scathingly about the self-satisfied ways of men; to fail to get lunch on the table by the stroke of noon was quite another thing.

Even in the nineties, when I look at some of the works of humour I (and other women writers and performers) have produced, I sometimes wonder how far we've come from our listening posts under the neighbour's kitchen table, literally at our mother's knee. Although I'm pleased to note in my own writing that the satirical thrust is evident here and there, I notice, too, how often I fold in the comedic stretch, when it comes to using humour as a blunt object with which to beat the world into better shape.

Perhaps one of the reasons for that is the fact that, along with underdog wisecracks, there is something else girls of the fifties learned at Mother's knee: that if you're going to be a smartass, you must also struggle to prove that you are nice. That velvet gloves were invented to conceal mailed fists. In the case of our mother this meant that, before you told a joke at your husband's expense, you had to make damn sure only the little kids were there to overhear. In my own case – speaking out boldly here, as a product of my times – it means, in my work, a slight case of arrested feminism. The comic criticality is allowed to be there, so long as it's sugar-coated with liberal doses of self-deprecation, as a way of signalling the harmlessness of my actual intent.

By which I am not trying to suggest that I have, at my beck, a whole fund of boffo one-liners that would tear the lid off the patriarchy once and for all, if only I possessed the courage to let 'em rip. Or that I have created one type of material, sanitized for mixed company; and keep another, unexpurgated set of gags in reserve, to trot out when it's just us girls. I mean that whether my intended audience is female, male, or permutations of both, whether the subject of levity is the vagaries of men or the vanities of women, I find myself, by long-standing habit, practising the politics of ingratiation rather than confrontation, by opting to use humour as a footbridge to other people's affection and approval, rather than as intellectual dynamite to blow their presuppositions sky-high.

While we're on the subject of presuppositions, you may think it's utterly out of line of me to assume that the cautiousness of my comedy has anything to do with being a woman at all. I mean, perhaps my behaviour is merely the automatic functioning of a born sycophant. But if only to humour me, let's suppose that it's not: let's pretend that I'm a typical female product of a persuasive culture, who's taken to heart the notion of getting love by getting laughs – so long as they are the right *kind* of laughs, that is. Warm, approving, full of approbation for the geniality of my mild self-mockery. After all, the comedy of women has never typically been the comedy of antagonism, or scathing satire, or out-and-out scatology. So far as I know, nowhere in the ranks of female comedy (not in the "mainstream," anyway) has there been a distaff equivalent of Lenny Bruce. (Not even the badmouthed Sandra Bernhard, who is much more brattish than brutal.)

The humour that I practise is, I think, fairly typical of humour practised by so-called "mainstream" women. It's the humour of the selfstyled *schlep*. Not surprisingly, the female characters I create in plays and essays are often *schleps* too, just like me, their literary mum. They are angry, of course, edgy, with the occasional scathing quip. But for every dart they stick into society's hide, they are as careful as their creator to aim a sling or arrow in their own direction.

Even when dishing it to other women, as my characters sometimes do – using as comic foils women who are too pretty, too perfect, too pliant, or too pat – they do so with the implied acknowledgment that these other women are the *true* women, the ones who know what real femininity is all about. Not only does this serve the purpose of keeping the mask of *schlephood* well in place, it serves to enlist the reader or audience as a fellow *schlep*. "Don't you just hate those women who are too thin and too rich?" my characters tacitly demand to know. "The ones who can walk in high heels without turning an ankle, and know where to find a clean kleenex in their purse without turning a hair?"

The level of my characters' lives, however, is not so utterly trivial as that. I am enough of a "moderate" (read: middle-class) feminist to endow them with worthwhile careers with good financial return, and to make it clear that whatever romantic blunders they may make will result in developments of a positive kind. At the same time, these are characters who do not joke from motives of mirth. Instead, they use comedy as a way of fencing with their feelings, or of signalling that they are perfectly all right, and cannot be hurt.

Again, I think about the limitations of that old notion that humour operates as an index of on-top-of-it-ness. Characters can (and mine do, in fact) make jokes precisely *because* they are hurt and hope to cover it up with a laugh and a quick getaway. The real agenda is to fend people off, while appearing, deceptively, to invite them in. There's something about humour that makes that trick possible, something about the mere appearance of accessibility that funny people advertise which lulls us into believing we've been, unlike Sam Goldwyn, included *in*.

The accessibility, of course, is an illusion, and the much-vaunted "laughter of recognition" is elicited by the character in order to preclude the recognition of pain. You can laugh with me Argentina, these kinds of jokesters seem to say, but don't you dare cry for me if I cry.

This species of humour is, above all, I think, the product of nice girls (like me, like my characters) who were raised to be polite. But by bringing the phenomenon to your attention, I am by no means insisting there's no such thing as feminist humour of a fewer-holds-barred kind. Some of the best and most political of feminist one-liners come from a more blatant recognition of women as an underclass. Instead of those fifties mothers pretending they had the right to josh their husbands behind their backs, instead of comic characters such as the ones I create, who insist on refusing to bum you out, take a look at the great found maxim uttered by the American female taxi driver who authored that legendary line: "If men could get pregnant, abortion would be a sacrament." This is a truth that goes beyond a mild *kvetch* about male attitudes, and gets to the heart of what keeps men in charge: their skill at putting both biology and religion into the service of their politics.

Here is humour administered as a social emetic, in line with that old "Laughter Is the Best Medicine" heading that *Reader's Digest* coined. When I put my own female comedy up beside such a medicinal quip, I see the extent to which what I write functions only as an anaesthetic, to dull the pain rather than purge the system.

I suppose my worst fear about humour generally is that, in a perfect world, there would be no need of jokes, and therefore those of us who traffic in titters may have a vested interest in keeping things rotten. My worst fear about myself with respect to humour is that I unwittingly serve the cause of rottenness by sometimes making light of what should be mirrored in only the darkest shades. I have no conscious wish to render bearable that which should not be borne. And yet, by rendering it laughable, I fear sometimes that this is the result.

It's a situation that the mums, back in the fifties *kaffeeklatsch*, might easily recognize. Whether their response to my dilemma would be – or even should be – the laughter of recognition is another question altogether.

Finding a Voice

On May 12, 1989, a few months after my sixtieth birthday, I stood in Tiananmen Square, Beijing, China, among thousands of students, workers, and whole families, conscious that I was seeing history in the making. Colourful banners with their slogans were hung on pillars and carried by waves of students on bicycles arriving at the square. Some young people were crouched on the ground arguing with an older man in the traditional drab Mao garb, and there were other groups engaged in discussion. It was the day that Mikhail Gorbachev was to arrive in Beijing and it was the day that journalists and writers joined the students and others in the square. Something was in the air, and we knew later that what was being planned was a hunger strike. Before we left Beijing two days later we would see ambulances taking to hospital fasting students who had collapsed and groups of medical students in white marching to the square to aid their comrades.

It was exhilarating to be there, but underneath the excitement as well as the physical fear of being in the midst of a huge throng of people, I had the ominous feeling that the situation could not last, something was going to happen. This was a totalitarian regime; those at the top could not allow the crowds to get the upper hand. They could not lose face before Mr Gorbachev and the rest of the world.

With a friend who was also a train buff, I had joined a three-week tour, London to Hong Kong by train. Our main goal, discussed tentatively for several years, was to travel on the Trans-Siberian Express. I had prepared for this trip by studying Russian and reading accounts written by others who had travelled this route through the years. I had not prepared myself for landing in the middle of a revolution. Little did we know that our trip, planned months in advance, was going to take us across Germany and Poland and into the Soviet Union and Outer Mongolia at a turning point in the history of these coun-

In Tiananmen Square (May 12, 1989)

tries, and into China at a time when thousands were trying to find a voice, to be listened to by those in power.

We crossed Germany by night, arriving in Berlin in the early morning. A few months later the Berlin Wall would come down, but here, at the wall, we met for the first time the realities of a totalitarian regime where the unsmiling East Berlin border guards with their brusque "*Guten Morgens*" confiscated the film of one of our fellow passengers, who had dared to take their photograph. From the windows of our train we saw the poverty in Poland, where workers in the fields used horse-drawn ploughs while dozens of new Massey-Ferguson tractors lay idle in a yard beside the track on which we were speeding by, no doubt because they lacked a vital part or fuel.

The sun never shone the whole time we were in Russia. We left the drabness of Moscow, and crossed Siberia where the only relief from the scenery of trees, trees, trees was the station stops where the people came from their run-down black tar-paper homes to the train to sell their wares, which included hot meals. On the train, a young woman, a "*provodnik*" or attendant in one of the sleeping cars, was eager to speak to us and practise her English. She had been a secretary but had taken the job on the railway because the pay was better. We have been corresponding ever since. On the train she told us that she never expected to leave the Soviet Union, but since that time she has made two trips to England. She has also had a child and told me, after the end of the communist regime, that she felt he would have a better and more tolerant life and education. I ask her how she is getting on in the difficult times but she does not answer that question.

We left Irkutsk and crossed the Gobi Desert through Outer Mongolia. At the border with Russia were barbed wire and guard dogs to remind us that we were entering the second oldest socialist republic, also to move towards democracy in the months ahead. As we reached China the sun came out and the weather became warm. Ironically, in light of what was to happen a few weeks later in Beijing, a group of soldiers waved at us in a friendly fashion as we crossed the border.

From Beijing we travelled by train to Shanghai and arrived on the day that Mr Gorbachev was to come here. Again the students were out in the thousands. It was impossible for our tour bus to move, but who wanted to see past history when living history was being made all around us? My friend and I walked and talked with two students who, on hearing our English, spoke to us, asked us many questions including what was democracy, and explained that what they too were seeking was a voice, to have their views and concerns known, and to have opportunities for jobs that were going exclusively to the children of the bureaucrats. It was the same story in Guangzhou, and in Hong Kong students were marching in sympathy with their fellows in China. To us, who take freedom of speech and access to information about what is happening throughout the world for granted, it was an eye-opener to talk to people who had neither.

Three Sundays after my Sunday in Tiananmen Square, we were devastated when news of the massacre reached us. A short time after, my friend and I attended a vigil in Toronto outside the Chinese consulate. A Japanese Buddhist monk played on a drum, and two mounted policemen stopped the traffic from time to time to allow us to cross, lay flowers outside the consulate, and stand silently for a few minutes in respect. At such a time quiet prayer and meditation mean more than words.

I start with this story because it represents probably the most adventurous undertaking I have ever embarked on, leaving husband and family behind and going off on a trip that turned out to be an unforgettable experience. I had never before encountered drabness and poverty such as that in Poland and Russia. I had never before seen, even though only as a tourist, life in totalitarian regimes. In Russia our guide was clearly uncomfortable discussing any subject on which she was not briefed and claimed she did not see a railway car full of young men guarded by a soldier with a rifle at one of the station stops in Siberia. And I had never talked to people who did not have the right to communicate or the means to tell the world what they

Judy aged four

needed and who were prepared to die in the attempt to achieve these freedoms.

I grew up in Toronto, the oldest of three children, in comparative comfort even during the Depression. My parents had moved there from Ottawa. My paternal grandparents' ancestors had come from Ireland several generations back. My mother emigrated from England when a small girl with her Scottish father and her mother, who was from Lancashire. I remember my grandparents well, especially my two grandmothers, who lived long enough to know my older children.

My father's mother had, under an imposing figure and manner, a kind concern for others and a sense of family and tradition. I enjoyed being with her and she was interested in my life. My Lancashire grandmother was a "no nonsense" sort of person. She was one of thirteen children, seven of whom were girls, and whose father saw to it that each of the girls learned a profession that she could fall back on if necessary. My grandmother learned to be a seamstress; she taught me to sew on her treadle sewing machine and to do embroidery and cutwork. She always came and stayed when my parents had to go out of town and she made dresses for my sister and me.

I went to high school during the Second World War at Havergal College, a private school for girls in Toronto. As it was wartime, we were expected to take St John's Ambulance courses in first aid and home nursing; in morning prayers we sang hymns for those in peril, and, of course, some of the girls had brothers, fathers, and uncles overseas. There were several dozen "war guests" in the school, girls who had been sent away from their families in Great Britain for safety for the duration of the war. How sad this must have been for them. A friend and I lied about our ages to be able to work in a canteen where soldiers came for rest, relaxation, and hot meals. We felt this to be patriotic and glamorous. The work consisted of drying dishes, peeling vegetables, and sweeping floors. The chance occasionally to empty ashtrays and make milkshakes put us in contact with the soldiers, but they paid little attention to fifteen-year-old schoolgirls.

My father was away for most of the war, as he, along with other businessmen, worked for the war effort seeing that the allied forces received the supplies and weapons that they needed. On a trip to England, he was on a boat that was torpedoed, and my mother bravely consoled my sister, brother, and me while we waited for news. Dad was saved after several hours in a lifeboat, but one of his party and many others were drowned; this was my first encounter with war and with death.

We were living in the country just outside of Toronto when the war began. Dad was sure there would be a food shortage and bought two Guernsey cows and arranged for a farmer to milk them. My mother, who had been brought up a city dweller but was always a good sport, pasteurized the milk; I can remember the large metallic containers she used and the bright yellow butter which we children hated because it had a "taste." For a while we had chickens in the basement, but at this my mother put her foot down and the chickens were removed. It was years later that I realized how fortunate we were to have gone through the war years with only minor discomforts.

At Havergal the teachers, all women in those days, encouraged us to think for ourselves, to set high standards, and to consider university as an immediate goal. Even today it seems that young women in high school tend to turn away from mathematics and science, intimidated by the feeling that boys do better in these subjects. There are

Judy (centre back row) at McGill (1947)

many arguments against schools for just girls or just boys, but at an all-girls' school, then as now, girls were never discouraged from pursuing the sciences and maths and doing well in them. At Havergal the chemistry teacher was Helen Reynolds, who later spent several years as warden of Royal Victoria College. She loved her subject and made it come alive, and I decided to continue in chemistry when I went to university. Most of my friends were going to the University of Toronto, but I had already decided on McGill. My father was a McGill graduate, and one day I travelled with him to Montreal and we walked through the campus. There was something about it that appealed to me. It still does today. That and the fact that Dad was a graduate as well as the idea that it would be a good experience to be away from home and in a different city helped to make up my mind.

In those days, the last half of the forties, women undergraduates living away from home were expected to stay in residence, Royal Victoria College, where men were not allowed past the front hall and had to wait for their dates in a gloomy room we called the "morgue." We had to sign out when we left in the evening and sign in when we returned, always by a certain prescribed hour. To my daughter going to university thirty years later, these restrictions seemed incredible, but the truth is that it was a satisfaction to complain about them and a challenge to try to circumvent them from time to time. In residence, I met young women from all over the world. Dr Muriel Roscoe, the warden of RVC, made an effort to get to know all the students in residence, and she tried, not always with success, to get us to mix with everyone and not just our best pals. In spite of the rules and regulations, these were good times. I started out in honours chemistry, but then switched to chemistry as a major and took some arts courses along with maths and physics. I remember with pleasure Dr Duthie's course on Shakespeare and that Professor Fieldhouse did not approve of the science students in his history classes because we couldn't possibly be serious about his subject. In the science and maths classes there were only a handful of women; in one maths class I was the only woman. I do not remember ever being made to feel awkward or out of place by the professors or by the male students, but the women in these classes did tend to stick together and were lab partners and friends outside of class.

My life and the lives of my friends were centred around the university: we never ventured far into the rest of the city either literally or in our thinking. There were politics on campus, there were clubs that represented the federal political parties, and there were some interest groups. For a time I worked on the *McGill Daily* and enjoyed life as a cub reporter, but, for the most part, we concentrated on our social life and our studies, the former often to the detriment of the latter. Sometimes we raised money for good causes, but, in general, our days were relatively carefree compared to the seriousness and concerns of campus life today.

After graduating with a BSc, I returned home to Toronto and got a job as a chemist in the Banting Institute. My boss, Dr W.R. Franks, was doing cancer research. He had invented the pressure suit, used by pilots during the war and the forerunner of the pressure suits used by astronauts today. The institute was a fascinating place to be working in at that time. Dr Best, who had worked with Dr Banting in the discovery of insulin, was there and would stop and chat occasionally, and, down the hall from my lab, work was being done that would lead to the first heart-lung machines. But I had left my heart in Montreal. In the last few months before graduating I had met John Mappin; we became engaged, we married, and I moved back to Montreal.

If this were happening today I feel sure that I would have continued working in the field of chemistry and taken a further degree. In those days, middle-class women who continued careers after marriage were in the minority. I was happy to follow the traditional pattern of bringing up a family. Unlike today, also, there was not always the financial need to have two breadwinners in the family. Then as now there were women who did not have this choice; they had to take their children to "day nurseries," going on to what was usually a menial job. I feel that I was privileged to be able to be at home with my five children, four sons and a daughter. I felt there would be opportunity when the children were older to do other things. The times were different. I admire the couples today who manage two careers and a family. But it is the woman who must stop and have the children. Society still has not come to grips with allowing women to put careers on hold for several months or years without penalty.

While my children were growing up, I took the occasional night course and did volunteer work. It was a library technician course at the Loyola campus of Concordia that made me start thinking of getting involved in books, and I looked into the possibility of working towards a degree in library science. I realized that the world of chemistry had changed too much over the years for me realistically to expect to be able to catch up.

One day in the spring of 1974 I learned that a writer friend, Hélène Holden, and an American friend of hers, also a writer, Joan Blake, were thinking of opening a bookstore selling only the works of Canadian writers. One such bookstore, "The Longhouse," had opened in Toronto two years before. Hélène and Joan were looking for a partner and I joined them. Canadian writing was starting to blossom at that time, small presses publishing Canadian fiction and poetry were starting up, but few Canadian writers' works were to be found in bookstores.

We made some plans in the spring but decided that we would wait until the children (we had fourteen between the three of us) returned to school in the fall before getting to work. Hélène said we had to open by October 17 because Margaret Atwood, whom she had met at meetings of the Writers' Union of Canada, was coming to Montreal to give a reading on that date. Already well known, Atwood would be a star attraction at our opening. Joan and I shook our heads and said it was impossible, but we found a store-front on St Catherine Street in Westmount, Joan and her children built shelves and painted, I took a business course, and Hélène, who knew some of the publishers, persuaded them to let us open accounts and order books. We opened on October 17, 1974 with Margaret Atwood in attendance. We had decided to call the store "The Double Hook" after the novel by the western writer Sheila Watson, which was published in 1959 and is described in the *Oxford Companion to Canadian Literature* as the "first truly modern Canadian novel."

The past eighteen years have been busy, exciting, at times worry-ing, but never dull. Canadian writing has flourished and has become respected internationally, and Canadian children's books are among the best in the world. My two partners, to whom I owe a debt of grat-itude for having the idea and the vision, now take a smaller role in the bookstore, but for me, after my family, The Double Hook has be-come an important part of life.

Quite often people will say, "Oh, aren't you lucky; I always thought I would like to have a bookstore." It does seem that to some "having a bookstore" implies spending the days talking to customers and dis-cussing books. While this is certainly part of what is involved, and a most enjoyable part, like any retail business, or any business of any kind, there is a great deal of "backstage" work that is far from glam-orous. The people who have worked in the bookstore over the years have been mostly, like myself, middle-aged women with grown chil-dren as well as younger women and men, usually college students completing degrees. Some of the older women have been with The Double Hook for many years and have developed their own areas of expertise. We find our customers interesting and loyal. We "mums" feel that working with the young people helps to keep us up to date, and we hope that they benefit from working with us.

In days gone by, when many doors were closed to women, booksel-ling was considered an appropriate occupation, like teaching, for "respectable" women of small means. That is, if they did not have husbands to support them and had not received an inheritance suffi-cient to live on, they could seek employment in a bookstore without causing tongues to wag. I suspect that the managers of these stores were men, but now I find in the book industry that women and men are involved at all levels and that gender does not seem to be an is-sue. In the immediate past, women writers have had to struggle to have their voices heard, and while in the nineteenth century in Can-ada almost half of the published poets were women, many would write under pseudonyms or publish the work as "by a lady." Today women's voices are heard more, there are anthologies of poetry, fic-tion, and non-fiction written by women, and some of Canada's best-known writers are women.

Now in its nineteenth year, The Double Hook has become a fixture in the community of Westmount and in the wider literary community. The *Westmount Examiner* once referred to it as a "venerable institution"! We host readings and book launchings and have welcomed dozens of writ-ers passing through Montreal on promotional tours. One well-known Quebec writer met her translator for the first time one day in the book-store. Our premises were once used as the setting for a movie.

Literacy, censorship, and taxes on books are three issues that occupy the book industry. The Canadian Booksellers' Association (CBA) is an active organization that works to help its members in their professional development and to work with the other groups within the book world on the above issues. Our membership in the CBA has been more than worth the annual fee for the support and advice we receive from the association, and the annual convention is an opportunity to meet booksellers and publishers from across the country. I served for one term on its board of directors, one of our staff is now on the editorial board of the *Canadian Bookseller*, which is published regularly by the association, and I am a member of a task force that is looking into the future of bookselling. As well, I am actively involved in QSPELL, the Quebec Society for the Promotion of English Language Literature, which works to promote awareness of the fine writers who live in Quebec and write in English and to give awards for the best of their writing.

I have also been, since its founding in the mid-eighties, a member of Westmount Initiative for Peace (WIP). Started at a time when the cold war was still a preoccupation, WIP, like other peace and environment groups in Canada and throughout the world, now works to convince people, and especially governments, of the necessity of turning arms into ploughshares, of requiring companies involved in the manufacture of the weapons of destruction to convert to the manufacture of useful consumer goods. We concern ourselves also with the problem of conflict resolution by means other than aggressiveness, with the international arms trade and Canada's role in it, and locally we try to dissuade toy stores from selling war toys and parents from buying them. The eradication of war and poverty seems further away than ever today, and it becomes more and more obvious that we in the Western world must start to rethink our personal priorities and that countries must rethink national goals. One thing for sure is that it must be made possible for more women to seek and obtain public office. Women's voices must be heard in the legislatures. It is up to all women and men who agree to work towards this, and especially people such as myself who have had an easy ride through life.

I was blessed with parents who were able to bring their children up comfortably and give them a good education, and who always supported our various activities and career goals. Then I have had over forty years of a good marriage with a fine man. Our five children are all engaged in interesting and diverse occupations and are considerate of their parents. And now we have a baby grandson who is a great joy.

The merging of past into future became especially real for me one beautiful fall day when I had a picnic lunch with my youngest son on the McGill main campus. We sat on the grass just outside what used to be the chemistry building when I was an undergraduate. My son is a graduate student in the School of Urban Planning, which is now housed here along with the School of Architecture. In my days at McGill I spent many hours in this building, which was then rather dilapidated. Now it has been beautifully restored. Revisiting the campus and touring the old building, I was filled with a sense of history, of continuity, and a feeling that, at that moment, all was well with my world.

But I cannot forget those students' faces in Tiananmen Square and in Shanghai. I cannot forget that, in the countries through which I travelled in 1989, students, writers, and all people had had their voices stifled for decades. Even in Canada there are people desperate to be heard, and we must always be aware of how fragile a freedom is freedom of expression. I feel enormously lucky to have been able to find my voice.

FREDA L. PALTIEL, CM

Quest for Equality

The invitation to write this essay arrived at a propitious moment, a time of major transition. I was about to leave the home my husband and I had built a quarter of a century before, redolent with memories, crammed with defining possessions; about to lose an aspect of my identity. Moreover, I had just announced my voluntary retirement after some twenty-six years in public service. These major *rites de passage* characterized a new phase of the life course, with all the uncertainties of adolescence, but without its capacities and promises – a period I have termed senelescence.

A child of immigrants, the only member of the family born in Canada, I have always been a "Canadian celebrationist." Not a chauvinist, not "my country, right or wrong," but proud of our cultural pluralism, our linguistic dualism, our unique mix of private and public enterprise; and above all of our basic decency, the relative transparency and permeability of our government structures, and our painful strivings to define and achieve democracy, with justice and equity. It has always been a privilege to represent our country when called upon to do so; to benefit from and, at times, contribute to its reputation. It has been an even greater privilege, for a period which spans a generation, to have been involved in the shaping of our public policy. How did it happen, how did I get there?

The most profound, most abiding influence in my life has been my beautiful auburn-haired, brilliant, resolute, industrious, generous, dignified, unschooled, and unlettered mother. She arrived in Canada from Russia with my two older brothers, having been separated from my father for ten years by war, revolution, and pogroms. I was born a year later, a very much wanted child. Indeed, my mother believed that I brought luck to people, and she always managed to find examples to support her conviction. With so much faith and confidence invested

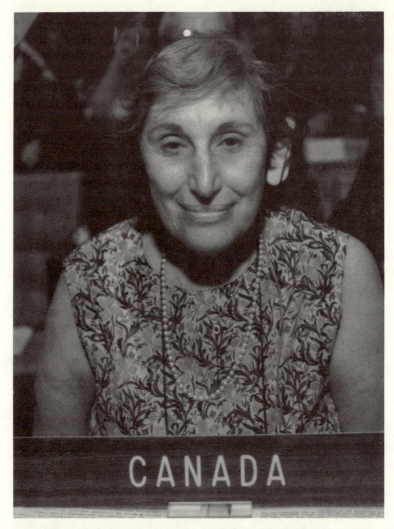

Representing Canada at the Pan-American Health Organization

in me, I somehow internalized the belief which became a mission. I could make a difference in people's lives. I had an obligation to do so.

The uncommon exposures and experiences of my childhood in the thirties laid the foundation for a personal life and career, which, if not exceptional, were certainly out of the ordinary. In grade school I was almost invariably the only Jew in the class. Giving too many correct answers, too early or too eagerly, or memorizing and reciting with feeling too many poems, brought penalties from bullies lurking around corners. While not muted by their aggression, I often ran home, my heart beating wildly with fear. We lived in the outskirts of town. When I was six, my mother was advised to send me to Hebrew school on St Joseph Boulevard. Thus began a childhood of city travel in buses and streetcars to study elocution and dancing, to rehearse and perform in children's plays. My instruction from eavesdropping and observing the surrounding multicultural adult behaviour on public transportation equalled my formal schooling. I was never without a book in my lap, while my ears were attuned to intriguing human disclosures.

There was no high school in my Catholic working-class neighbourhood (which also included a Protestant Italian community), and I had hoped to go to Montreal High School for Girls, which had a reputedly good drama program. I was, however, cajoled into attending Baron Byng High School (immortalized by Mordecai Richler) because it was attended by most of my new friends, who belonged to a club with strong ties to the Israel Kibbutz movement. It was a claustrophobic experience (boys and girls had separate entrances, yards, and classrooms) redeemed only by the saintly art and music teachers, Ann Savage and Mr Herbert; by my representation of the school in the Inter-High School Model Parliament; and by an oft-frequented library, full of inspiring biographies and books about science and philosophy which never made it into formal school curricula.

This was the only period in my life when I participated in organized sports, basketball, badminton, and, after school, mixed softball on Fletcher's Field. Some years later, I played some tennis and skied for a while, but like so many women I neglected to follow active sports and fitness. A pity! Later, at Queen's, I wrote a verse about this period.

Why even back in grade school you were the Hebrew Joan of Arc.
You sang and danced and speechified and prayed to God in the dark.
Then you painfully staggered through high school loathing your Latin and Math.
And in lieu of divine revelation you incurred the Almighty's wrath.
For you no longer sought for Messiah, the Saviour.
With Freud and Karl Marx now to guide your behaviour.
So you steadfastly marched in flat heels and man's shirt.
Suppressed the bourgeoise in you, deep, till it hurt.

There could not have been a more dramatic contrast between my ghettoized early adolescence of political arousal and my entry into the folkways and mores of small-town Ontario at Queen's.

At Queen's too there was a price to pay for being intense, audible, and visible, for daring to ask questions in the introductory political science class (and probably others). The hazing committee made me wear a sandwich board for a week stating "the prof has the floor." This time I learned a lesson. At Queen's I would major in casualness, in practised nonchalance, clad in pastel tweeds, like all the others. Despite my membership in something called the Social Problems Club and some voluntary war work, my political consciousness was on hold. Outside, a war raged and I ache at the memory of Joe, one of the two overseas soldiers who wrote to me far more than I responded, who died on the beachheads of Normandy. In addition to the social life at Queen's, I gained an appreciation for liberal democracy from Professor Corry, the foundations of empirical and educational psychology from Professor Humphrey. I also gained from Professor Tirol an admiration of Victor Hugo, consummated years later by visiting his home in the Place des Vosges, in Paris.

Returning to Montreal after Queen's, I suffered culture shock in reverse. I presented myself to the CBC; the personnel office asked if I could type (I couldn't). I presented myself to the *Montreal Herald* as a budding drama critic; the editor was amused at my "chutzpah." And finally, I failed to convince Dr Silverman at the Mental Hygiene Institute that he needed my talents. But fate or serendipity took a hand. I accompanied a close friend to the McGill School of Social Work, which was embarking upon a government-sponsored program for an accelerated course to provide services to the families of the armed forces.

I sat in the corridor waiting, and as my friend came out of the interview, I rose to go. The casework professor asked whether I was applying and when I demurred, she insisted I explain why. I was not interested in "keeping children off the street," I replied. Incensed by my wrong image of the profession, she painstakingly explained its mission and methods, and handed me an application form to be returned within several days. Seizing the opportunity to return to my by now beloved Queen's, where my current crush was still at medical school, I went in search of references from three professors. These were generously given, and within a week I became a social-worker-in-training, placed at the Baron de Hirsch Institute, with bus fare and a seven-dollar-a-week allowance. It was hard to face my disappointed friend.

Today I shudder at the marital counselling I did as a twenty-two-year-old, harshly judging a pregnant bride who refused to accompany her husband to live in a rooming house in Halifax, pending his sailing orders. The high point of this period was successfully placing and counselling war orphans who had survived the Holocaust and Displaced Persons camps in Europe.

After three years I returned full-time to the McGill School of Social Work to complete my studies, where Caroline Elledge influenced my entry into medical social work. I completed all my requirements for an MSW, except the thesis, received my BSW but acquired a skeleton in my closet, one shared with many others of my age cohort, that of "the feminine mystique." I started to work in the pioneering medical social work department at the then-called Children's Memorial Hospital, under the noble direction of Christina James. In this period I married Khayyam Paltiel and worked until about a week before the birth of my first son Ari (now a demographer). When Ari was six months old, we all moved to Winnipeg, for my husband's employment. I had an unfinished thesis in my luggage.

In Winnipeg, I was given the opportunity to develop community leadership skills. I organized a national art exhibition, was active in the Community Welfare Council, directed mental health plays, served on the board of SHARE, a predecessor to the Manitoba Mental Health Association, and did a telephone survey of rehabilitation needs which helped bring the first provincial rehabilitation counsellor to Manitoba. I also had a second son, Jeremy (now a political scientist/sinologist), but did not complete my thesis. McGill rejected my inspired suggestion for looking at the personal and social factors which impelled persons to pioneer in founding voluntary organizations. Among my papers was a third attempt at a thesis, a nearly completed study of the perception of the medical social worker's role by medical students, nurses, and physicians. There it is, my skeleton laid bare.

In Windsor (1953–58) my two daughters were born, Candida (now in film and TV production and teaching) and Ora Beth (now a haemotologist/clinical epidemiologist), and I carried out extensive voluntary social and cultural functions.

There has been considerable synergy between my domestic and international activities, with moral suasion going both ways. The international sphere of my activities has been profoundly rewarding and I hope to continue aspects of it in retirement. It began accidentally. After an invited trip to Israel in 1957, my husband decided to complete his interrupted doctoral studies in Jerusalem. Having joined him for about a week there, I too was transformed by the experience. I knew it would not be an easy life, with four children and a poverty-threshold income in a strange country, but I also know that a suburban split-level house, a station wagon in the driveway, and my husband's executive position in Windsor in an era of "The Man in the Grey Flannel Suit" could be the point of no return. So I said yes and changed the course of our lives.

In Jerusalem I carried on as a volunteer and an "acculturating" mother until I was "discovered" by a World Health Organization pro-

Freda, Jerusalem (c. 1961)

fessor. After reading a pamphlet I had written for volunteers, he invited me to join a tutorial team teaching family health to medical students at the Hebrew University Medical School. I proceeded to establish and direct the professional medical social services in Hadassah Hospital and also obtained an MPH degree, which, particularly in my training in epidemiology, laid the groundwork for my future role in health policy development.

On my return to Canada, I was discovered once again, this time by the research director of the Royal Commission on Health Services, who learned that I had just completed a case study of the Rheumatic Fever Society in Israel. He recruited me to do a chapter on voluntary health organizations in Canada. The prevailing view was that Medicare would kill them. I held that it would enable them to carry on public education, advocacy, and support of non-establishment research. It did.

So I am not a congenital public servant; much of my working life, paid and unpaid, has been in the voluntary sector. I was recruited by and hesitantly joined the public service in my mid-forties, after completing the chapter for the Royal Commission, following the publication of a book on poverty, and a chapter on "Research" for the Senate Committee on Aging.

In 1968–69, on a grant from the Canada Council which took me to Geneva, I undertook a study of labour force attachment of European women with family responsibilities. (I found that ideological supports and available child care were the most salient factors.) Later, I had just completed a report on rehabilitation services in Canada for the UN when I was summoned to the Privy Council Office and handed the newly tabled report by the Royal Commission on the Status of Women. I took that historic document home for the weekend and realized the values it contained were far ahead of prevailing views in Canadian society and that implementation would result in a transformed Canada. I also realized that timely implementation would require a pragmatic approach to policy development rather than a full-scale debate on principles. Subsequently, one of my conditions for undertaking the role of Canada's first coordinator, Status of Women was that not only public servants but also citizens be invited and remunerated for sitting on working groups. This was unprecedented. The position of a status of women coordinator in the Privy Council Office was crucial, enabling the integration of a gender perspective into all policy issues. As an "eminence grise," it was sometimes possible for me to have "a last word," scribbled in the margins of documents, destined for the Cabinet or the prime minister.

International Women's Year (IWY), 1975, was a Canadian turning point in two major respects. The first was pension reform for gender equity in the Canada Pension Plan, the second a major breakthrough in federal granting to women's organizations. The concepts underlying the pension legislation set the groundwork for subsequent reform towards gender equality. The UN Mexican Conference for IWY was overshadowed by the cold war, north-south conflicts, and adoption of the heinous "Zionism is racism" clause, now finally revoked. The good outcome was the International Women's Decade, which forged inseparable bonds among women around the world.

In 1979 we developed Health and Welfare's first Plan of Action (1980–85) in which family violence/wife abuse was addressed. In 1980, I criss-crossed the country talking to many groups and learning among other things that some people perceived social workers as secondary victimizers. When the Canadian Association of Social Workers (CASW) invited me to chair a national task force on interspousal violence I was glad to be able to help sponsor a national symposium on the subject. We drew together grassroots shelter workers, crisis intervention workers, researchers, policy makers, and other concerned citizens to propose strategies for action. The establishment of the Family Violence Clearinghouse was announced at this symposium.

That year I also advised the Canadian delegation to the Copenhagen Mid-Decade Conference to place two items on the global agenda: family violence/violence against women and women's occupational health. The second item was incorporated into the UN Convention on the Elimination of All Forms of Discrimination Against Women, while gender-based violence was not. Today international experts are producing a draft declaration on violence against women for the World Conference on Human Rights. I recently organized Canada's first research round table on gender and workplace health. These challenges have long incubation periods.

My retirement is scheduled to occur three days before my sixty-ninth birthday. Few public servants last that long and I did not anticipate outlasting anyone. Had I left at age sixty, however, I would have missed out on representing Canada at many international fora and making contributions to many international instruments. At meetings of the UN Commission on the Status of Women, preparing for the Nairobi World Conference, in 1985, I proposed the concept and was a drafter of the Nairobi *Forward-Looking Strategies for the Advancement of Women to the Year 2000.* I have represented Canada at the World Population Conference in Bucharest, the OECD, the UN Commission on the Status of Women, the International Social Security Association, and others; have served as adviser and expert and been a Mental Health Fellow of the World Health Organization.

For more than a decade, I enjoyed a happy and productive relationship with the Pan-American Health Organization, serving on the directing council and as a member and chair of the Women, Health and Development (WHD) executive subcommittee. I was dubbed the "Godmother of WHD" and my office was the Canadian focal point for WHD. I have personally established WHD endowments at my three alma maters. I also served at various UN expert group meetings, e.g., one on social supports and one on women and aging, and chaired a WHO interregional conference on women, health, and development. In 1990 I was named the academic chair at the Salzburg Institute for study seminar on "A Caring Society in a Threatened Economy."

The development of new perspectives and new paradigms for women's mental health has been a major focus of my recent lectures and publications, nationally and internationally. I believe the nineties will be the decade for women's health. A major domestic achievement was the pathfinding 1988 National Symposium on Changing Patterns of Health and Disease in Canadian Women, and its *Proceedings.* It presaged the establishment of a federal-provincial territorial working group on women's health, which I chaired. We produced *Working Together for Women's Health: A Framework for the Development of Policies and Programs.*

Despite my fully engaged life, the love of my children and grandchildren, the devotion of my friends, I find widowhood very hard. Though

En famille, Passover (1988) – just days before Khayyam's sudden passing

hardly serene, my union was an intense, intertwined existence with a husband, Khayyam, who was my best friend, my lover, my severest challenger and critic. A complex man of towering intellect, of unswerving integrity whom very few could know fully, he had a temperament ranging from utter solemnity to surprising *joie de vivre*. We enjoyed marvellous holidays in France and Italy, always in fine, but lesser-known, Michelin-featured "birdie in a rocking chair" hotels. It is nearly five years since I lost him so suddenly. The painful disentanglement is nearly complete as I now live in my small condominium, surrounded by those possessions I chose to keep. I am grateful for a unique marriage which gave me four gifted, ethical, exceptional children, so much encouragement, a seamless interdependence and a cherished intimacy – but oh how I miss the latter two!

I am also the last member of my family of origin. My gentle, good-humoured, blue-eyed father died at age ninety-four. My brothers both died tragically, but one left a thriving family.

What of the future? After addressing the Commonwealth Medical Association in Jamaica, I toured the health centres and was struck by the girls who become mothers before they may become women; and I thought about our young girls who choose to starve themselves to death rather than become women. I now have a new mission – to produce a global report on needs, risks, and tasks of peri-menarchal girls, ages ten to fourteen, the most neglected, overlooked members of the population upon whom our future societies will depend. I hope that my message can be conveyed, if not sooner, at the Beijing 1995 Women's World Conference. That is my rendezvous with the future.

Prelude

Every so often I need to scream. I guess I have a lot of anger within my being, something that propels me into a state or anxious frustration. How can I help it? This world is full of violence and it scares me. To be honest, complacency unnerves me.

When I was five years old, I discovered my clitoris. It was quite accidental, really, since I thought it was my penis (or penis-to-be) and I was standing on top of the toilet seat trying to urinate like my brothers. My mom caught me and calmly told me that I can't pee like Rhys, Greg, or Rick. She also told me I was a girl and I would not develop a penis, in fact. That same year I signed up for figure skating because I was told I could not play hockey since girls can't play hockey. Instead, my brothers played while I learned how to do three-spins and waltz jumps. I have always felt robbed.

Mom was always in pain, yet she was the strongest person I have ever known. She worked two jobs (waitress and janitor) and was home for us whenever she could be. Consequently, my brothers and I learned how to take care of the house because she and Dad were tired from working all day. Oddly, we didn't really mind. (It was exciting to learn how to use the washing machine at nine years of age.) My parents shared everything equally and taught us that realistically there was no difference between men's work and women's work. I thank them for that.

In 1979, Mom started going to the local hospital for traction exercises for her "pinched nerve." Eventually, doctors sent her for testing in Sault Ste Marie and Toronto. The day the doctors rendered the biopsy results was the most confusing day in my life. Cancer: I thought that

Mary-Margaret (1992)

people could live with cancer. And I could not understand why my brothers cried. About a week later they explained that she was going to die in six months: it took eleven. I watched Mom deteriorate from the epitome of strength into an anguished woman. She cried because her big toe hurt and I could not help her. No one could. And then she died in the hospital while everyone else in my family was there that day except for me. I still hurt.

Dad became an alcoholic. He always drank a lot, but he lost control of his life after Mom died. Yet during the year after (during sober periods), Dad and I bonded a lot over burgers at Harvey's. I distinctly remember discussing my period with Dad, not feeling uncomfortable, and drinking a chocolate milkshake. He really wanted to be a mother to me: we became close and he treated me with a great deal of respect.

Dad married Jeanne about one and a half years after Mom died. It was four days after my thirteenth birthday and my gift was the dress and shoes for the wedding. I did not approve of the marriage. Jeanne is twice divorced, eleven years older than Dad, and quite "prissy." Maybe it was jealousy ... for over a year, I cooked and cleaned and took care of my father while he drank himself into a stupor. The marriage immediately suspended the freedom and independence I gained from responsibility. I became the family scapegoat. When things went wrong, it was always my fault – and of course, Jeanne was never wrong. (It was easy to blame me since I was the only child of both families who lived with them.) All our old furniture and customs were abandoned for Jeanne's traditions. I had to become a lady – learn how to eat properly, set the table correctly, and serve the men before the women. In other words, my father and Jeanne forced me to forsake everything I knew from before Mom died in order to facilitate Jeanne's ambition to civilize me.

("*Fat girls don't wear mini-skirts.*" "*Don't put the fork and knife on the same side of the plate when you are setting the table. Who cares if it's just the three of us.*" "*Boys might be attracted to you. They like girls with large breasts.*" "*You are too aggressive for men.*" "*You shouldn't become a lawyer. Become a legal secretary.*")

Jeanne overruled my mother: my mother became taboo. I became a slut, a thief, and unruly. I was kicked out of the house three times as a teenager for general disrespect. Once, it was for having tea at my minister's house, which caused me to be late for dinner. Another time, for yelling at my stepmother for falsely accusing me of stealing her Christmas ornaments. The last time was for having a party while they were in the Dominican Republic.

Maybe I don't respect my father and stepmother, but with the emotional abuse they delivered to me as a teenager (which I am only beginning to deal with now), I frankly do not care. They assumed I was promiscuous (four and a half years before I lost my virginity) because I was caught necking with the minister's son. The four-year trauma that I experienced after Mom's death was deemed illegitimate for some unknown reason. Although I was an "A" student, and went to every leadership conference my school offered, I was never as bright as Jeanne's children (neither of whom finished university and both of whom regret their life choices). I will never be Jeanne's child, therefore I am a failure. From what I am told, I look exactly like, act similarly to, and have the same ambitions as my mother. I am not embarrassed or ashamed. It is the greatest gift God ever gave me.

University was a scary trek. My oldest brother, Rick, drove me to Montreal. The prospect of going to the "best school in Canada" thrilled, motivated, and terrified me. I moved in with two people from Timmins with the impression that I could get along with "northerners" much better than other students. Of course I was homesick for a while. I loved my brother intensely, and I loved living with him and his kids the summer of 1988.

September 22, 1988 changed my life forever. After my women's rugby initiation I was gang-raped. In many ways, it marks my formal introduction to many feminist issues: rape culture, patriarchal structures, violence against women. In retrospect, all I can remember distinctly is that I was not in control before, during, or after the rape. Previous to the assault, I was too drunk to walk straight, or talk coherently. I don't remember walking outside between the main house and the carriage house. During the incident, I was assaulted by three unknown men while being watched by eight others: all are faceless to me. I could not articulate my fear. Afterwards, the media decided to determine what my privacy was, and constantly infringe upon my civil liberties. The Crown Prosecutor's Office played judge before my case could even see the courts, therefore de-legitimizing my entire complaint. I cannot explain how much it bothers me to hear the word "alleged" preceding the "gang rape at Zeta Psi." I want to scream, "That's me! It's not alleged: I am real and what I experienced was real!"

For a while, women's organizations used the "victim-me" as a martyr to the greater quest. Trying to manipulate my "cause," the Concordia Women's Collective (CWC) told me that I basically had a duty to all other women to adopt ardent feminist politics, when I was not at all concerned about other women. Rightly or wrongly, I was my own primary concern, and they had no concept of what my "cause" was. For approximately two years, I viewed the Women's Union and the CWC as full of "dykes," women who were not realistic about their feminism, and all of whom I wanted nothing of.

For years I have been dealing with my sanity as well as my sexuality. Every time I believed my life was becoming smoother, something happened to counteract my hopes. In October 1988, my father disowned me because I brought shame to his family by being gang-raped. (Thank God that my "parents" are the only ones in my family who see it that way.) My decision to deal with my assault proactively influenced my approach to rediscovering my Self immensely. Men could no longer define who I was to them. For too long, I let either my father or eleven faceless men determine my sexuality, my fate, and ultimately they became me. In order to transform my notions of self, I had to define myself against them. I am autonomous ... I am moral and intelligent ... Men who rape, who harass, who abuse, are not qualified to determine my life. Only I am.

Exactly four years after the event, I can see the changes in my attitudes towards women, all of which are positive. It did take some time for me to accept that all feminists in feminist organizations were not "dykes." Along with this awareness, I have found a comfortable place within a community. I do not have to explain my personal actions or beliefs: women accept me. Perhaps this influenced my decision to "come out" as a lesbian: I can no longer deny my innate orientation to both sexes, or my attraction to a community that embraces diversity and change. I can no longer disavow my pubescent fantasies about women as normal teenage homoerotic dreams, and then pursue relationships exclusively with men. Men have censured so much about me that I can identify my self contrary to their notions of me. And if I scream, it is because I am angry: if I cry it is because I am scared. They cannot – will not – silence me again.

Priestesses, Goddesses, Witches, and Whores

I remember the first time I told someone that I was thinking of becoming an ordained minister.

We were standing at the top of a hill looking down across the lake in Neuchatel, Switzerland. I had just successfully completed grade 13 and was saying farewell to one who had become a type of mentor, confidant, and counsellor. She was, or to my eighteen years seemed, the archetypal wise woman. I was probably so open because at that point I thought this would be the last time we would meet, since she lived in California and I in Quebec. Talk of the events of the past year inevitably led to thoughts of the future, and I spontaneously blurted out, "I want to become an ordained minister."

I had never mentioned this to anyone before. Fortunately, she responded as if it were the most natural thing in the world for me to do. There was no tone of shock or surprise or disapproval in her response, just a rather matter-of-fact acknowledgment that the path would be difficult, given that I was a woman. We have met since, only once, and I have long lost touch with her. But I will always have the deepest respect for Muriel Haskel because, far from ridiculing my sense of call, she took it seriously. Little did I know then that her response was far from typical of what I would meet from others.

My upbringing had not alerted me to the notion that women could be disbarred purely on the grounds of their sex. My parents had always encouraged both my brother and sisters to believe that aptitude, skill, and training were the principal criteria for any career, not gender.

Of course, as the daughter of a lawyer I was not so naïve as to believe that in some professions the road was equally obstacle-free if you are a woman. But in my innocence I thought that most of the pioneering work had been done by women in previous generations. That may well be true in law and medicine, but what I had not appreciated

The Reverend Doctor

was that when the Church claims that the ordained ministry is not a profession but a vocation, all too often what is meant by vocation is one in which the laws of natural justice are suspended, so that sexism may reign unassailed.

This was brought home to me when I attended a meeting organized by a group of Anglicans calling themselves the "Council for the Defence of the Faith." My father, innocent of the stance of this group, had heard that it was to discuss the issue of the ordination of women to the priesthood within the Anglican Church of Canada and suggested that I might go along. So one cold and rainy November afternoon I set out, all bright-eyed and bushy-tailed, for the church where the meeting was to take place. Nothing could have prepared me for what I was about to hear, unless I had had a knowledge of the workings of the Ku Klux Klan. The small room was filled and, within minutes of listening to speeches being given, I realized that this group was anything but sympathetic to the idea that women be allowed to seek training for the ordained ministry. For one hour I sat listening as we were told that the idea of a woman being ordained would lead to the downfall of the one true catholic church. Women who wanted to become "priestesses" were a perversion and, akin to witches, would quickly transform Christianity into some sort of goddess worship. Any woman who aspired to ordination was obviously unnatural and was nothing better than a whore. After all, we all knew that a woman's role was intended by God to be that of a loving and faithful "helpmeet" to her husband, and homemaker for the family.

I remember leaving that meeting in tears, not simply because my vocation was called into question, but because of the vindictive and venomous way in which the speakers described women. They were talking about me. Yet nothing of what they said had ever occurred to me. I had never thought that I was perverting the gospel of Jesus Christ, or that I would become the cause of schism, or that somehow the whole natural order was about to collapse because I was responding to what I perceived was a "call" from God. Then and there I realized that the playing field was not level and that it was going to take a great deal of fortitude and resolve to continue in the face of this kind of opposition. Finally I began to understand what Muriel had intimated. It was 1975 and yet with regard to the Church's attitude to women it might as well have been 1875! Ironically, this first occasion on which I encountered prejudice against women was in the Church. Unfortunately, it was not to be the last time.

Undeterred, by the following year I had discussed my calling with Reginald Hollis, the Anglican Bishop of Montreal. With his support and encouragement I decided to anticipate the acceptance of women for ordination to the Anglican priesthood and begin my theological education. This brought me to the Faculty of Religious Studies at McGill. I had been studying in the honours English program. Now I changed course and enrolled for an honours BA in religious studies.

Some of my courses were shared with the Anglican, United, and Presbyterian church ordinands who were enrolled in the BTh program. Needless to say, with the exception of one other woman, all of them were men. Heated and often acrimonious debates in the Junior

Common Room did much to "heighten my consciousness." Had I expected strong support from my peers, I would have been disappointed. If anything, it was the members of the faculty who seemed to be the progressive ones, not the students. There may have been faculty members who opposed the ordination of women, but they kept silent either from politeness or discretion. There were certainly no overt comments of disapproval. Those who were in favour of the ordination of women, however, were consistent in their support and helped many of us, both women and men, to build the necessary intellectual models which helped us recognize that the issue was not simply one of ordination but rather of authority and identity.

As an intended ordinand, I was expected to gain practical experience in a local parish. Given the dissension within the Church over the issue of the ordination of women, it is not surprising that the parish to which I was assigned was divided. Fortunately for me, the group which opposed my presence was a small one. Only much later did I discover that they had attempted tactics which could only be described as blackmail to try and keep out, as John Knox once said, "the monstrous regiment of women." The rector, Archdeacon Jack Doidge, was made of sterner stuff, however. I owe him and the vast majority of that congregation a great debt. Then as now, it has been my experience that opposition to women priests/ministers constitutes the minority of the Church's membership, albeit the tail which seeks to wag the dog.

By 1977 I had been accepted as a postulant for holy orders and, because I was now showing interest in pursuing graduate studies, it was suggested that I spend the next year and a half studying languages and Bible at the Hebrew University in Jerusalem. The diocese was able to offer me a small grant and it seemed the perfect opportunity to test both my vocation and my academic potential in a totally unfamiliar environment: one in which I was known by no one, and in which there would be no preconceived notions of what I should be or do. I left with my bishop's blessing and a letter of introduction to the Bishop of Jerusalem. I took up my studies at the university and shared a self-contained apartment in the back of one of the original houses in Kiryat-Moshe with a Jewish woman who, having been brought up in an atheist home, had come to Jerusalem in search of her religious roots.

There was so much to discover in Israel by way of different cultural and religious groups: so much to watch and hear and touch and taste that was new and different, that I had very little time or at least was unwilling to spend my time with the Anglican community in Jerusalem. Indeed I grew most ambivalent towards the Church, preferring instead to deepen my appreciation of my new-found Jewish and Arab Israeli and Palestinian friends. Which is not to say that I abandoned my "call." I prefer to think of this period as a time in which I situated my sense of calling in a broader and less parochial context.

It is impossible to live in a land so small and yet so diverse, one that has inspired such passionate and violent loyalties, without being affected by them oneself. It was here that I began to understand the process of dialogue and a respect for the "Other" which did not demand that they become like me. I also learned how soul-destroying is religious chauvinism. I became first sceptical about and then positively opposed to notions of evangelism if by these was meant an attempt to convert others away from their own religious tradition to Christianity. To this day I remain confident that God is more all-encompassing than this.

I determined not to stay in Jerusalem for my postgraduate studies but instead accepted the offer of a place at London University in Old Testament studies with special emphasis in Aramaic. The change from Jerusalem, Israel to London, England was, needless to say, dramatic. I by no means, however, had ended up in paradise. For here I was in Heythrop College, composed mostly of Roman Catholics, in a country where the Anglican church did not ordain women, and where I found my greatest spiritual support from a congregation of British Baptists! Which is not to suggest that I was left without support. As at every other stage in my life, there were others who generously shared their vision and experience of God's grace. Britain made me aware of the existence of women in churches other than that of the Anglican communion who had responded to the self-same call to ordained ministry and who had been exercising that vocation for many years. One such was The Rev. Dr Marie E. Isaacs. She opened many ecumenical doorways for me which led to conversations both with women in the Roman Catholic tradition and with women in the many Protestant and Free church traditions. Not all of these were necessarily ordained or intending to be ordained. All of them, however, were committed Christian feminists, propelled by a sense of urgency that some radical changes were going to have to take place if the Church was going to survive into the twenty-first century.

Even within the Church of England in Britain, I met communities who were not only willing, but yearning, to experience the ministry of ordained women. One such was a small inner-city parish church which had seen better days in terms of its affluence and influence. To the outside observer the smallness of the congregation could be read wrongly if taken to indicate the size of its heart. This small group accepted me and what talents I had to offer with a warmth and generosity which contributed both to my personal maturity and professional skills. At the instigation of their young priest-in-charge, they wel-

Patricia G. Kirkpatrick, D Phil (Oxon)

comed me to their pulpit and made me feel, whatever the official line, that I was their ordinand. It is good to know that with the outcome of the vote taken in their synod this past February, should I return, my status as a priest will at the very least be legal.

In 1980 the first woman to be ordained priest in the Diocese of Montreal was Lettie (now Canon) James, another woman whose influence upon my life has been very significant. She it was who bore the greatest burden in Montreal in defending the ordination of women to the priesthood. Throughout the diocese she defended the issue with dignity and no small amount of humour and with an energy that at times even exhausted me, someone thirty years her junior.

Having completed my doctoral studies at Oxford, I returned to Montreal to embark upon further pastoral training. During this period I was appointed at McGill as sabbatical replacement for the professor of Old Testament studies.

In his wisdom, the director of studies at the Diocesan Theological College decided that I should run the gauntlet of opposition to women in ministry by serving this period of my training in a parish whose rector had been, and to a lesser extent still was, a stalwart opponent of women's ordination. The extraordinary outcome of this baptism by fire was that I learned not only more of the ways of the male clerical club but also that there is no situation beyond God's redemption. It is wholly attributable to God's grace that at the end of my time there the rector and congregation had moved closer to the realization that both male and female are made in the image of God and may be used by God in whatsoever capacity God chooses.

I was ordained deacon in the fall of 1985, and continued what has been the pattern of my life since, attempting to combine what is in many ways the two careers of university teaching and priesthood. Anyone who has tried this will know not only the exhaustion of half-time jobs (which demand whole-time attention), but the guilt which is fostered by the respective institutions which set themselves up as rivals for your attention. The Church is accustomed not only to total allegiance but to full-time appointments. What were they to do with someone like me who felt called to serve both the parish in a priestly capacity and the university as an academic? Had I been a man this would not have been posed as a problem. As I was a woman, however, it could be used as another reason why women were unemployable. My part-time appointment at McGill meant that I could continue my training in parish ministry and still keep very much in touch with the world of academia.

Given the particular history and perspective of the Faculty of Religious Studies at McGill, my colleagues did not see any dichotomy between my two callings. I must acknowledge also that the church of St James the Apostle was willing to break out of the normal bounds of church appointments by creating a part-time position for me as their Christian education director. Had they not been so imaginative, it is highly unlikely that my ordination would have come about.

My ordination to the priesthood in 1986 brought together a number of strands in my life. I was particularly touched that six of my British friends came over for the occasion, including Anglicans, Roman Catholics, and a Baptist. Coinciding as it did with my full-time appointment to the Faculty of Religious Studies, my ordination signalled the Church's recognition not only of my priestly call but of my academic vocation. In a period in the Church's history in which intellectual life has at best been placed on a siding, and at worst positively decried, such recognition of the value of academia seemed to me then and now more than timely.

Since then I have continued as a full-time academic who is now tenured, and have continued my association with the church of St James the Apostle, now as honorary assistant priest. I have been blessed by the fact that the person who first set me down the path of Old Testament studies, Professor Donna R. Runnalls, is now dean of the faculty. The perspective that she has brought to bear on the running of the faculty has definitely been informed by feminist thinking. We do not ignore issues of women in the work force, and to my knowledge the dean has worked long and hard over issues such as employment equity here at McGill. Of the two spheres of my professional life, the church and the university, I say with some regret that the one in which I have experienced sexism is the church. Hence the experience with which I began my story has been repeated throughout my life. As a Christian, I find this difficult to admit, let alone publicize. It would be false to infer from this that the Church in all its communions, and in every land I have experienced, has not provided people who have nurtured and supported me as a woman. It is not only in the world but in the Church that we find wheat and tares growing together.

The male clerical club has seen the advent of women to their ranks as a threat. And at a deep level they are right. The debate concerning the ordination of women to the priesthood has raised issues far more profound than whether as women we want to become honorary males. Inevitably it raises questions about the very nature and character of ordained ministry. Is it a priestly caste, determined by genetic or social factors? In what ways is it an elite cut off from the rest of the people of God? What are the appropriate models of leadership for a community which claims to pattern itself upon the life and teaching of Jesus? Many years ago I was introduced to a very eminent dean of a British cathedral. When he was informed that I was an ordinand he remarked: "I don't approve of women priests." This conversation stopper was followed by a pause, after which he added, "but there, I don't believe in Christian male priests either. In my opinion priesthood is sub-Christian." Perhaps I should add that he too was an Old Testament scholar. His words remain a challenge to those of us who have joined the "club." If we do not continue to question its constitution and rules of membership then we can rightly be accused of "selling out" the values of the Kingdom of God.

Of course the positive side to this change in membership is that many provinces in the Anglican communion have had to re-evaluate their understanding of the ordained ministry. In the light of much feminist thinking, churches are once again redefining structures of hierarchy and choosing to govern in more egalitarian ways. Congregations are once more discovering that God is not a static entity to be defined by professional theologians. Those who were once seen as being more interested in priestcraft and status are themselves discovering the liberation which is afforded when the experience of God is not restricted to outdated models of authority. Part of this feeling of liberation is due to a growing rejection of Aristotelian modes of thought which pit man against woman or that see in woman the privation of man. The world is no longer defined in terms of competing primary elements but rather as a place where all of God's creatures must learn to live in mutuality and interdependence.[1]

In 1973 Mary Daly, in her book *Beyond God the Father*, argued the problematic of a deity which was defined solely in male terms. As one of many conclusions she stated that "If God is male, then the male is God."[2] Her analysis was insightful and highlighted the tremendous force symbol systems exercise in our constructing of reality. I think it significant that, with the advent of women into the ordained ministry of the Anglican church, there has not been a co-opting of women's talents into the established male role definitions. Rather, the very presence of women in the ordained ministry has forced the institution to rethink some of its basic paradigms for talking about God. In so doing, it has had to rethink its liturgy so that it not only incorporates gender-inclusive language in prayers and hymns but also finds the metaphors appropriate to speaking about God in non-gender-specific terms. Even the very translations of the Bible have been radically altered because of a new-found sensitivity towards inclusive language. All these things have happened since I first felt called to the ordained ministry. In less than fifteen years, people have been obliged to radically rethink their notions of authority, tradition, and identity regarding the nature of God, the Church, and its membership.

When the Holy Spirit blows, she blows, and it would seem that there is no holding her back.

To be sure, there are still places of resistance, places that do not want to rethink their theology, places where such a rigid understanding of tradition is held that people dare not disturb ancient practices. But such places are a minority and, by and large, people are realizing that we cannot continue with the dualisms of the past which sustained systemic inequalities between the sexes, races, and classes. Whether or not St Paul meant his words of Galatians 3:28, "In Christ there is neither Jew nor Greek, there is neither slave nor free, there is neither male nor female; for you are all one in Christ Jesus," to be taken literally, it would seem a new generation has decided that they should be, and that therefore every effort should be made to guarantee that this vision of equality come to pass.

There are voices that speak hauntingly of a backlash against the feminist movement in various secular institutions, and sometimes people ask me if I think we are headed for just such a backlash in the Church. I have no crystal ball and I do not like such idle speculation,

---

1 Prudence Allen, *The Concept of Woman. The Aristotelian Revolution 750 BC-AD 1250.* (Montreal: Eden Press 1985), 83–103.

2 Mary Daly, *Beyond God the Father: Toward a Philosophy of Women's Liberation* (Boston: Beacon Press 1973), 19.

as it tends more often than not to feed our over-exercised paranoia. This I will say, however: as we enter now into the "post-Christian" era we are watching the last remnants of Christendom gasp their last breaths. But Christendom cannot and should never be equated with Christianity. The former includes a vast complex of socio-economic and political structures of domination, the latter a commitment to the values of the kingdom as exemplified in the life and teachings of Jesus, a life of servanthood. It is far less difficult to work towards an egalitarian ideal when you are not so concerned to retain the hierarchies which have been created by an institution in the past. The real test will come when, as members of the body of Christ, male and female, we stand by the poor and the disenfranchised and do not allow ourselves to be tempted to retreat into the shadows of privatized religion.

Although there have been times of tears and frustration, and no doubt more yet to come, I remain convinced by and gain strength from the numbers of women who will not be silenced in their search for a more just and virtuous vision of the values of the kingdom of God. At the heart of most feminist philosophical and theological debates lies the question about the relationship between dependence and independence. In my reading of the gospel, I have come to understand that our humanity is only realized when we allow ourselves to be interdependent and interconnected with all of God's creation. It is this interdependence that I will continue to work for, and with God's grace I will encourage others to do likewise.

At present I am a member of the Anglican Church of Canada's Doctrine and Worship committee, and have been appointed by the Archbishop of Canterbury onto the Inter-Anglican Commission, which was established in order to study the issues of authority and identity in the world-wide Anglican communion. One of the consequences of my membership on these committees is that I have become increasingly convinced that our strength as a communion is found, paradoxically, in our many differences and our willingness to listen to each other's, at times, contradictory stances over various and sundry moral and ethical issues. I have sat and listened to Asian bishops and laity argue that their culture would never accept the ordaining of women to the priesthood. I have sat and listened to African bishops and laity state categorically that lesbian and gay rights have no place in the church. I have sat and listened as British bishops and laity have made light of the attempts many have made towards the use of gender-inclusive language. Needless to say, I have found myself more often than not arguing against these views. But the point here is that at least I am able in Anglican circles to debate and discuss issues of authority and identity without fear of sanctions being brought against me. The notion of interdependence relies on the ability of each partner to hear the other's fear and joy.

Across Cultures

Among the several messages I picked up as I walked into my office one morning recently was one from a journalist of the Montreal *Gazette*. Before I could think much about it, he called back and we set up a time later that afternoon for a phone interview. It was to be on the subject of the employment equity policy at McGill. This policy was still being formulated at McGill to satisfy the Federal Contractors' Program, whereby institutions which obtained federal funds were to demonstrate they had made efforts at hiring women, visible minorities, native persons, and handicapped people.

I spoke about equity policy that afternoon from my condominium in Old Montreal. The panorama of spectacular changes to the Old Port which I could see from all sides had been created to celebrate 350 years of this beautiful city's founding. It was also the year of Canada's 125th birthday. Coincidentally, it was only now that some teeth were being put into social legislation to provide equality for Canada's original inhabitants and newer groups which had built the country but had been historically discriminated against. I wanted to make clear the difference between equity policy (which is a Canadian concept and does not involve lowering of standards – the usual argument used against preferential treatment) and affirmative action (which, although identified with the U.S., started in India and involves hiring minority group members with minimum qualifications). The journalist had done his homework. He asked me, a woman and a member of a "visible minority" who is a professor at McGill, why I would think there is a need for such a policy. Would not young white males feel discriminated against if minority members (such as women) of equal qualification were to be given preference in hiring? The article, which appeared a few weeks later, said: " 'in order to bring everything to a level playing field' ... said Ratna Ghosh, a McGill professor of education. ... 'young white

Dr Ratna Ghosh with husband, Dr Ashok Vijh

males [may] have to hold it for a while, until others catch up.' " The colour photograph was not bad, but I hadn't singled out white males, the reporter had!

The interview was not long, but I sat near the window and reflected on my career at McGill as I watched the gorgeous cruise ship the *Royal Princess* dock as if in our front yard. Was it already fifteen years that I had been at McGill? Two of those years stand out most in my memory. In 1982, my first sabbatical, I was appointed by the Shastri Indo-Canadian Institute (SICI) to be their resident director in New Delhi, India. I left my post as director of graduate studies at the Faculty of Education, to take up the tremendous challenge.[1] A presti-

---

1 At that time a consortium of twenty-one major Canadian universities and the National Library of Canada, SICI had its head office in Canada (now located at the University of Calgary, it had been originally housed at McGill). The Delhi office was a much larger establishment than the Calgary office.

gious institute, SICI enabled scholarly exchanges between Canada
and India. I had been awarded a senior research fellowship from SICI
for a project on Indian academics, but as resident director I would assume the responsibility of the Delhi operation.

That year changed my life. It gave me back the confidence I had
had as a child but had largely lost during a marriage (my first) which
succeeded to a great extent in demolishing my ego. To be a woman in
charge in India, meeting academics from Canada and India, diplo-
mats from many countries, bureaucrats at the highest levels, artists,
and business people was a most heady experience. It was a lucky coincidence for me that many of the key people I had to negotiate and
deal with in the Indian government were women – the minister of education, the secretary of the Department of Education (the top civil
servant), and the chairperson of the University Grants Commission.
In addition, I had the privilege of meeting Indira Gandhi, the country's prime minister, on several occasions. I was fortunate to meet dynamic women academics, some of whom were directors of centres,
some of whom were well-known scholars, and yet others who were
beginning their careers.[2]

The other year that stands out since my appointment at McGill is
1988. This was a very eventful period for me. I was promoted to full
professor and elected as President of the Shastri Indo-Canadian Institute, both in May. It was my privilege to go to India in that capacity to
sign an addendum to the Memorandum of Understanding with the
Government of India and be with Prime Minister Rajiv Gandhi, who
came to lay the foundation stone of the institute's new building in New
Delhi.[3] In August, my son Partho finished his M Phil degree in Cambridge, England,[4] and joined the international investment banking firm
of Salomon Brothers in New York. In November I married Ashok Vijh,
a scientist who has introduced me to another world of intellectuals.

It is said that writing a book is one of the highest forms of indulg-
ing in one's ego. So, writing an autobiographical account surely must
be an over-indulgence of one's ego. I undertook this task not as an exercise in indulgence but rather as an expression of how my life has
evolved across two continents, and my efforts at synthesizing two
cultures which are in many ways so opposed. This synergy enables

2 It so happened that, at the time, a senior police official in Delhi was a woman, although I never met her.
3 It was almost exactly a year later that Rajiv Gandhi was assassinated. I heard the
news with shock at Indira Gandhi International Airport as I was leaving India after a
short trip.
4 At Cambridge, Partho and his Australian partner became the first non-British de-
baters in history to win the British Debating Championship. The *Times* called it a sign of
the times.

Ratna aged four, Calcutta

me to continue feeling completely at ease both in the land of my birth and in my adopted country.

I grew up in the beautiful hills of Shillong in the north-east mountainous region of India wedged between Myanmar (Burma), Bangladesh, and Tibet. The breathtaking landscape combines rolling hills, sleepy valleys and spectacular waterfalls, pine forests, velvety meadows, and blue skies, in sharp contrast to the rugged and majestic snow-capped Himalayas to the north. Although it is a hundred kilometres from Cherrapunji, made famous through geography books as the wettest place on earth, the micro-ecology of Shillong is such that it concentrates the rainfall in bursts of heavy downpours over four months.

A hill station which the British called Scotland of the East, Shillong was famous for its elite boarding schools for boys and girls who came from many parts of India. It served as the capital of the province of Assam (known for its tea) and was a curious mixture of civil servants, army officers, British expatriates, and a matrilineal tribal group, the Khasis, for whom it is the homeland. Missionaries had made a strong mark through schools and hospitals, and the Khasis are almost totally Christian as distinct from the other Indians, who are Hindus, Muslims, or Sikhs.

Strict discipline was what the nuns emphasized at Loretto Convent, and this influenced us throughout school in everything. In addition to memorizing Shakespeare and Shelley, we learned sewing from the nuns, who also insisted on team games such as cricket, field hockey, and basketball. We diligently practised the piano for hours, long before the examiner visited from the Trinity College of Music, London each

November. My real interest was mathematics, but I was unable to take higher maths because the nuns did not feel they could teach at that level. Like many females of my time, I ended up with English literature for my bachelor's degree, not because I wanted to but because at that time it was the only course in the college I attended.[5]

My mother took over where the nuns left off. As Bengali girls, my sister Swapna and I were expected to be able to sing the songs of Bengal's Nobel Laureate, Rabindranath Tagore. That was not enough, because Indian classical dancing was a must, and we were trained in the gentle movements of Manipuri classical dance. In addition, my mother had us learn what she said her son (had she had one) would have learned – how to drive a car, shoot a rifle, and ride a horse. We teased her, and asked her if she would have taught her son to sew? The one thing we were not taught was cooking. As a matter of fact, the kitchen was not a place we were encouraged to visit. My mother's elder sister had died of burns when her saree had caught fire. The kitchen was too dangerous for us. In any case, she pronounced, we would not have to cook ourselves, only supervise the cook. And if worse came to worst, we knew how to read recipe books, didn't we? I learned the hard way years later that reading recipes does not guarantee ability in cooking when one does not know the basics – like boiling water! I have grown to enjoy cooking and supervising Ashok's attempts in the kitchen.

An excellent cook herself, my mother, Indira, picked up cooking after she was married. I am most impressed now with what I remember of her organizational abilities. As the wife of a prominent ophthalmologist in north-eastern India, she did, as was expected of her, a lot of social work. She was founding president of a girls' school. She was a perfect hostess during my father's various honorary positions as president of the Rotary Club, president of several medical associations, and so on. On the one hand, there was perfect and harmonious separation of roles – my mother ran an efficient home and my father was able to concentrate on his profession. On the other hand, my mother helped with the administration of my father's private nursing home. Mother did the job of bringing us up. She kept us very sheltered and our world was one of reading and music when we were not absorbed in the massive amounts of daily homework. High academic achievement was what we were taught to value. Among the first women to graduate from university in the British Empire were two Bengali women, we were reminded.

---

5 Undergraduate teaching in India is done through a system of colleges affiliated to a university.

We loved hearing stories of mother's school and college where she and her two sisters were in residence because their parents lived in Burma, then part of British India. My grandfather was a lawyer and member of the legislative assembly for fourteen years. Mother graduated with a BA in philosophy from Bethune College during the struggle for independence. The story of an event at her convocation had a particular impact on me. A young graduate woman from another college fired a shot at the British official who was giving out the degrees when she went up to him to get her parchment. The official ducked and was not hurt. The pleas of the nuns from the woman's college prevented her death by hanging, which was the usual fate of freedom fighters, and the young woman was transported to the Andaman Islands for life. She was set free, of course, with independence in 1947. I still remember meeting her many years later in Calcutta: a fragile woman who did not know that she had influenced my thinking about powerlessness and vulnerability – of colonized situations whether they be countries or individuals.

The dominant emotional and intellectual presence in my life was my father, Dr Gauri Sankar Guha. He came from a family which traced its roots back to King Pratapaditya of Jessore (one of the largest and most important of twelve principalities in ancient Bengal). The family had migrated to Assam in 1826. My great-grandfather, an attorney, died young, leaving my forty-year-old grandmother with eight sons and a daughter. I remember my grandmother as a small but strong woman who wore only white clothing and absolutely no jewellery, as was expected of widows at the time. She read extensively and brought up her children, some of whom became internationally known. She had outlived several of her sons when she died at the age of 103.

As one of several children who was still in school when he lost his father, my father completed his medical degree with considerable difficulty and got himself to Germany with a Humboldt Scholarship. He had completed his MD in ophthalmology in Berlin when the war broke out. He came back to India and was inducted into the British army (with the rank of major), which he left as soon as he could. He wanted to practise among the people, often without charging fees even for operations in his nursing home. He was honorary consultant in the government hospital. I remember his telling us that for him religion was serving people who needed help. He had a profound impact on the development of my social consciousness, not only through our discussions at the dinner table but also through his exemplary life. It was unusual to have that influence in such a hierarchical society where class and caste divisions are still strong. In our conversations we often compared women's position in patriarchal Hindu society with their status in the Khasi matrilineal system[6] which surrounded us. His sense of internationalism had an impact on our lives. We travelled every year during winter break to many parts of India, and spent a year in my early teens in Europe, where we visited many countries after two terms in school in England.

It was my father's sense of compassion and his commitment to developing one's potential to the fullest that are at the root of my later intellectual interest in equity in education for historically disadvantaged groups. On the other hand was the striving for excellence which he illustrated in his own life. He was, perhaps, the only practitioner I knew who was also a scientist and researcher. After Berlin, he had studied in Hamburg, Oxford, London, and Paris. He published articles in some of the major journals, both national and international. He had grown up speaking Bengali, his mother tongue, English in the education system, and Assamese, the provincial language, and he made considerable effort to learn Khasi. In addition, he read German and French after his daily early morning walks, so he would not forget them. We lost him twenty-five years ago. My memories of him are his gentleness, his quiet strength, his warmth, but also his discipline and total devotion to his work. His sharply sculpted features, sensitivity, and pleasant personality made a strong impact on people with whom he came in contact.

Looking back at my teenage years I now see the contradiction in female roles to which I was exposed. On the one hand, there was my grandmother's matriarchal presence, my mother's strength, charm, and outgoing personality, the Khasi matrilineal system. On the other hand, there was the social ideal of the pure and chaste girl which propelled my mother to keep us sheltered to the extent that she would not let my sister or me go to Presidency College in Calcutta for our undergraduate degree because it was coeducational. Although I had won a merit scholarship to study out of province, letting me go to study in Calcutta was a major concession. While my father would have liked me to study medicine, the nuns discouraged the study of science or maths, nor were they competent to teach these subjects at the "A" level. After much family deliberation I was allowed to go to Loretto College in Calcutta, an extension of the strictly supervised environment of the nuns in Shillong. My sister, who also received a scholarship, followed me a year later. While there were several bright students there, and while it was the place where Mother Theresa had begun her

6 The youngest daughter inherits the property. In turn, it is her responsibility to look after her parents. Upon marriage, her husband moves with her into her parents' home.

A traditional bride (1960)

life as a nun, Loretto was better known for moulding young women into socialites who were destined to be wives of top executives of business firms or of bureaucrats.

I studied there with honours in English literature and minor in history and education. Still very sheltered, I was, as I look a back now, too naïve and immature to really enjoy English literature. The examination system did not require much creativity, and I was fairly good at performing within its parameters. In any case, my mother felt that it was time to marry me off after a BA degree, and I enrolled in short courses in interior designing and Ikebana (Japanese) flower arrangement, and at the Alliance Française to acquire the rudiments of French. This was a "finishing-off" stage while marriage arrangements were being finalized in Calcutta with a person whom I met only a couple of times, but who was considered to be suitable in terms of looks, education, and socio-economic background. I had very little to say. It was the thing to do. I felt guilty the moment doubts entered my mind as to whether that was what I wanted. How could I be so selfish as to think of what "I" might want? There was no question. My mother knew what was best for me. Father was in Shillong at the time and was consulted on the phone. He, too, was caught up in the momentum of events leading up to the wedding to which about a thousand people came for dinner.

Within a short time I found myself in Germany – in a strange land with an unknown language and a strange man. I felt so alone. Not only did I not know this man, I did not really know males. I had no brother and had been kept away from other young males, as all "proper" young girls were at the time. It was a traumatic experience to feel so helpless, so totally overpowered in a traditional marriage to a chauvinistic man (and I am being kind here) where the wife is vulnerable. I was not prepared for this complete reversal in situations from a peaceful and happy childhood to one of a suppressed young adulthood. Yet I accepted it. The reason, I feel now, is best explained by the Indian psychoanalyst Ashis Nandy. He points to a "pseudo-innocence" which leads Indian women to an unawareness of their power to intervene in the real world because of the indirect psycho-social benefits of being a victim.[7]

We went back to India within the year, and I thought things might change with the birth of our son, Partho. They only got worse. Then we moved to Canada, but no sooner had we done so than my father died. Partho and I went back to India for an extended period. I returned to Canada devastated by my father's death but determined to do something with my life. I started university in Calgary (after ten years as a housewife) when my son started elementary school. Other than my times with my son and interactions at the university, I have blocked out from my mind the sixteen-year period of my first marriage. Alberta Government Graduate Fellowships, the Canada Council Doctoral Fellowship, the Killam Doctoral Fellowship – all enabled me to go through graduate school. Writing my Ph D dissertation on development theory focusing on power inequality between industrial countries and the Third World was like tracing the theoretical aspects of the personal dynamics of power which I was experiencing – the powerlessness of the Third World countries was similar to my own powerlessness.

The stress of my personal life made me physically ill by the time we moved to Ottawa. My sister and her husband Ashis (both doing their doctorates) were in Boston at the time with their children, Arjun and Shona. Neither they nor my friends could understand why I stuck to the situation. My self-esteem had dropped to zero and, given my cul-

7 Ashis Nandy, "Woman versus Womanliness: An Essay in Speculative Psychology" in B.R. Nanda, ed., *Indian Women from Purdah to Modernity* (New Delhi: Vikas Publishing 1976), 160.

tural baggage and lack of confidence, I just did not think of alternatives. It was when I realized what the strained home situation was doing to my son that I decided to leave.

This was the first major decision I had made in my life. I drove all the way to Calgary from Ottawa with my son, having a one-year appointment at the university, and no money. I informed my mother by letter. I have never looked back. I vividly remember my feeling as we drove west – was this how a bird feels when let out of a cage? Can freedom be so wonderful, I wondered? I know now that freedom is the most basic need of a human being. For me, all things worth having involve freedom – freedom to be oneself, freedom from oppressive people and oppressive structures.

The first thing I did in Calgary was to enrol my son and myself in a Taekwando (martial arts) course at the university. I needed to be free of fear – fear of staying alone at night, fear of walking home alone. I was still vulnerable. I wanted to be able to defend myself. Taekwando did wonders for me (even though I cracked a toe)! The physical skills which give the power to defend oneself also give psychological strength. Imagine my surprise when, in a class demonstration, I split a one-inch-thick, twelve-inch-long wooden square into two with one swift kick! Partho has continued with karate, but I stopped after three years of training and a restored self-image.

By the end of the year in Calgary I had four job possibilities. I came to McGill because I had known of its international reputation and wanted the stimulation it had to offer. Montreal was another important reason (although French is acquired through hard work, not osmosis as I had hoped). In choosing both I have been lucky.

McGill has done much for me, and I have, in turn, tried to do what I could. I have had the opportunity to serve on several interesting committees in the university and work in local and international projects. I enjoy teaching and have had the freedom to pursue my research interests in Third World development, and in educational issues for subordinate groups in society – specifically those defined by gender, race, and/or class. The rewards have been in various forms: in signing a book contract, in having an article published in a good journal, in getting a research grant. Perhaps the greatest satisfaction is to see a doctoral student make the Dean's List, to hear of a master's student getting a job in an international agency, or to receive appreciative letters from former students.

My years in Montreal have been fun. I look for the art, the music, and the theatre it offers. I have enjoyed showing off this beautiful city to the many friends and relatives who have visited me from all over the world. I have been enriched by my many friends and enjoy our small dinner parties over Indian food and scintillating conversations. I continue to look forward to dancing the salsa and the samba on Friday evenings. I have shared the excitement of being with Ashok when he has received many scholarly awards and national honours. We have done crazy things such as driving from the airport in Montreal after an international flight straight to Quebec City in the nick of time for his Order of Quebec. I remember my dilemma when he became an Officer of the Order of Canada in Ottawa the very day I was faced, as president, with a crisis in the Shastri Institute (and solved it long-distance). Little did I know when he became a Knight Commander of Merit that I would be honoured in the same Order this Fall as Dame of Merit, Sovereign Military Order of Saint John of Jerusalem (Knights of Malta).

Like the cruise ship docked in front, I have been on an exciting journey, frequently across several continents, and hope there will be many more stimulating ports of call in the years to come.

Excerpts from My Life

There are many things that come to mind as I recall my youth. There were the good times and the not so good times. Most people say that they can only recall the good memories. Why is it, then, that the not so good times seem to dominate my memory when I try and recall my youth? Why do I remember all the things that frightened me? All the circumstances that caused me to feel intimidated or insecure?

As in most native families, my parents had numerous children. There were twelve of us, six girls and six boys. I was the eighth child. My mother used to tell her family and close friends that she wanted to have a boy so much. She ended up having three girls before the first boy arrived and then she had two more girls before she had another boy. Then I came along. Probably my mother thought that she'd end up with mostly girls, but she was blessed with four more boys one after another, after my birth.

My father, Matthew, has always been a very overbearing figure in my life. We never had a close relationship, although I craved for his attention during my youth. Matthew was the authoritarian, and, although my mother had a fighting spirit, in the end she would succumb to his wishes.

The bits of memory I recall begin around the time my brother Joseph was born. I must have been two years old. I remember being weaned from my mother's breast. We were living in a tent that was shaped like a cross. On the arm to the left, that's where our family lived. On the next arm, which is the head, lived another family, then again another family lived right across from us. The fourth arm was the porch, which was to our right. There were three stoves, one for each family, which were situated around the middle of this complex. It felt very cosy when all the stoves were ablaze with fire. I'd be mesmerized when I saw the mouth of the stove where I could watch the

Annie Neeposh Iserhoff, B Ed (McGill, 1992)

fire as it snapped and crackled. On one of those days, I remember going over to sit on my mother's lap and pulling her blouse up to
nurse. She pulled her blouse back down and looked at me and said,
"I can't nurse you any more, you have a little baby brother, who
needs to nurse more than you now. How about going to Mary? She
volunteered to nurse you if you want." Mary was the neighbour. All
I felt was dejection and it sure didn't feel right to go to another
woman to nurse. From then on, I was weaned. It was hard to accept
what had happened, not because I loved to nurse but because that
was when I felt close to my mom. But, anyway, it was time to be independent.

Then I remember the times we travelled from the old camp to set
up a new camp or in search of food, animals that is. I recall being laid

down and wrapped in blankets and a tarpaulin and being strapped to a sled or a toboggan. There would be enough space for me to breathe and see the sky, the clouds, and the tops of both coniferous and deciduous forests when we were travelling by land. I remember feeling so helpless, so out of control, so claustrophobic. I wanted out. Finally, probably because of my fuss, someone decided to sit me up on the sled even though I was still tied down. That felt a lot better and I was able to observe what was happening all around me.

As in all societies, there were a lot of superstitions. It was hard not to be affected by them, and some stick with me because they were instilled in me when I was a child. It seemed that many of these beliefs were directed more towards the girls or women. This used to vex me or make me feel vile, although more than likely, I'd succumb to them.

The girls were not allowed to play with boys' toys and vice versa. The toys both the boys and the girls had were always made of wood, hide, canvas, or cloth depending on the toy. The girls were told, if they ever played with the boys' toys, that when they grew up they'd be dragging their breasts and that would be a horrendous burden. The boys were told that they in turn would lose their strength and would become very poor hunters if they played with the girls' toys. Another superstition was that if a girl or woman stepped over a boy's or man's legs, he would become an incompetent worker and hunter.

Our parents used to tell the boys to run out in the nude during the winter, hit their chests with their fists, and cry out, "Giiwedin, giiwedin," which means north wind, north wind. Then they'd come running back in within a few seconds. This was meant to bring on the wind so the men could have a better hunt. During one of these times, a girlfriend and I decided to beat the boys to it. We got undressed as fast as we could and ran out, beating our chests and yelling, "Giiwedin, giiwedin." As we ran out we heard our mothers and older sisters yelling, but it was too late, we were out there already. Did we get the lecture of our lives! Of course, we hadn't realized that only the boys could do something like that. It had looked like so much fun. We were told, "Now, we are going to have a real bad storm because of what you two did." Sure enough, there was a terrible storm, and the two of us felt we were the cause of it. However, afterward some of the older people thought it was very funny, and even to this day, one woman laughingly reminds me of this incident.

One day our parents were talking about a place called Mistissini. They said we would be travelling there as soon as all the lakes and rivers were clear of ice. They talked about seeing all their friends.

My first experience upon arriving in Mistissini seemed like waking up from a dream. I had been sleeping at the bottom of the head of the

canoe covered with some blankets and a tarpaulin to keep out the water. The humming of the motor had lulled me to sleep during most of
the travel by water, which was a good three-quarters of the trip. Each
time the motor would stop, I'd wake up, get up, and look around to see
if we were there yet, but I'd end up being disappointed. However, this
time when the motor stopped, I got up to see a whole bunch of tents,
and people swarming towards the bank where we were to beach. I
couldn't believe my eyes. Who were these people? How come I hadn't
seen them before? Had they lived here all the time? I couldn't wait to
get off the canoe and venture to their tents.

Somehow, I don't have any recollection as to when I first saw the
Hudson's Bay store. The only thing I can recall was it was different
from the tents we lived in. Every part of the building was made out of
wood, including the floor, and you could see outside through the glass
(windows). That was the only thing I remember, that impressed me.
Oh yes, and the Englishmen who worked there spoke the language I
used to hear from the talking box (radio). Some had hair the colour of
the sun during the day, others had hair that nearly matched the colour
of the sky at sunset. Oh, and their skin was so white. I was a little leery
of them because they looked different and they spoke in a language
that I couldn't understand.

Summertime was when the nurses got flown in. Parents were told to
bring their children to the nursing station for their annual check-up and
immunization. My mother took us there one morning after giving us a
bath in a washtub. She was saying that we must be clean and put on
clean clothes before we saw the nurses. On this particular morning, my
mother mentioned that she had seen worms in my stool. She described
the worms. The interpreter translated the message to the nurses. The
nurses had a little conference on the side.

The next thing I knew, my mother said I was going to be shipped to
the hospital. On that day, there were at least half a dozen or more of us
being shipped out, adults, teenagers, and children. As we boarded the
plane, I heard my mother say to one teenager, named Caroline, "Take
care of my daughter, don't let the French convert her to their church." It
sounded like something terrible was going to happen if this happened
to me.

The departure was a very traumatic experience. I cried until I was
exhausted and probably fell asleep after a while.

There was a whole world out there. Everything we saw was new. It
was beyond our comprehension. There were moving vehicles, of all
sizes, big houses, huge buildings with many floors. Everything was so
overwhelming. It felt as if I was being kidnapped to an alien land and
that I would never see my family again. I voiced my terror, and the girl

who was to look out for me assured me that I would be going home soon.

We seemed to be travelling forever, then one or two would be dropped at a certain town or hospital. By the time we got to our destination, there were only a few of us left. A nurse took me to the children's ward and it seemed like a long time before I ever saw a familiar face again.

There was one very frightening experience. A woman, whom I believed to be a nurse, was bathing me. She held my head under water until I struggled, swallowing some water while gasping for air. I cried and I'm sure she shut me up somehow for a while, because it happened more than once, before this stopped. She must have been caught because after a while this treatment finally ended. It was such a relief not to have to be bathed by this person again.

One morning, the nurses were fussing over me. Somehow, I knew they were planning to take me to the chapel. I recalled my mother's words to Caroline. I cried, asking for "Caroline, Caroline!" The nurses didn't know why I was so upset. So one of them went to fetch Caroline and she came. I was hysterical and told her what I was afraid of. She must have picked up some French because she was able to translate my fear. Caroline calmed me down and told me they weren't going to take me to their church after all. I don't know what other message Caroline told them, but I know I never did go to see the inside of the chapel.

Fall came and went, winter set in and I sensed panic setting in on me. Again, I carried on calling for Caroline. Finally they brought her to me and I told her I was terribly homesick and I wanted to go home. I said I'd been in the hospital long enough. It was time to go home. She told me it was too late, we were all stuck there for the winter. She reassured me that we would all eventually go home, the next summer. I must have cried for days. After many months, one bright sunny morning, Caroline came to see me and told me we were going home. It was the best news I'd ever heard and I felt so light and happy. Within a few days we got ready and as before we travelled by car first, then we took a plane which landed in Mistissini.

Fall came and it was thrilling to know that I would be going to the bush again. My father received his food voucher from Indian Affairs. He and my mother went to the Bay and got all the basic foods, such as flour, lard, sugar, baking powder, tea, coffee, powdered milk, currants, raisins, yeast, rice, oats, beans, and a few little surprises. Plus, he would buy on credit the essentials he needed to replace for hunting, fishing, and trapping. Most families had at least two or three canoes of various sizes to accommodate their different needs while hunting. These canoes were all very useful during the transportation from the village to one's hunting grounds. Everyone travelled by either paddling or using a two-and-a-half horsepower motor if they had enough money to spare to own one. Somehow, we were lucky enough to share our hunting grounds with someone who owned a motor. Anyway, we travelled into the bush in style that autumn. There was a whole string of canoes as we left for another ten and a half months in the wilds.

One day, I overheard my dad say to my mom, "Let's make some fire-water. We'll need raisins, beans and sugar." The first time, I was very curious and watched the process, not realizing that it was going to cause me terror when they consumed it. They said it would be ready a couple of weeks after it was made.

The day finally arrived when it was time to drink the homebrew. Needless to say, I wanted to try it. I was flatly refused and was told it was only for grown-ups. I asked why, and I was told that I'd get drunk. I didn't know what they meant and I managed to sneak a sip that was left at the bottom of a cup, just to taste it. It had a sweet, strong, pungent taste, yet it was pleasant enough. The grown-ups were laughing and seemed to be enjoying themselves.

However, as the evening wore on the adults seemed to get louder and louder. I realized they were arguing. The children were told to go to sleep. I guess I slept. Someone stepped on my feet and it woke me up. There was a lot of arguing now. Some of the adults were ready to punch each other. I couldn't believe that my parents sounded so hysterically loud and unreasonable. Children woke up crying. My heart was beating fast with fright. The adults seemed to have gone crazy. Suddenly, a fight broke out and I saw my parents involved in it. My young brothers and I started to cry. We were told to shut up while one of my older sisters took the youngest child and tried to calm him.

On later occasions, my older sisters and oldest brother were permitted to drink too and I felt like all hell broke loose. The early memories of the terrible drunken fights amongst my father, mother, sisters, brother, and other adults haunted me for a long time. We, the young ones, soon learned fast what it meant when our parents talked about making firewater. We learned to detest these events and hated the mention of such a drink.

On one such day, my older brother and I conspired to do something to stop these events. We decided to tip over all the pails containing the firewater. When we finally got our opportunity, we fulfilled our decision. Boy, when our parents found out, they were beyond reason. They quickly deduced who the culprits were. I can say now, if I had known then what judgment day meant, that's the term I would have

Annie at six or seven

used to describe my brother's and my predicament. With the use of a burning branch, we had one of the major tannings of our hides. It was terrifying to feel the extent of our parents' anger. This was the first of a few beatings that I recall vividly.

When I was six years old, the Indian agent came to the community to visit all the parents. He informed the parents that he was enlisting all the children of school age to go to school at Moose Factory. Moose Factory is in Ontario at the tip of James Bay. It is about 450 kilometres by air west of Mistissini, which is in central Quebec.

My family did a thorough cleaning in and around our tent. This was their way of showing respect for the Indian agent. It was almost like receiving royalty, and I never questioned it at the time. Finally, the agent arrived at our tent. There was a lot of apprehension and I felt it. After his greeting to my parents, he started to read off the names of their children, their birthdates and their ages. My heart was beating fast as he read my name. He asked, "Where is Annie?"

I had been hiding behind one of my sisters' skirt, hoping against hope that he didn't have my name. Who was I kidding? My sister pulled me out and around in front of her and replied, "Here she is!" The agent looked at me and said a few words which I didn't understand. Then one of my sisters, who had been in school for the last few years, translated his speech. He said I was old enough to go to school, but that I would never make it because I was too skinny and too small for my age. For all that was worth, I was relieved to know I had more time to live with my parents.

Two summers later I wasn't so lucky when the Indian agent came to our tent. He stated, "Annie looks ready for school now." My mother spoke up and said, "I don't really want her to be sent away to school because I need to raise and prepare her to take care of us when we get old."

The agent responded that if they didn't let me go, he would have her family allowance revoked and their food vouchers for basics cancelled for the year. My father spoke to my mom and tried to convince her that I must go to school. My mother didn't relent at that time, but my dad told the Indian agent to put me on the new student list. My mom was very upset with my father.

They argued for days about my situation. Finally my dad said, "I'm going fishing for a week or so. When I get back, I don't want to find Annie here." That was the end of the argument. My father had had enough and he was gone the following day without so much as a good-bye.

Someone from the village heard the plane as it headed towards our tiny settlement on the day the students were to fly out. A lot of the parents were very unhappy. Children were trying to hide because they hated the thought of leaving their parents for another ten and a half months. My brother Murray ran into the bush and tried to hide. He had been doing this time and time again.

He had told stories about the place. The terrible way they were treated both by the staff and their peers. The food, which made one puke. He used to refer to it as dog food. The many times he went to bed hungry. We all had heard horror stories of the place. Our parents felt helpless because they couldn't do anything about it.

This was to be the most powerful memory of my youth. I begged and pleaded with my mother not to let me go. She braided my hair. Then she asked one of my sisters to help get me dressed up and ready for the plane. All the while, I sensed her sadness as she was sitting there in the middle of the cabin floor. Meanwhile, my oldest brother, Philip, and one of my sisters were still looking for Murray. Philip finally found him and dragged him back to our cabin. By this time, my mother started to sniffle and I knew she was crying. Murray saw my mom sitting there crying and he felt he was the cause of it. He cried out, "Don't cry mom, I'll go to school, just don't cry." I threw myself beside her and grabbed her waist crying. I held on tight for dear life. My sisters were told to unclench my hands from my mom's waist. They dragged me out of the cabin and dragged me all the way to the plane. I fought them for all I was worth. Someone lifted me up and pushed me into the plane and closed the door. l cried, and realized that nearly all the children were crying except maybe a few of the older boys.

We all tried to look out with our tear-streaked faces. I noticed that some of the parents were crying. The picture of my mom sitting in the middle of the floor crying kept appearing in my mind and I'd burst out crying again and again. The plane smelled strongly of gas and it was making most of us sick. Some children were stuffing themselves with sweets to console themselves. It was a devastating sight. The plane started. My head was aching as the plane took off and most of us started to cry all over again. Finally, one by one, pupils fell asleep from exhaustion.

I woke up with the smell of vomit and I couldn't go back to sleep. Children were getting sick all around me and I got sick too. We all must have longed for the plane to land.

This experience was new to most of the youngest children. Some like myself had been exposed to these types of surroundings before. I sensed the overwhelming effect it had on all of us, especially on the inexperienced.

We arrived and got into a snowmobile and were driven to the residence. Some youngster translated what we were expected to do. We were told to go to the shower room, undress and shower. A couple of the counsellors came into the showers and helped us wash. Afterward, we were all herded into the washroom. Everyone was given a delousing treatment which left our skulls burning. This treatment was very degrading.

The first month or so was the hardest month for all of us. There were nights we would be crying ourselves to sleep. Some nights the counsellor would hear us and threaten that if we kept it up we would be spanked. Many of us young ones got a good spanking because we got caught crying from loneliness. Finally we learned to muffle our cries.

Everything my brother and others said about the school became a reality. Most of the time we all hated the place. However, there were a few happy times when we forgot our homesickness. Times when we were involved in organized activities such as movies, picnics, walks, canteen, or Brownies.

We heard that some of the older girls tried to run away, but got caught. They got the strap when they got caught. We also saw the older ones get humiliated, until they finally fought back physically. This again would require another strapping.

We, the younger ones, were informed that we were not allowed to speak our mother tongue. It was hard to follow such a requirement, since we didn't know the second language. Many a time did we get a spanking for getting caught speaking in Cree. For a while, we, the first year students, only spoke in one-syllable words, then short phrases in English.

Whenever we were out of sight or out of hearing from the counsellor we would speak in our native tongue. After a while, we learned to treat this requirement with a bit of play and humour. Some of us would compete to see who couldn't be caught speaking their language or who could pick up the English language fastest.

The first summer we went home is one of the saddest memories I have. The plane landed in our community. There were a lot of happy faces, both in the plane and on the dock where the parents and siblings were waiting for the airplane. Each of us was eagerly looking for familiar faces. My sister Helen had come to meet my brother and me. Her face shone with excitement as she came towards us, as I'm sure all our faces were shining. I was thrilled to be home again.

My father was at our tent and he greeted us with a handshake. I felt shy, a little weird and uncomfortable. Where was my mom? I thought, she probably went to the store to buy us some goodies and stopped to visit some of her friends along the way like she used to do. I waited for her to come home.

Helen prepared a meal for us and we all sat down to eat. Still, my mother hadn't come home. I was starting to get anxious, but finding excuses for why she wasn't home yet. After supper, I sat by the doorway, waiting and watching out for her to arrive any moment. Finally, my father said, "Annie, why are you sitting by the door? It's getting chilly. Get in and get your blankets ready, so you can go to sleep." I asked, "When is mama coming home?"

That's when they told us that my mother had been taken away to a hospital in Quebec City late last fall. I didn't ask any more questions. It hurt too much, but there were no tears that night. Somehow, I felt a premonition that it was worse than I wanted to find out. As the summer wore on, and the years came and went, little by little I was told all about my mother's situation.

For a long time, my siblings and I all felt we were the cause of my mother's condition. Each of us had been carrying a guilt that was heavy in our hearts. Of course, we weren't aware that we all had this guilt until many years later, after each of us led separate lives.

For seven straight years my mother was in that hospital and was never home. After her seventh year she finally came home, but she only lasted a couple of weeks. This time, they sent her to the Roberval Institute. She was there for the next five years. They'd release her for a couple of weeks during the summer and then she would go back.

Finally, after much negotiation, the family persuaded the Chibougamau hospital to keep her there. Now it wouldn't be so difficult and complicated to go and visit her. My mother has been kept there ever since. Once a year, she would be home for a few weeks and then would want to go back.

Today, it seems it would be impossible for her to come home at all. She is in a wheelchair and is now a wisp of a woman. Each of us, her children, find it almost impossible to be in her presence. It is unbearable to have seen her wither away all these years.

For the first five summers that I was home from school, I would beg my father not to let me go back to that horrid place. It was torture to have to go back there. During that time he never budged once.

In my fourth year, in midwinter, a group of us decided to run away from the residence to Rupert House, where we hoped to take a plane back to our community. The planning took about a month. One of us drew a map of the region, and mapped out where we would be going. There were a few students in the school who were from the Moose Factory community. We depended on their help and they gave us information on what we wanted to find out. Also we felt the native people in the region would help us. Some camps were placed on the map on the route we planned to take.

Towards the last couple of weeks we would store food, such as peanut butter and jam in plastic bags, apples, oranges, cookies. We were planning to ask a native family to provide us with bread and some sleeping bags. Of course, we were very naïve, but we didn't know it then. We felt we would succeed.

The time arrived when we were planning to leave. It was during the evening, after the night watchman made his first rounds. We were to leave in two groups of about six. My group was the first to go. We sneaked downstairs to the playroom, where our lockers were, to get our coats. However, one of the girls accidently slammed her locker door and we all were deathly quiet for a few seconds. We heard footsteps and we all got into our lockers hoping against hope that we wouldn't be caught. There was no such luck; someone had heard the noise and reported to another person who spread the word. Within minutes, one of the counsellors came into the playroom and started to open the lockers one at a time. One by one we finally all got out of the lockers.

We were told to wait in line. There were about five staff members. Four were female and one male. One stood in the playroom, one, the male, at the bottom of the steps, one at the top of the first set of steps, another at the top of the second set of steps, and our counsellor was waiting at the door of our dormitory. Every one of them had taken off one of their shoes or slippers, and the male counsellor had taken off his belt. We were all terrified of the male staff member because we all knew he would hurt us the most. As we arrived at each staff member we each got the spanking of our lives. Our bottoms must have been black and blue, for it hurt to sit down for days. All our privileges were taken away from us for at least a month.

Although I understood after a few years why we got punished, no one ever spoke to us about it. All we knew then was that we had done something that was bad in their eyes. However, we felt justified by our actions. All we wanted was to see and live with our parents.

There are a lot of horror stories that I can recall, during the time we spent in Moose Factory. We lost a lot of pride, self-confidence, and self-respect, and we developed an identity conflict. The separation of brothers and sisters drew families apart. We became like strangers to each other. We no longer knew or confided in each other. We all lived in some kind of shell. We only came partly out when we found someone who genuinely seemed to care. Even then we needed a lot of coaxing. Our bond had been broken.

In the fifth summer, we were informed that we were going to be sent to a new residential school in La Tuque. This time all the students who were still in elementary would be transferred to this new place. Everyone hoped it would be a better place for us, and the Indian agent assured us it would be.

Our parents were beginning to realize that we were developing different life attitudes and habits from theirs. They felt we were becoming a problem in the community. Many students in their early teens were starting to drink, especially the boys. The elders felt they were starting to lose control of their schoolchildren.

The students were being criticized that they didn't know how to work. The boys didn't know how to pitch a tent, how to set up nets, or how to hunt. The girls were being told that they couldn't handle a woman's work, such as getting boughs for the tent floor, washing clothes as fast as the bush women, chopping wood, or lugging pails of water. Soon we were referred to as the lazy school kids. These comments made us feel even worse about ourselves than before. It seemed that everyone was disappointed with us. We got the impression that we were failures. Some of the students were able to persuade their parents into letting them quit school. After a couple of years, it seemed that these adolescents had regained some of their self-esteem, whereas the schoolchildren were getting worse.

After a year in La Tuque, a lot of the students said that, for the first time, they actually enjoyed being in school. I was one who felt that way. Although we still got the most demeaning punishments when we were in trouble, it was a lot better than Moose Factory. The food was more edible. We could interact more with our male siblings and the activities were more coeducational with more variety. The seniors had more freedom and responsibilities. For the first time we actually filled out more and gained some weight. That summer when we came home, my father made a comment that I had grown up a lot and that I didn't look too skinny any more. It made me feel good to finally receive a positive comment from my dad, however small. By then, like all the schoolchildren, I needed and was starving for positive reinforcement, but words of praise came few and far between.

For the first time, in the summer when I was fourteen, I didn't ask if I could quit school. In fact, most of us were looking forward to going back. When my father returned, he made little hints on how much I was improving in doing the housework. Finally, he said, "You can quit school and go in the bush with us this winter."

It was my moment of triumph. I responded, "I asked you, year after year, if you would take me in and each time you refused me. Now, it is too late. I like going to school now and I'm going back. You cannot hold me back. I want to finish school." My father looked at me with a weird smile and didn't say anything. He never made a comment, not then or afterwards. I went back to school that year.

In our third year in La Tuque, we were informed that about fifteen students, both boys and girls, would be placed in private homes. These students would be: senior group, promising pupils, and ones attending the La Tuque High School. The housemother (staff member in charge) read out the names and my name came up. It was an exciting time and we all looked forward to a new experience and a more homelike environment.

The French people I lived with were a very close-knit family. Mme Beland was sixty-two years old and separated from her husband. Her eldest daughter Micheline, about twenty-seven then, was confined to a wheelchair, and her youngest daughter, Pauline, who was fifteen, lived with her. There was another sister, Diane, who was about twenty-three, a nurse working in Montreal.

Without realizing it, this family was a great help to me both socially and psychologically. The healthy attitude I developed was all due to their way of life and what transpired between us. I realize how lucky I was to have been a part of their family. To this day, I still have a very close contact with Pauline, who is like a sister to me.

Pauline is a very special person. In her mind, she adopted me as her sister, as she told me later. The first year it was difficult for me to get used to Pauline. She tried hard to be a friend, but I wasn't very cooperative. I had a few hang-ups that I couldn't cope with and I felt she was interfering. As months went by, I got settled in. Pauline began to seem less of a nuisance. We had our fights and disagreements like any healthy siblings and we learned to forgive and forget.

Since then, Pauline has always been a big part of my life. She was and is my salvation. She has shared and been with me through happy and traumatic times in my life. Because of Pauline and her family I was able to put my life into perspective.

One summer, I invited Pauline to spend a few weeks with me at home. She accepted my invitation. This was a wonderful experience for all concerned. We spent a week in Mistissini. By this time, my father had stopped travelling. This was his second year running a sturgeon camp, within his hunting ground. Pauline and I flew in and she spent a couple of weeks in the bush. Many a time, Pauline retells the time she spent in the bush with my family.

To this day, I believe my life is intertwined with the Beland family's. My experience living with them prepared me for my present situation.

In my last high school year I went home at Christmas. On New Year's Eve my girlfriend and I, like every teenager, had a few drinks. We decided to go out and find a party. Of course, we headed straight to the place where there seemed to be a big drinking party. Someone was playing fiddle music and we heard people step dancing. When we entered, the place was very crowded. The floors were wet and slippery because of all the snow the people tracked in, combined with the drinks that had been spilled. We saw many friends there. They were all drinking with bottles in their hands. We were offered a sip, which we took. One of the boys, Matthew, had never drunk before. Matthew was receiving his education in the States. He was in his last year in a prep school and was also home for the holidays. He was an Iserhoff, one of the non-status people in our village. My girlfriend and I both found him very attractive.

Tonight Matthew looked like he must have had too much. He fell to the floor. My girlfriend and I helped him up, before someone toppled on him. We took Matthew outside so the cold fresh air could sober him up a bit and sat him up on a skidoo that was stationed there. We told him to stay there until he felt better. Matthew asked me to stay with him and I was happy to comply. However, I asked him why he drank. He said his friends offered him the alcohol and he wanted to try it. He said he didn't enjoy it because it was making him quite sick and he didn't plan to try it again. That was how our relationship started.

The year we were to graduate, a friend of mine and I didn't quite make it, but our counsellor had faith in us and told us we were bright and had a lot of potential. He did a bit of research and found out that Brandon University was training native students to become teachers. These students didn't necessarily graduate from high school and some were even mature students.

Of course, this came about so fast. I never thought I could ever be a teacher. It was a real shock to realize that this counsellor had such unattainable ambition laid out for us. My ambition had fallen along the lines of secretary, hairdresser, or interior decorator if I was lucky. In my wildest dreams, I wanted to be an actor, in plays or, if I had a chance, in films. My counsellor got the forms. I was planning to apply at Banff Fine Arts University, but I chickened out. I thought I'd die of loneliness if I went that far alone. So I never fulfilled that dream.

Meanwhile, the counsellor kept encouraging us to go for the training. Finally, we were brave enough to consent although we didn't feel all that confident. It turned out to be an experience which would be engrained in our lives forever, a time when harsh realities hit us full force on our faces. We had encountered prejudice many times before with our peers and some authoritarian figures, but it seemed subtle compared to what we experienced in Manitoba. It was like a brutal awakening and rape of our innocence.

People on the street were rude and called us names in public even if we were minding our own business in broad daylight. Violence erupted between the natives and non-natives at dusk. Someone always got hurt and it was usually a native. It was a very painful experience.

The professors and our student counsellor were not aware of what was happening to us. They tried to make us change our minds, once we decided we were going to go back to Quebec. We couldn't cope with the circumstances that were arising. The natives there had never known any other way of life, so they were coping better than we could. That is, if drinking is one way of coping. My friend and I left and only wondered what happened to the friends we made. J.J. Harper was one of the close friends we made there. He had always been very supportive, although we saw what racism was doing to him. It was a real shock to see his name in the front pages: shot by a policeman and later in the same night declared dead.

After I went back to Mistissini that year, I called the Indian Affairs and asked if I could apply to study at O'Sullivan College in Montreal for the fall term. They gave their consent. So, I applied and I got accepted. However, fate had other plans for me, which were not visible right away.

In summer my father arrived from the bush. Then my mother came home from the hospital. For a little while everything seemed normal. The family was all together.

Finally, our differences arose. We had been scattered too long and our personalities had developed into the different lives we had experienced. Apparently, I had become very independent and I expected my younger brothers to be the same. However, they and my parents expected me to treat them in the traditional way, to serve the men. It was infuriating to be expected to do every little thing for them around the house. After a while I retaliated. It was a "no no" and I paid for it.

At the time, I felt like I was no good for anything or for anybody and I wanted to disappear. These types of words had been thrown enough into my face and I was beginning to believe that it was so. It seemed like everyone was venting their anger at me. Many hurting things were said and I knew my people felt justified, but their values were not mine any more. I was a lost cause as far as my grandmother and parents were concerned.

I gathered some stuff and ran out of the cabin. I didn't know where I would go. I felt like the world was against me so I didn't feel like seeing anyone. Finally, I headed for the houses referred to as student residences, which were supposed to be closed for the summer. I checked one door and it was unlocked. I went in and locked the door. I hid in there for two or three days but no one seemed to realize that I wasn't around. I cried and cried for hours at a time while I was in there, feeling like my whole world had crashed around me. I felt I didn't belong anywhere any more. Finally, I went back out. I hadn't eaten anything during that time and I realized I was hungry. However, I had made a decision. It was time to leave the community.

Most of the younger members of my family seemed to have disowned me as well as my grandmother, my parents, and my unmarried siblings that summer. I left the community as soon as I could and headed south to Montreal, hopefully to prepare for my future.

The following year, after a negative experience at O'Sullivan College, I ended up at McGill with other native students who were undergoing teacher training. We were being trained to be teacher aides within our prospective communities.

Most of us finished the year successfully. That summer, I worked at the Chibougamau hospital as an interpreter for the native people. My French was quite poor, so I had to make do with the little I knew and picked up a little more French while I was working.

Meanwhile, I, along with other native teacher trainees, had applied to be teacher aides. The interview took place that summer, in our community. A few days later, we found out we were hired, not as teacher aides, but as teachers. I was going to teach pre-k and kindergarten.

That summer was 1973. Matthew had asked me to marry him and I consented. Finally, the good times had come back.

JANET G. DONALD

Sketches for an Autobiography

An autobiography is a tale of personal development, of the choices one makes or the paths one follows, of coming to terms with the context or breaking barriers, of confrontation, accommodation, and assimilation. For a psychologist, a tale of personal development must also take into account the effect of the topography or setting at each stage of development. To write this essay, my first task was to find a way of capturing the psychological setting or lifespace in which I grew up.

The title of this book posed a second dilemma for me, since, in the forties and fifties in southwestern Ontario, having an agenda was not part of the topography; adaptation was the ethos of that era. We were expected to care and to adjust; having an agenda was suspicious if not aberrant. Would I have dared to have an agenda? Would it be recognized if I had?

Autobiographies are more frequently romances than histories, works of fabrication and concealment rather than expositions. Understanding the limitations of memory and the tendency to elaborate, I needed a method which would enhance impartiality or control bias. Added to this problem was the sheer number of roles I remembered playing as a child. Virginia Woolf said that we talk of six or seven of our thousand selves. Which of the multiple personae or roles I had played as a child, adapting to parents, siblings, aunts, uncles, cousins, or in school, ballet class, or at a party, would I describe?

The cognitive limitations of self-disclosure and my being a novice in the domain of biographical writing prompted me to begin my investigation for this essay by reading a series of biographies and autobiographies (Bair's of Simone de Beauvoir, Rollyson's of Lillian Hellman, Ayre's of Northrop Frye, Greer's of her father, Steinem's *Revolution from Within*, Heymann's of Jacqueline Kennedy, Hepburn's *Me*), a mixture of kind and unkind reviews of lives. Although Frye insisted that he had unconsciously arranged his life so that nothing had ever happened to him, a common theme in these books was the quest or task orientation displayed by each biographee. The only exception to the rule was Germaine Greer's father, but she compensated for his lack of purposive behaviour. Generally speaking, my reading suggested that having an agenda might be a *sine qua non* for landing in print.

I learned from a radio symposium of biographers in June 1992 that the current mode in biographical writing is to "bare souls" and reveal real, flawed persons and society's reaction to them; for example, Marie Curie's affair, or Sartre's alcoholic demise. Revealed faults in biographical writing raise the issue of privacy or taboos, one of which provided a rationale for my doubt about having had an agenda. The controlling ethos for many of the women written about in current biographies, women of the late nineteenth and early twentieth centuries, was that respectable women did not work. The symposium participants pointed out that although work is now central to women's lives and is seen as necessary, it was only around 1960 that it became acceptable to talk about women working, hence having agendas, or careers. This explains why the cohort after mine, now in their early forties, readily use the terms "career" and "career planning," while members of my cohort do not, even though many have led accomplished lives. The symposium participants saw 1960 as the beginning of an era of openness. It was about that time, when I was in college, that "role playing" became a mildly pejorative descriptor of classmates who had so-called hidden agendas.

The solution to the problems of establishing lifespace influences, determining whether I had had an agenda, and controlling for subjectivity or fabrication lay surprisingly close to home. During the last seven years I have employed ethnographic methods in studies of the learning task in the university. These methods could be used to establish the setting in which I had grown up and to consider its effect on my development. Visits to the sites of my development, and interviews of those who had known me, "key informants," matched over time periods, would, I reasoned, allow me to accurately depict my lifespace and set parameters for my memories. The outcome would be a series of sketches from different perspectives as for a portrait. I decided to interview friends from school, college, and later life, as well as family (father, brother, sister, cousin, aunts). I began with the question "Did I have an agenda?," and I took notes on my laptop computer. My informants' replies began conversations which at times continued for several hours. In the process of interviewing, I found myself gathering both family and local history.

One of the most revealing findings about the interviews was that people did not speak of actual events or occurrences, which would pro-

Janet as babe in arms (1941)

vide a setting or empirical proof, as much as they spoke of personal at-tributes. Memories were stored within a conceptual framework of a person rather than of happenings. Second, the memories said more about the relationship between my interviewee(s) and me than about me. Often, memories were of unexpected or individualistic behaviours; the unusual was salient and therefore encoded. My interviewees' re-flections were frequently comparisons of the ordinary with the extraor-dinary. They thus resemble snapshots and viewpoints rather than a coherent narrative.

I began by travelling to my childhood home in Riverside, Ontario and asking my father if I had had an agenda. A person of few words (the fifth of nine children), he replied in the affirmative, but also rec-ognized that it might have been unconscious.

You sure did. Because everything you did, you had to be tops. You were all agenda. You may not have known it, but you had it.

He then gave an example of an incident that occurred when I was four or five.

Go back to your ice cream cone – that's what your whole life has been like – you were going to do it.

One Sunday afternoon, desiring a chocolate ice cream cone, I care-fully went through the entire household, some five bigger people, asking each in turn if he or she would walk to the drugstore with me. This strategy was essential because I was not allowed to cross the street by myself and I had to cross the street to get to the drugstore. Unsuccessful in finding an escort, I went to my piggy bank, extracted a nickel, and walked down the street to the drugstore, where I pur-chased the desired cone. Unknown to me, my father had trailed me to the store. I think this incident encapsulates my family's perception of my personality.

I was more surprised by my father's next comments, startling because I had a picture of myself as the quiet middle child who had not occupied the limelight.

More competitive as you grew up: competitive in Sunday School; having your own way of doing things.

Took opportunities; had your own ability to think things through.

Too aggressive, that is, took a project and ran with it. Got it from your mother.

My parents were community leaders, my father the superintendent of the Sunday school and chair of the school board, my mother the district commissioner of Girl Guides. My dominant childhood memory of both parents is of their chairing meetings. I found my father's evaluation of my being "too aggressive" inconsistent with the inscription he had put on the family tombstone – "Let your light so shine before men that they may see your good works and glorify our Father which art in Heaven" – so I asked him what he meant by the term "aggressive," and if his "doing things" meant that *he* was aggressive.

By aggressive, I mean you were going to do it. Aggressiveness means push. You had energy, and leadership qualities.

So the definition of having an agenda includes aggression, initiative, independence, and some degree of interpersonal authority.

The following day I visited my three aunts, my father's younger sisters. I had happy childhood memories of staying with each of them when I was a pre-schooler. Their view of me was much more similar to my memory of my childhood persona than my father's was.

Blonde, very tiny, graceful – dancing; shy, well mannered; had a very close relationship with your father – his pride and joy. Beamed when he saw you.

You go for the top; have to be the top, the very best of what you're trying to do. Very shy, not bold.

I found their description more authentic, although being the "best" and being "shy" seemed odd co-descriptors. I think, however, that this is what the topography of my early childhood allowed me to be.

My brother has given me some of the best educational advice I ever received: to take physical sciences and three maths in grade 13, to accept each year as a new and different learning experience, and to be observant (and quiet) going into a new situation. Five years older than I, he also has the most immediate memory of me as an infant, so I was interested to see if I would get corroborating evidence from him. I preface his remarks by saying that the position my brother played on the high school football team was tackle.

You had a will that could be interpreted as having an agenda. You had always the attitude of being a winner, no matter how many times I knocked you down. You were going to succeed, that is the term I would use.

It sounds as if my earliest childhood lessons might have been in survival techniques. When I asked my brother where he thought I got my winning attitude, particularly since I would never have described myself in that manner, he replied:

It was obvious from a very young age. You walked along the top of the furniture; you were going to do it.

I began a habit of crawling up and along the back of the chesterfield when I was a few months old. I still like hilltops.

We in the family had an expression, "But that's Janet." That meant you were going to do your own thing. You were independent and you are independent still.

Here was another reference to an inherent personality and the recognition of considerable determination, even to the identical phrase "You were going to do it." The definition of having an agenda has enlarged to include having a will and the attitude of being a winner. Why do I remember being the quiet child, when others in my family see me as active and self-confident? I gathered further insight from my younger sister.

You always have a clear agenda; it may not be clear to those around you, but you go for what you want and you get it. "Just Janet" meant the rules were not going to apply to you. You stepped outside the prescribed role.

My sister's suggestion that I go for what I want and get it strikes me as inaccurate to the extent that there are many universally desired things – love, fame, power and money – which I think I would enjoy more of. The "just Janet" phrase developed, I believe, quite innocuously, from a favourite story book entitled *Just Mary Stories*. But my sister's comments about doing my own thing were consistent with those of my father and brother. It seems that my immediate family held the view that I was a very independent child and that this was not wholly approved of. How did I come to be that way?

I asked a close girl friend, first met at Edith Cavell School in grade 4 when we were nine, what she remembered.

You had objectives; you always seemed to me to have a plan. Going over and buying material in Detroit, and whipping up outfits, skirts, and outfits made to match. There were always plans.

I remembered being told by another close girl friend in high school that I was two different people in school and out (adaptivity again), so I asked my friend if this was so, but she replied,

No, because we were in school together, had been in school for a long time. And you were not competitive. When you got to university and into the

Air Force, it was for a reason. It was not that you did things deliberately, but you did them.

Once again, competition was given a negative valence. Agendas were not conscious. I asked my school friend if she thought that other classmates had had plans. Did the boys have plans? Speaking with thirty years of experience as a secondary school teacher, she replied that we had not had much guidance compared to what there is now. She continued:

Likeable, I don't remember ever arguing with you. Good discussions, and not agreeing with what you said, but a sense of acceptance. I think you have a great mind, and you always had. It's nice to have friends who are smart. When you had a viewpoint, you would stand up in class; you would ask why? You loved to challenge the teacher.

Great times together – always loved going to your house – playing croquet in the backyard, your mother was so nice. It was a very calm relationship ... many visits over the years.

One definition of a friend is someone who approves of you. But I did not remember challenging my teachers; I do remember differences in points of view. I contacted my intellectual rival in high school, now a consulting engineer, and asked him if I had had an agenda in high school.

Yes, you did. You were always pushing for excellence, determined to make a career for yourself: qualities and determination were there. They would have led you to college. You were enthusiastic about psychology. I don't know why you made that decision, other than that you were always interested in what people were thinking.

The teenage personality begins to gel, and the contrasts among family role, public persona and friend are once more enunciated.

My closest cousin (I have eighteen first cousins), one year older than I and a confidante from early childhood, provided a synthesis.

Conformist on surface – tiny, blonde, pretty, cheerleader, prom queen, bright and not the oldest. Always the sense that there was something else: this is not enough; this is not where I want to be; looking for something more. Now you are less a surprise, because you are doing something you are good at and enjoying it.

Thirtieth homecoming in October 1992 at the University of Western Ontario provided the opportunity to review the university setting which I entered in 1958. I asked two of my fraternity sisters (we were members of a women's fraternity), one my big sister and the other my roommate, if women at Western had had an agenda. My roommate, who had entered Western in the same year and graduated with me in 1962, replied:

Mother had an agenda, for me to do journalism and business. After graduating (in journalism), I wanted to go into teaching, so that was my agenda. I now teach language disorder kids. I was not materially driven, I did what I wanted.

My big sister, who had entered Western in 1957 and graduated in 1960, replied:

Hard question. I don't think that I had an agenda. I was in journalism for one year, then switched to English and history. The thing I got most out of university was the opportunity to join organizations and to learn and develop skills that I have since used, for example, as first woman chair of the United Way and as manager of two political campaigns. So it was the skills I gained that were important. At Western, girls in medicine were hassled but lasted it out; one girl in engineering lasted two years.

The chilly climate extended after graduation. My roommate remembered her first job:

At Canadian Press the men put the playgirl pictures up on the wall around my desk. They were crude and insensitive.

These comments reminded me of an experience in my sophomore year, in 1960, as a member of the Undergraduate Women's Organization. Throughout the year, representatives from Canadian corporations conducted job interviews on campus, and my task was to talk to the representatives about interviews for women. After many phone calls, three agreed to speak to me. One showed up, and bluntly said that Canadian corporations were not going to interview women because they were not going to hire them.

I asked my fraternity sisters what they remembered of the atmosphere at Western. My big sister replied:

Revolutions in Hungary, Cuba, wearing black armbands, "Better red than dead," the cold war. Most girls were spending time looking for boys and worrying about their relationships with boys.

When I juxtaposed my memory of Western being true to its epithet "the country club" with our fraternity being intellectual, my big sister remembered:

It was too intellectual, the other two sororities looked down on ours because it was so intellectual.

She had been our fraternity vice-president and pledge trainer, teaching us the Greek alphabet and fraternity lore, and nine of eighteen pledges that year had A averages, extraordinary at that time. I think our year was the watershed cohort, although we did not flaunt our intelligence. At the end of third year, a friend on the University College Council with me expressed fear to his fraternity brothers that I might fail my year: that year I had received a prize for top grades in psychology and I held a major four-year scholarship.

Was the atmosphere different for young men? I asked a close friend who had met me during my first year at Western if he had had an agenda.

I had a minor agenda, business then law.

He became a gynecologist and a pathologist on his way to becoming a cardiologist.

You were much more one to have an agenda: wanted things your way, in your career or self-worth; self-assured: much more a sense of yourself and what you wanted to do.

You wanted to save the world, had important things to do in it.

You had an idea of the future, ability to accomplish something.

I had not hidden my light under a bushel with this friend, but would it carry through to adult life? Graduating from the honours psychology program in 1962, I did a clinical internship at the 999 Queen Street Mental Hospital in Toronto, where I learned a new criterion for human capacity which has served well over the years: the ability to cope. I returned to Western to complete a master's degree in 1963 with help from a Canada Council pre-master's grant, married a graduate of Western's MBA program, moved to Toronto where I worked in the research department of the Board of Education for the City of Toronto for a year, began a doctoral degree in applied psychology at the University of Toronto in 1964, produced a charming infant in 1965, and graduated in 1968. One week after my thesis oral, I loaded child and cat into car and headed to Montreal to join the transferred spouse.

My first job in Montreal was as a tests and measurement specialist for the Protestant School Board of Greater Montreal. I asked a friend who was headmaster of one of the schools in the Board at that time if I had had an agenda.

Yes, the impression I had was that you knew where you were going. I sensed it in your detachment. You appeared to be observing and biding your time.

Why would a sense of detachment, which could be interpreted as a form of non-engagement, be a sign of having an agenda? Was I simply being cautious in a new setting? When I asked for an example, my friend said:

You appeared so poised and so aloof. Most people would recognize that you were different from the people working there. You were better dressed. It was a male bastion.

I then asked him if what I had done in the intervening twenty-five years was consistent with his early impression.

Very much so. You became part of the Montreal establishment profession-ally, where the work that you do would be recognized, both externally and internally, perhaps more externally than internally.
In 1970 at the opening of Vanier College, I became coordinator of psychology. In 1973 I joined McGill's Centre for Learning and Development, which metamorphosed into the Centre for University Teaching and Learning in 1984. I became director of the centre in 1982. I asked the former director, who had hired me, if I had had an agenda.

A written plan for your life? I don't think so. Some things you wanted to do or be or have? Yes, there are lifestyle things. You seemed to go after a life that is – adventurous. You like intellectual adventuring and exploring; you like to travel but you like to travel in your mind as much. The kind of work you have been doing has been a cumulative exploring of the whole area. So I think you must have an interest at least if not an agenda to go deeply enough into the area you are studying, not to pop around. You were the first female in the Centre; that was a little bit of a struggle at the time.
I asked if he noticed changes over the twenty years.

There was an evolution, a slow, gradual change rather than some revolutionary change. You have probably accomplished the construction of the world in which you live. I don't think you are simply reactive, and I think that is quite an accomplishment. There are a lot of other accomplishments, in terms of a position of leadership at McGill and in the profession itself, your research work.
Constructing one's own life is a powerful metaphor, an immense challenge, and, according to my reading of the Judeo-Christian heritage, evil. My sister talked about the challenge.

What I also learned from you specifically was that you could do it on your own, you could travel, create your own space, and that was ok. You did not always have to be a mixer. There were things that you could do on your own, enjoy by yourself. There was a great deal to be said about having your own career, the fun of it, the feeling of being successful.
It is a finding of the self and finding that doing that is not selfish. That is one of the critical messages that one has to get through. We have been so socially conditioned to do everything for everybody else that we forget about ourselves ... Going away with you was a holiday: I could become curious. You encouraged my curiosity, it was like finding a new world, a new self, taking off the chains.
I don't know how much you reveal about your experiences to other women to enable them to get through the system, to give them courage to carry on, but it certainly helped me.

What have I learned from this study? I see immense changes in the topography since I was a child. The direction of change appears posi-

Dr Janet Donald, director, McGill Centre for University Teaching and Learning

tive and supportive. "Having your own agenda" was described in the forties in terms of "being tops," "competitive" and "too aggressive," then as having a "will," "being a winner" or "doing your own thing." In the fifties, terms like "having objectives," "having plans," "deter-

mination," "looking for something more" were used. By 1960, the
phrases become "self-assured," "wanted to save the world," "an idea
of the future," and "knew where you were going." More recently, the
descriptors are "intellectual adventuring and exploring," and "construction of the world in which you live." The terminology is not only
more positive evaluatively but more active and engaged.

The results of the interviews were, to say the least, unanticipated. I
expected to hear about the events that made me what I am. According
to my "reality controls," I had an exploring and independent personality which was predetermined rather than learned, inevitable rather
than responsive. Corollary to this finding is that initiative may be
viewed as aggression and may not elicit support within one's family.
The interviews suggest that the opportunity to observe within the family and my success in learning science and mathematics in school contributed to my choice of psychology as a field of study. But my choice
was an independent one. My mother was appalled by my preference
for science; my high school teachers decided that I would enroll in the
English language and literature program at university. There is consis-
tency in my level of determination. Success occurred when I did not
"buy in" or accommodate. Reading this essay, I am reminded that one
of the first things I was conscious of learning as a child was that other
people, well intentioned as they might be, either do not "get it quite
right" or are only too willing to make decisions for you that do not take
completely into account your needs, attributes, or desires.

Although by doing this study I have learned something about myself as a developing individual, I have told but one small tale. Anaïs
Nin remarked in her highly explicit journal that there were still many
omissions. I recognize that there are many other tales to tell about my
life, and that this essay is confined to a very specific area of it. I do not
believe I would have told this tale if I had opened my notebooks, archives, or my memory.

As premise or guideline for autobiographic writing, I deduce that
the "baring of souls," if trendy, is naïve. The interviews and my ex-
planation of them *are* in one sense revealing, although there are no
bare shoulders. The most personal and dramatic stories of my life
have not been registered in this essay. This is partly due to the use of
biographical interviews, but I surmise that, paradoxically, fiction may
be a more appropriate mode to tell one's most dramatic and truest
tales.

The stories that I would write are stories of how pathways diverge,
what directions are considered, of Canada's urban culture, of relationships of many kinds, of the course of intellectual and personal development. Stories of how that leads to a change in direction, what is

constant, all these interest me. I think we need to tell and to read more of these tales. In *Women Who Run with the Wolves*, C.P. Estés says that tales are, in their oldest sense, a healing art. I perceive that as society in general deconstructs, as authority is more universally questioned, we shoulder greater responsibility for the construction of our lives and the need to tell our tales becomes an imperative.

Becoming Feminist

Tracing my feminist development back to its sources means going back to my childhood, and to the profound influence exerted upon me by my mother. My mother was (and is) a brilliant woman who was told half-way through her doctorate that – despite her scholarships, awards, and accomplishments – she would never receive tenure because of her sex. I was raised by a woman who realized that it would be more practical for her to type and edit her husband's doctorate than to complete her own; by a woman whose husband left her and who raised three young girls alone; who endured the prejudice and hostility of a close Catholic community whose members whispered "divorce" as though it were a dirty word; who was independent, took lovers, and painted the front door of our stolid house a bright, fire-engine red; who worked two jobs and finished her degree; who kept her girls fed, cared for, and loved, who taught her daughters that women were worthy, capable, and strong; who led us by her own example.

I grew up in house filled with women: my mother, two sisters, cats (always female), and visiting aunts. I was the youngest child, quiet and introspective, and I learned my lessons by watching and listening. I listened as my mother described how her father had called her "useless" and had discouraged her throughout her university career. I watched my eldest sister try her hand at everything – music, art literature, science. I watched her dye her blonde hair black, tear her clothes, enrol in the almost entirely male field of computer science, and graduate at the top of the class. I saw my second sister play the role of blonde bombshell; watched as she streaked her hair, worried about her clothes, her weight, her makeup. But then I saw her at night, without makeup, as she pored over the advanced calculus and geometry which came so easily to her, and I learned how false and exhausting play-acting could be.

Emily White and friend

I learned to read at an early age. I read everything and anything: adventure stories, cookbooks, histories, travelogues, pet care manuals, romances. I never read *Nancy Drew*. I developed a dangerously fertile imagination, and would spend whole days in my make-believe worlds, worlds in which I was a princess, a private eye, a movie star, or a lionhearted adventurer. Always worlds and roles in which I was powerful, independent, and in command.

I was a good student. My grades were consistently high and I won the awards that they give out to girls: best girl in math, in reading, in French. Never the best student, just the best girl. I was a naturally conscientious pupil and throughout my grade school and high school careers I applied myself diligently to the material that was taught to me. I learned men's histories, I adhered to male epistemology, and I studied male writers. My grade 13 English textbook was entitled *Man and His World*; women's role and treatment in history were not addressed; women writers were not read. I went to a highly conservative school in which "feminist" was a term of disparagement and the word "lesbian" too embarrassing to utter even as an insult. I memorized and internalized a curriculum based upon a tradition in which women had been denigrated, erased, silenced. I was a straight-A student.

By my last year in high school I was starving myself. I lost thirty pounds and spent my days delirious with hunger. My teachers said nothing to me; my principal called me to his office, congratulated me on my fine academic performance, and recommended that I represent my high school at three board-wide functions. My anorexia was an attempt to assimilate into what I knew was an acceptable mould; my ideas, independence, and ambition otherwise contradicted what I had been taught was proper and valuable in a woman. Denial not just of my needs and wants, but of my very self, seemed, at the time, a viable solution.

I did not come to McGill as a feminist. Older students jeeringly warned me that the Women's Union was just for "ugly dykes"; I did not know that a women's studies minor existed. I took the large, first-year survey courses, in which my high school lessons in men's history and men's literature were covered more thoroughly. I lived in a dormitory which featured "Eat the Cock" parties, which did not warn women of the ghetto's high rates of rape and assault, which was run entirely by men, and which catered almost exclusively to male behaviour.

I cannot recall when or why I started to read feminist theory, nor can I remember the first "feminist" book that I read. But I do know that the books began to show me a world which I had not realized existed. The voices of women such as Adrienne Rich, Mary Daly, Joanna Russ, and Germaine Greer rang out from the pages – harsh, angry, brilliant, and incisive. Their voices began to clear away the clutter which had accumulated through years of schooling and years of living in a sexist society. My reading provided me with a genuine awakening which allowed me to see myself, my life, and the roles of other women in new, clear light.

I have been writing this autobiography in a chronological manner and have brought myself up to the present, or at least to the recent past. And I seem to have come to a bit of a standstill. The last three years of my life are still too fresh and new – too blurred almost – to permit me to write about them in any sort of systematic way. Events and influences merge and overlap in a way which defies categorization. There have been Take Back the Night marches and Pro-Choice demonstrations; the December 6th massacre; poems by Audre Lorde; the rising rate of violent assaults upon women in my neighbourhood; pamphlets and magazines from radical feminist presses; conservative attacks upon abortion rights; glorification of the nuclear family; *Notes on Lying* by Adrienne Rich; travels on my own; classes in feminist theory; investigations into witchcraft; the Women's Union; talks and arguments with friends; and all of the other minutiae of daily life – the wolf whistles, the jeers, the discrimination and bigotry – which serve as constant reminders that ours is a profoundly sexist society.

I have just reread this "autobiography" and I realize that the first few pages read more like a litany of complaints and abuses than as the orderly presentation of events for which I had been aiming. But it is precisely my anger which is the primary force behind my current, highly politicized, feminist frame of mind. My anger and my convictions are inseparable. I have had to fight against the enervating influence of the androcentric culture in which I have grown up, and any and all feminist work which I pursue in the future will be devoted to reviving what my mother taught me: that women are strong, brilliant, capable, and worthy, and that nothing should ever prevent any woman from realizing the richness and potency which she possesses.

Humour and Death

Kwey.

This story about my life and my family relationships cannot be told without talking about humour and death. To link them may seem paradoxical, but both have significantly shaped how I view life and the world around me. What has emerged is a woman who is now on a spiritual and emotionally satisfying path; I'm walking the walk instead of talking the talk. Former preoccupation with the end results has given way to simple daily mindfulness. I take nothing for granted anymore. Resentment, quiet rage, blame, and bitterness towards certain people, situations, and attitudes no longer erode my soul. The spiritual, emotional, intellectual, and physical component parts of myself are more balanced and, consequently, I am becoming teachable. This flexibility allows me to share with you the personal experiences and perspectives that have affected how I think and feel today. Humour and death have shaped my life, contrasting the Aboriginal culture of my mother's family, which has sustained me, and the francophone culture of my father, who died when I was nineteen.

I am an Algonquin (Anishnabe), the first-born daughter of a first-born daughter of a first-born daughter, and I am the mother of a first-born daughter. Yet, I come from a patrilineal Aboriginal society. This inheritance has made a strong impact on my life, and I cannot separate myself from my family and its complex web of interrelations or my story will be shallow and incomplete. As a result of my upbringing, my attitudes, beliefs, values, and subsequent choices in life, as a female, are closely linked to my very large extended family on my mother's side. Allow me to walk you part-way through some of these people and places, starting with my maternal grandparents, who had a huge influence on my life.

My grandfather, Nona Manatch, was adopted and raised as an only child in the Rapid Lake area, in Parc de la Verendrye, Quebec. He was raised in the traditional ways of the Algonquin people; family groups travelled and set up camps where the hunting, trapping, and fishing were considered to be plentiful. They hunted moose and trapped fox, wolf, mink, marten, and various other small animals for their furs. They fished sturgeon, pike, trout, whitefish, doré, and barbottes. I'm told by many that Grandpa was a favourite guide – he delighted the tourists because he had an infectious laugh and was always good-humoured. One elder I interviewed, for a monograph I'm in the process of writing, told me about my grandfather's legendary laugh. He said that if you were on the same lake as my grandfather and his tourists, you could hear his belly-laugh for miles, and hearing it would make you laugh even though you didn't know the joke. We grandchildren worshipped him and loved his company because he never got angry and was always an uplifting person to be around. Life to him was serious, but he never took it seriously. He believed in providing for his family, but found time to get to know his many grandchildren. What I found endearing about him was that he couldn't swim and his livelihood was guiding fishermen, and he had a morbid fear of snakes and the woods were full of them. But these fears never prevented him from doing what he had to do to provide a good living for his family, and this included a good education.

The women set up the camps, which involved airing out and cleaning the log cabin that was usually situated on the family trapline. Canvas tents were set up if they were off the trapline and hunting big game. The surrounding bush area had to be cleared to make place for busy camp activities like cooking, washing, and working. The women (grandmothers, mothers, and older daughters) cooked, sewed, took care of the children and elders, helped repair fishing nets, traps, and hunting gear, and tanned animal hides. As a rule, the men did the hunting, fishing and trapping, but it wasn't unusual for some women to go out with the men and work alongside them. Camp activity was busy and the work was hard, but leisure times were filled with laughter, music, teasing, cajoling, and lots of talking and story-telling. Dogs and puppies were a common sight at camp, and some dogs proved to be useful in the winter when they were harnessed to pull sleds when men went out to hunt or check a trapline.

My mother told me a story about one of their dogs, Rags, an intelligent mixed husky who actually earned some money. My grandfather had been hired as a guide by an American and Grandpa needed Rags to help him bring the supplies to the designated camp area. The American was impressed by Rags's work and put him on the payroll; he even got a cheque. Mom's family still laugh about the meal they enjoyed in the restaurant "on Rags." This is the same Rags who took off with my mother's hand-made doll, patiently crafted by her mother, shook it to shreds, and buried it in a hole. But he had left part of the doll sticking out of the ground so Mom found it and ran crying to Nanny, who had to suppress a smile. It was funny to hear both of them telling the story; Nanny enjoyed remembering what a character Rags was and how amusing the incident, Mom remembers how upset she was but also remembers how kind Nanny was to make her another doll.

I really like the way past events are discussed in my maternal family – there is a genuine openness with the feelings that are evoked. I've witnessed crying, laughing, whimsical smiling, the whole range of behaviour associated with emotion. Stories are sometimes embellished, or reach mythical proportions, but the core feelings remain and I never tire of hearing the many stories told and retold at family gatherings.

Children were central to camp life and were present at all activities. The toddlers learned by participating in the various duties by playing and imitating the older ones. When they were older, children were gently guided and initiated into their roles; little girls helped and worked alongside the women and the little boys did likewise with the men. My mother was about eight years old when she learned how to bake bread and bannock (an Indian bread made without yeast), and was already taking care of her younger siblings. Babies were never far from the action. Aunts, cousins, older sisters, grandmothers, great-grandmothers, and mothers held them constantly, or they were bundled into "tikinagans," cradleboards which were made of wood, cloth, or felt and hide. Mothers or favourite caregivers would add their personal touch to the tikinagan by sewing on lace, braid trim, or special fabric. The babies looked like little cocoons, laced up to their necks, in their cradleboards, which were leaned against a tree or a rock. Very few mothers use a tikinagan today, although many of us own one; there are still a few people who know how to craft them, but they are dying. Fortunately, the craft is being passed on in some homes or in culture classes at the school. My grandmother and grandfather made little ones for me and my sisters to put our dolls into and we still have them. I treasure mine, for it reminds me of times past and how the Anishnabe traditionally lived.

News of pregnancies and babies is met with great joy and excitement in Indian families even today, and family activity centres around children. On the reserves I've lived on and visited, children are omnipresent. They are rarely excluded from events like weddings, funerals, parties, bingos, pow-wows, and feasts. They are equally present at traditional rituals like sweat lodges, naming ceremonies, mixed circles, or school events like meetings, parents' nights, report card nights. Babies have a lot of physical contact and attention is lavished upon them; they are cuddled, teased, and sung to.

There is a traditional singing ritual that is still practised in our family today, and we are passing it on to our children. It is a peculiar and private custom: as the baby's character emerges, a chant or type of song is composed by those closest to the baby. It's hard to explain how these chants are made up. They just happen, but they are directly related to a personality trait that the baby has, and this manifests itself when the baby starts to actively communicate with others. Once everyone agrees that the song fits the baby, it is chanted often. Soon the baby recognizes it and delights in hearing it. We all love to sing it and laugh at the baby's reaction. If we were feeling bad, our personal song would be sung and we would feel better. The song was never chanted if a parent was angry at me, and I knew I was forgiven if I heard the song again. Being ignored or excluded from an activity is the worst way to be reprimanded because inclusion is considered very important in the Anishnabe culture. If we were ignored for a long period of time, we knew we had broken a social taboo or convention. To feel left out is about the worst feeling I can think of today. I, and my brothers and sisters, have our own songs, and we have songs for our own children. They are kept within the extended family and are never chanted in front of acquaintances or strangers. I think that our stories and songs strengthen familial bonds. The retelling of a familiar story or the singing of a childhood chant enables the participants to transcend the present (at a funeral, for example) and live in the moment of a past amusing event. It helps the grieving process and is comforting for the loved ones left here on earth. Hearing our special song chanted by a relative really makes us feel unique and needed. It's much more personal than a name and gives you a true sense of belonging to the clan.

My grandparents' marriage was arranged. My grandmother, Josephine, wasn't aware of this arrangement, and she only found out when the banns were read in church. After the marriage, she and her husband moved to Rapid Lake. As I understand it, Nanny had many adjustments to make. She was very young when she married, the Rapid Lake dialect was different from the Algonquin spoken in Maniwaki, and the lifestyle was different in Rapid Lake.

Grandpa was about fourteen years older than my grandmother when they took their vows. My mother, Daisy, was born about a year later. She was born in the bush in Lac Barrière; my grandfather (and godfather) helped my grandmother deliver her. It was windy that day and she was given the Indian name "maiden of the wind." She was baptized "Marie-Lisa" because the Roman Catholic missionaries did not consider her parents' choice, "Daisy," to be a valid one as it was not in the Bible and, therefore, not a Christian name. The family were devout Catholics, so I don't think this rule bothered them, although she has been called "Daisy" anyway since birth. Grandpa and Nanny had a son after my mother, two daughters, another son, and their last two daughters when Nanny was well into her forties.

My grandparents' children spent their precious early years with them until it was time for the youngsters to go to school. They were placed in different French- or English-speaking convents and boarding schools. I can only imagine what this might have been like for my mother, aunts, and uncles. I hear only snippets here and there at family gatherings or when I'm alone with one of them. Little is said, the topic of conversation is usually avoided, but I sense some of the experiences must have been gut-wrenching. One night my mother could hear her brothers crying in the boys' dorm and she went to see what was wrong. They had all been beaten, because one boy left the light on to read. Her brothers told her of other beatings; one of her brothers used to get beaten in the bathtub. He had trouble learning: because he was blind in one eye he had trouble keeping up with his classmates. My mother told my grandmother about the abuse and they were promptly taken out and moved to another school. Fortunately, this school was in the town of Maniwaki and they were near their parents.

I think that separation from loved ones is agony enough; the other things have to be blocked out in order to survive. I taste bile when I hear and read about some of the horrid experiences countless Indian children have endured in those "educational" institutions. I only hope and pray that my relatives were spared the beatings and abuse. But even covert racist behaviour towards them has had a negative impact on those of my generation. It hurts me to hear that my mother had been called "maudit sauvage" when she was younger, and I'll never forget the sting I felt when my sisters were called "Chinoises" (my sisters look more "Indian" than I do) when we first moved to a suburb in Montreal in the mid-sixties.

For years the "residential school syndrome" was not talked about. How can anyone possibly come to terms with the horrors of it? I don't know how I would have survived such an ordeal. I feel blessed and fortunate to have had the opportunities in life that I've had. It's comforting to talk to members of my nation and other First Nations who are starting to heal from their past "educational" ordeals by actively seeking help through counselling programs. Subsequent problems like alcoholism, drug addiction, and family violence are finally being brought out in the open and are being dealt with on many reserves and in urban centres. We are now seeing that drowning the pain with alcohol and abusing other substances to escape is not the traditional Native way. I grew up to witness and become part of the drinking cycle and the devastation it causes. I cannot name names, this would be too hurtful to those concerned, but I can say that those in my direct line (mother and grandparents) were non-drinkers and I feel lucky. Many of my people cannot say this; personally, I have given up drinking totally because I am afraid of what alcohol could do to me. I want to be a responsible, adult role model for my daughter, my nieces, and my nephews, as well as the ones yet to be born.

My initial reaction, as an adult, to the economic and social problems that the majority of Aboriginal peoples are struggling with was shock and outrage. I wanted retribution and revenge. But the enemy is elusive, cunning, and very powerful. I believe now that violence begets violence and I am deeply hurting myself if vengeance is my sole motive. But I think it was a feeling I needed to recognize, understand, and address before I was spiritually able to move on to other productive ways of dealing with injustices. I cannot change past wrongs, but I can work on changing negative attitudes that only frustrate me and bewilder and push away others. When I started to study full-time for my master's degree in September 1990, I remember that I felt I had a mission to inform my colleagues and certain professors about the Native situation in Canada. I remember feeling frustrated and angry towards some people for their racist, ignorant beliefs. My early academic papers definitely had angry overtones, and when I was told that everything had to be documented from the literature (some of my research was based on interviews with prominent people I knew personally), I remember feeling defensive. I didn't feel I was in a position to argue with an established university academic, so I deleted some information that I thought was important.

There's another incident which bothered me greatly. Two researchers were in the process of trying to get funding for their research project and I had asked to read their proposal. I read it and saw that two Natives I knew were listed as research assistants, and when I saw them I asked them how they were enjoying working on this project. The three of us were shocked to discover that they were *not* working on it and had never even been asked to do so. They had heard about it but were never approached by the researchers, nor did the latter ever express an interest in having my two friends work with them. We shook our heads in disbelief and finally came to the conclusion that they needed the "token Indian" names as assistants. My two friends were strong students; one is pursuing his doctorate and will be teaching at another university this fall, and the other is finishing his master's degree and has since returned to his reserve to teach. They never pursued this falsehood and

we have all put it behind us, but at the time it galled us that the proposal went through the proper channels and was formally accepted.
I'm curious to read the study results and see what conclusions they arrive at because the three of us are familiar with the reserves they're
studying and we know some of the people they'll be working with. Reporting these people would have caused undue strife and bad feelings
for many people and I am not a judge.

I met people with backgrounds very different from my own in my
classrooms at McGill and I listened carefully to their points of views
and opinions. This in itself was a valid, mind-broadening education. I
learned about other "ways of knowing" from other parts of the country and the world. The face-to-face communication I experienced with
colleagues and some excellent professors is something I won't get from
books alone. And I'm a voracious reader. Academic reading has its
place, but to put faces and voices to new concepts has enriched my
learning experiences. I have these many people to be grateful to, for I
am more open to other cultures, ideas, and "ways of making meaning." As an Aboriginal woman, I feel it's more beneficial to work
alongside the non-Native people than to work against them. Fighting
against other groups of people only makes for distrust and suspicion
and I'm tired of blaming others. I guess I'm a quiet activist now who is
willing to listen and pull back the accusing finger. It can be a struggle,
but the rewards are greater in the long run.

Now, I'd like to share with you what my father's people are like
and how they affected my life. The death of my French-Canadian father, Renaud Joseph, when I was only nineteen, caused many years of
personal anguish and a deep sense of loss. As a result of Dad's death,
my mother, two sisters, and two brothers were only able to maintain
fleeting contact with his family and this brought me closer to my
matrilineal relatives. In all respects, even as a child, I found my Native relatives to be warmer, more humorous, and generally more loving. My father's family (Dad was the youngest of nine), most of
whom are very successful professionals or businessmen, were harder
to get to know, and I always felt I had to be conscious of my manners
and behaviour when in their presence. The annual or semi-annual
gatherings at "Mamère's" felt formal to me; but I fondly remember
the large house and the beautiful gardens full of fragrant peonies.

Dad's side of the family are good-living, upstanding, well-educated
people, and, in my heart, I felt they respected and loved us and looked
forward to our visits. Mamère, who had been widowed in the early fifties, wasn't even told of my father's, her son's, tragic death at forty-
eight. She was about ninety-three years old at the time and the family
had decided that it would be too much for her to handle. I always felt

that this wasn't right, but I never felt I was in a position to express my feelings about it. Mamère died shortly after my dad, in a seniors' home, feeling very lonely and broken, I would think.

There was always a sense of mystery when I think back to our visits to Mamère's: secrets (one uncle's marriage to his first cousin, my aunt's long stay in a mental institution, the sudden death of a nine-year-old cousin who was born before my dad); unexpressed feelings (hurt, sadness, anger, fear, exhilaration); unrequited loves (two barren aunts – or childless by choice?); tiptoeing (Mamère used to wander the halls all night with a flashlight, checking for fires). My uncles, aunts, and cousins were tightly self-controlled people and the demonstration of feelings was not considered acceptable behaviour. I quickly learned to adapt to this code of behaviour when I was in their company, for to rebel against these implicit rules or to let go was more trouble than it was to comply. I will demonstrate with a story.

Sometimes there was music played in the parlour where one of my uncles had his baby grand piano. He, and at times one of his brothers, would play a classical piece on the piano and violin. Family members would sit around, politely listen, and comment on how lovely the piece was.

One afternoon, I was sitting on the piano bench with my uncle, who was trying to teach me how to play a classical piece – maybe it was Beethoven, I don't really remember. One of my two frail, bespectacled maiden aunts was propped up with pillows in a wing chair with her tomato-soup-ringed mouth open – she was listening intently or sleeping. Every once in a while she'd emit a long, low moan, her head would bob, and her false teeth clicked. We, the five kids, started to giggle and were promptly reprimanded by the grown-ups for showing disrespect, but then roared uncontrollably with each increasing "sssshhhh!" We lost all self-control when Aunt ——'s eyes opened (her gaping mouth even wider) and her glasses fell to the tip of her nose. She surveyed the scene and slowly rose from her chair. I thought she was going to the bathroom to escape. Then she fainted, but she did it in slow motion. She didn't crumble, she sort of floated down and landed softly on her bum (we don't use this polite word when we retell this story) with her scrawny legs sprawled out, it seemed like five whole minutes. We all just stared at her in utter amazement; she looked as if she was on drugs and we felt as if we were, or maybe, by some mysterious force, we were suspended in time. It was surreal! You could hear a pin drop. No one was even breathing and when she landed, life went fast forward. The adults leaped from their seats, swarmed her, checked her, murmured consoling words, and she was pronounced alive and well. How hurt could a ninety-pounder be, falling so slowly from a two-foot distance? I thought. Knowing that she was a hypochondriac who behaved dramatically when she felt embarrassed or didn't get her own way, I dismissed this little episode as a put-on Victorian swoon. But that slow-motion fainting spell! It still perplexes me today. I thought they were so weird and uptight; everyone knew she was faking but played the ritual game and followed all the rules. They all had roles to play and rarely deviated from them.

After a stunned moment, to lighten the mood, I turned back to the piano and played a few bars of the military funeral song "Death Watch." Like the crack of a whip, I got the laughs from the younger audience but instantly shrivelled from the noise (clucking) heaped on me by the adults. I can still see their lips moving a mile a minute. This was immediately followed by their siren-sounding suppressed giggle noises. That was the only time, other than when the men had had a couple of drinks, that I remember seeing them loosen up. But they were practised at regaining self-control and managed to maintain their composure. Heaven forbid, we can't lose face, laugh at ourselves, or risk putting someone on the spot! Meanwhile, I lost it. I was laughing and crying, sputtering fluids all over the place. I was feeling scared, excited, and crushed at the same time. Being a twelve-year-old pre-adolescent, laughing at what was perceived as absurd seemed a natural way to react.

I learned early to wear a mask and play a role and, consequently, was led to believe that being "seen and not heard" and denying my self-expression were the appropriate ways to conduct myself when with my father's relatives. This restricted behaviour made me feel uneasy, boxed in, and suffocated. My emotional outlet was playing alone with my brothers and sisters.

We, the kids, would only let loose when we were alone out in the yard, the garage, or in the three-room attic. My brothers and sisters used to marvel at the treasures we'd discover piled in boxes on the floor, on and under the high brass beds, bureaus, settees and various pieces of furniture. We found antiques of all kinds: toys, books, clothes, school records and souvenirs. For my sister Ann and me, it became our favourite play place, so we spent a lot of time up there fantasizing and pretending that we were children from another era. In one of the attic rooms, there were large, framed photographs of our ancestors hung up on the walls; men with stern looks, beards, or moustaches and unsmiling women with high-collared blouses and hair buns. No babies' or children's pictures were hung up.

My second sister, Christine, used to go wild in the old garage with our two young brothers. She was the tomboy who took apart her Christmas doll carriage one year and built a go-cart to race down the streets with all her male friends. They considered her one of the "guys," and she later studied to become a cabinet-maker. Ann and I were more like the "girl" types and enjoyed the traditional "girl" things, so the attic was more fun than the garage with its cars, motorbikes, tools, and "boy" things. There were two or three porcelain-headed, soft-bodied dolls with frilly, lacy dresses and miniature furniture that I particularly loved playing with. I asked my parents if I could have one, but they said I couldn't ask for a present, it had to be given voluntarily. I wasn't even allowed to hint. I yearned for one of them for years.

Contrast these visits with the vacations spent in Rapid Lake. All my cousins, aunts, uncles, and other family members would descend upon my grandparents, great-aunt and great-uncle, and second cousins in the height of the summer season. Because there were so many of us, we would bunk up in the priest's house, cabins and trailers. It wasn't unusual to sleep with two or three cousins to a bed, but we didn't mind. It was a good chance to catch up on what had been happening in our lives. There was a lot of freedom. We ate outdoors, fished on the lake, laughed, and ran all over the place. In the evenings, we would make fires, eat some more, listen to stories, and my grandfather would take out his fiddle and get us up to step-dance. Our language was peppered with French and Algonquin words and was probably hard for outsiders to understand. We still talk like that today.

We all participated in the outdoor activities; the adults used to laugh at the young ones trying out new dance steps. There was no self-consciousness, and everyone joined in the singing and dancing. Nanny was special to all of us. She was much quieter than Grandpa, but we all revered her because she was gentle and treated each one of us like her favourite grandchild. She sewed us moccasins, made birchbark baskets, and I remember her as an attentive listener. She was never idle, but she didn't appear hurried or frazzled, she had a steady, untiring pace. She used to come to our homes and help our mothers with the new babies. I remember her coming all the way to Goose Bay, Labrador to help Mom when she had my two baby brothers. Nanny used to read a lot and she even taught my grandfather how to read. Nanny started the school in Rapid Lake and was their first teacher. Classes were held in the summer because so many families were away in the winter. She would start her school day washing and feeding the children because most of them would come to school hungry, tired, and dirty. Some of their parents drank a lot, and Nanny believed that the kids needed to have some of their physical needs attended to before they could start their lessons. She taught them the basics like reading, writing, and arithmetic. Some of the people in the settlement came to rely on her pretty heavily because she was a giving person and couldn't say no. She stopped giving drunk people money and would only give them groceries to feed their children. Nanny was a diabetic and her health was not very good as she entered her sixties. She knew she was dying and, shortly before her death, she pulled aside a widow friend of hers and asked her to marry Grandpa after the funeral. She was worried and didn't want to see Grandpa alone. Nanny died a year after my father and there were hundreds at her funeral. It was apparently 100 degrees that hot July day, yet many people from the States and Canada came to mourn her passing. Everyone took her death hard.

The women in my family are strong and resilient. Nanny started having children at a very early age and brought up seven. The women and the men had different roles, but the women worked much harder. Their work was often physical, and they got little rest. Even when they sat, their hands were busy; they sewed or rocked a baby. In spite of great adversity, Nanny endured; she taught school, raised the children, kept up two homes (one in the bush and one in town), took care of the finances, spent a lot of time with all the grandchildren, and "kept the fires burning." Even the smallest child's voice was listened to and considered. I see my grandmother as a great teacher; she held on to what she believed in and passed her teachings on to us. She was the keeper of our culture. In spite of the poor status of Indian women, even in the eyes of our Aboriginal brothers, she never let us forget how important it was to feel proud of our heritage. I was made to feel that I belonged to a great nation because I was taught the traditions, cultural values, and customs of our people by my grandmother, who believed in herself and her family.

I will always remember those summers in Rapid Lake as the best times I've ever had. I felt free and loved – the cameraderie was what made them so special. However, it has not been my intention to portray my father's well-meaning relatives as thin-lipped prudes. I relate what I perceived as a child, to contrast it with the way I felt with the Anishnabe side of my family. I'm not saying that the differences are strictly cultural either; many people come from two culturally different backgrounds. I think that it is natural to identify more strongly with one group. Maybe if my father had lived past my nineteenth birthday, things would have turned out differently. But he didn't, and was taken from us when we were all teenagers, and I'll never know what could have been. I think it is only natural for a family to dissolve if one parent dies. So my reality is what I'm living now. My affiliation is with my mother's people. I am legally and emotionally an Aboriginal person. I am much more comfortable with the Aboriginal "world view": the special type of humour, the easy laughter in the face of adversity and pain, family bonds and the attitude towards life and death.

I was the only child of my parents to be born on the reserve (Maniwaki), and they left when I was about a year old because my father was a young civil engineer who travelled with his work. We moved around

Lise (right) with her mother and daughter

quite a lot until we finally settled in Ile Perrot, near Montreal. We were
fortunate to have lived in remote northern communities, like Val d'Or
and Casey in the province of Quebec and in Goose Bay, Labrador for
eight years. My two brothers, René and Donald, were born in Goose
Bay and it was there we got to spend time with the Inuit and Naskapi
peoples. When I was ten, Dad got transferred to Montreal.

My secondary schooling, college, and university years were completed in Montreal. I studied one semester in Nice, France and travelled to many other places in the States, Europe, Mexico, and South
America. I have not travelled much since I've become a mother; mothering and working is more than a full-time occupation. Six of my eight
years teaching were with the Cree, Inuit, and Algonquin peoples. I
went back, as an adult, with my daughter, to my place of birth and
taught in the Kitigan Zibi (River Desert) school for four years. This was
an invaluable experience. We spent time in a traditional camp near
Rapid Lake, where a group of Barrière Lake Indians have left the settlement of Rapid Lake because of the social and political problems. We
stayed in the bush, one time, when they were tapping the sugar maple
trees with birchbark baskets instead of the modern tin pails. These are
experiences my daughter couldn't get in a conventional school. I hope
these will be memories that she'll carry with her into adulthood.

My grandfather had moved to Maniwaki by then because he needed
to be near the hospital, so my daughter got to know him and love him

as I did. In that way, she was able to live among our relatives and learn about her ancestral culture and language. We spent a lot of our spare time with my grandfather, her great-grandfather, something which few children have the opportunity to experience. It makes me feel proud and fortunate to know that we were able to spend Grandpa's last days with him. At the end, he died in the hospital, at the age of eighty-four. It was his time, and I felt relief when he no longer felt pain. We buried him at the traditional burial ground in Rapid Lake, after he was laid out in his own home on the settlement. He was prepared by the elderly women, and we kept twenty-four-hour vigils by his side. This was the only wake I've ever attended that was not at a funeral home; his body was laid out in the living room, a table and chairs were placed nearby, and people came and went as they pleased. We ate at this table, drank coffee, laughed, cried, prayed, and listened to the elderly women sing traditional Indian hymns. Children, babies, and dogs were all over the place, which brings me back to the beginning of my story. I sustain my culture by maintaining ties with my traditions and my people. I am part of a new generation of young Aboriginal men and women who refuse to passively let a dominant culture walk all over us; our voices are stronger, we are more vocal, articulate, and educated.

For a long time, I felt torn between my two equally strong cultural lineages. My mother's parents and some of her cousins and siblings speak three languages (Algonquin, French, and English), and I perceived the languages as simply different "ways of talking." This language situation posed less of a problem for me than the different "ways of knowing" between the two radically separate value systems and patterns of behaviour. Like the chameleon, I learned to adapt to the two culturally disimiliar environments. Unlike before, when I was younger and saw everything black and white, I now view both cultures non-judgmentally. I no longer feel the need to defend myself, explain myself, or answer to anyone about what or who I am. In the anthropological literature, I used to be defined as a "half-breed," but I am a Native woman who has "two-way" knowledge. I consider this to be a privilege for I can comfortably work and live in different circles, mindful of my Aboriginal heritage.

I returned to Montreal in 1990 to pursue an M Ed in second languages at McGill University. My monograph topic is a study of the Algonquin Immersion Program in Kitigan Zibi School. I'll be teaching full-time in Kahnasatake in the fall, in the "Year of the Indigenous Peoples."
Meegwetch.

MARGERY G. PATERSON

McGill Is My Life

McGill has always been a part of my life. My older brother attended McGill in the late twenties and early thirties, and I listened avidly to his stories of college life, exploits of the hockey and football teams, the *McGill Daily* and famous lecturers. No wonder I came to revere the Scarlet Key uniform of cream-coloured trousers and bulky red and white sweater. At school my one ambition was to go to McGill. Nothing further than that entered my mind. I finally achieved my goal in 1938 and the university was all I expected it to be and more. Coming from The Study, a private girls' school with small classes, I found the size enormous and somewhat bewildering until things sorted themselves out. After two years, I left to take a business course at the old O'Sullivan's Business College on Guy Street, where I found myself helping to correct spelling papers. From there I was sent for an interview for a job in the Registrar's Office at McGill.

In fear and trembling I approached Dawson Hall at the east wing of the Arts Building where the administration offices were located at that time and was directed upstairs to be interviewed by the Registrar, T.H. Matthews. Fortunately, a familiar face greeted me, that of Betty Weldon, Mr Matthews's secretary and a former student and teacher at my school. With great relief, I survived the interview and was hired as a stenographer in the general office downstairs at the magnificent salary (to me) of $15 per week of five and a half days. When I reported for work, another bit of luck was with me in the person of Virginia Cameron, who ran the general office and who, for a short time, had been a teacher at The Study. She started me off immediately by rapidly dictating short letters in answer to various inquiries until I had covered copious pages in my notebook with Pitman shorthand, which I hoped and prayed I would be able to decipher later. I ended by taking it home and writing it all out for typing the next day. Anyway, I survived the test and, although Virginia Cameron was a martinet, I found she had a heart of gold. We all liked and respected her tremendously.

Not long afterwards Betty Weldon left to pursue studies in physical therapy and I was promoted to secretary for Mr Matthews. An Englishman and former mathematics professor, he had a quick mind and a wonderful command of the English language. His letters were a delight to transcribe, always the right word used and the letter short and to the point. He was also secretary of the university Senate and his minutes were a marvel to read. Occasionally he would give me a letter to compose for him to sign and I was always thrilled to receive it back with "V. good" or "Excellent" noted at the top of the draft copy. We got along famously and I learned a great deal from him.

A bout of illness kept me away from work until 1945 when I returned part-time to the general office and was shortly put in charge of scholarships, bursaries, prizes, and medals. Mr Matthews was secretary of the University Scholarships Committee and I assisted him and was also responsible to the chairman, a faculty member. The chairmen were all outstanding, and I remember them all with enormous respect and admiration. To me, the greatest was Dr Roscoe. She always kept the meeting under tight control and got things done. The Roscoe Report on Scholarships was a milestone and was worked out at many delightful luncheon meetings at the RVC. I felt privileged to attend them and to get to know the wonderful committee members and specially invited guests in informal surroundings.

Scholarships assistant was a dream job and included looking after entrance scholarships. Applications for our first prestigious entrance awards such as the J.W. McConnell and Morris Wilson Memorial scholarships, which provided residence and tuition, were collected, and records and references obtained for candidates from all across Canada for consideration by a subcommittee of the University Scholarships Committee. The excitement of sending telegrams to the winners ran high and the replies were eagerly awaited. When the winners arrived, I tried to help them with any problems, and they would come in during the session from time to time just to have a talk. They were all interesting and I came to know some of them very well.

At that time, the Registrar's Office was the hub of the university. Many procedures originated there, such as admissions, records, registration, convocations, transcripts, school certificate examinations, production of university examination papers, Senate documents, calendars and announcements, scholarships and bursaries, duplicating and general information. In later years, as the registration expanded, separate offices were established such as the Admissions Office, Student Aid, and the Secretariat, all spin-offs from the Registrar's Office.

The post–World War II period was a very exciting one for the Registrar's Office. Student veterans were returning or starting university, and every month they came in to collect their Department of Veterans' Affairs cheques. The office staff, all female, vied for the privilege of giving out the cheques. We also liked registration for medicine, dentistry, and law, which took place in our office and was primarily male.

Convocation was, of course, the big event and the diplomas were all prepared and given out in the office. Graduation robes were stored in the basement in Dawson Hall and taken over to the Arts Building for distribution to the students. Academic robes for the platform party were selected and labelled for delivery to the robing room at the convocation site. I seemed to inherit this job and was named "Mistress of the Robes" by Dr J.S. Thomson, then dean of divinity. This was great fun, as those helping to robe the participants came close to the distinguished honorary degree recipients as well as to the chancellor, principal, deans, and members of the Senate and Board of Governors. I remember one harrowing moment when a gown had been forgotten and I was hurtled down University Street in a black limousine with motorcycle police escort to retrieve it in the nick of time before the procession moved off into the Currie Gymnasium. Another bad moment was when a large green plastic garbage bag containing mortar boards and velvet hats had been picked up by mistake by the garbage truck and had to be tracked over the bridge to the south shore dump to get it back. We also lost one heavy red doctor of laws robe to Emperor Haile Selassie of Ethiopia, who insisted on taking it home with him. We often wondered where he had the opportunity of wearing it again, and in such a hot country it would not have been very comfortable!

On Convocation Day in the spring, a decision had to be made whether the ceremony should be outside or inside, according to the weather. The registrar was up at dawn in conference with the meteorology representative and then telephoned the information to the principal. The platform seating arrangement was planned by the registrar and each chair had to be exactly at the right spot on the stage. The oriental rug in his office was always taken down for the platform and he paced up and down until the ceremony began. I soon learned to avoid Mr Matthews as much as possible on those occasions. He was totally occupied. As the diplomas were given out in the office after convocation, we could not leave for lunch, so Virginia Cameron arranged for a wonderful cold buffet to be brought over from the Faculty Club and installed in Mr Matthews's office where we could take shifts for lunch and talk about what had happened. A small amount of sherry helped things move along.

The registration gradually became so large that it was not possible to hold convocations in the gymnasium. Expenses also rocketed. Discussions were held with the Place des Arts until it was decided to use that complex, where the Salle Wilfrid Pelletier seated three thousand persons and the seats did not have to be installed on each occasion. Another labour saver was that the academic robe collection was sold to Milne's, which would be responsible for maintaining and distributing it. The university retained a small selection for the platform party.

At Convocation time I assisted the university marshals in preparing and putting on a long-playing show without a rehearsal. Instead of one ceremony in the spring we had progressed to six in order to accommodate the cast of thousands. With sincere affection and appreciation I remember Professors Svenn Orvig, Tom Pavlasek, John Elson, and Ed Furcha. Their unfailing good humour and support made it a delight to work with them to produce what we thought was *un grand spectacle*.

Dawson Hall was due for a facelift in 1947, and the administration offices were moved up to Duggan House, an old residence on McTavish Street, while renovations were made. This meant that our office had to be fragmented on several floors. The main office was in a former library on the mezzanine floor, filing on the floor above, and duplicating in the basement. Mr Matthews and his secretary were just above the mezzanine with Mr Matthews in one room and his secretary in a former bathroom adjoining. This meant that the order was reversed and one saw the registrar before the secretary. Not a very convenient set-up and sometime hilarious, but we all made do and enjoyed the lovely garden for lunch. When we moved back to Dawson Hall we found we had the entire ground floor, as the accounting department which had been on one side had moved upstairs to the third floor. Mr Matthews's and Virginia Cameron's offices were now on the same floor at the back of the building. No new furniture, however, and still the same straight-backed chairs with a cushion you recovered yourself if it wore thin. I finally asked if I could buy my own stenographer's chair. A second-hand replacement was found in due course. Funds were very tight in those days, as McGill was not able to use the federal university grants which were available in other provinces.

To add to the decor in his new office, Mr Matthews installed a fish tank complete with guppies and tropical fish on the window-sill. He loved fish and went to a fishing camp every spring with Professor A.S. Noad. He often brought back trout with which he treated the office at a luncheon at the Faculty Club. At one point, the guppies reproduced at an alarming rate, and, in order to prevent the babies being eaten by their parents and other fish, efforts were made to get them out of the tank. I remember coming to the door and seeing what seemed like hundreds of tiny, squirming fish all over the Convocation rug and was reluctant to come any further for fear of stepping on them.

When Mr Matthews retired and went to Ottawa to help set up the Association of Universities and Colleges of Canada, Colin McDougall was appointed registrar. We couldn't believe our luck in getting such a marvellous person as our chief. We gave a special party to congratulate him on his novel *Execution*, for which he won the Governor-General's Award.

One cannot write about Dawson Hall without mentioning Mrs Dorothy McMurray, who was like a Queen Mother to all of us. She was the principal's secretary and she ruled the building from his office. When a student's record card was needed for the principal, she requested it by telephone without giving her name and hung up without any "please" or "thank you." A new girl was apt to be completely bewildered by this. The principal, on the other hand, called and said "Cyril James speaking" in his beautiful voice and made his request most pleasantly. "Mrs Mac," however, was most protective of the "Ladies of McGill," as she liked to call us, and organized luncheons or get-togethers from time to time. At Christmas, we all went up to the principal's suite and were invited in, occasionally beforehand, to help with the decorations in which the principal was most interested. Legendary names among the "Ladies of McGill" were Audrey Hutcheson, who guided many deans of engineering, Merle Peden, who ran the Faculty of Medicine, Isobel Oswald, fountain of knowledge of arts and science, Mrs Gladys Murray, kindly secretary to the warden of the Royal Victoria College, stately Miss Janetta Pratt and quick-witted Betsy Holland of the Cashier's Office, quiet and knowledgeable Dorothy Asch, who was George Grimson's right hand in the Comptroller's Office, steadfast Kathleen Oliver of dentistry, and the wonderful Gwyn Williams of the Cashier's Office and Student Aid, to name just a few.

My first trip to England occurred one summer and, by chance, I departed at the end of June from Montreal on the same ship, the *Empress of Australia*, with the principal. He, of course, was in first class and I in tourist with two friends. He happened to see me on deck as we sailed and every morning came down to have a few words at the foot of my deck chair and to dance with me for a little while in the tourist lounge at night. The Canadian Cricket Team was on board and he held a reception for the players to which we were invited.

Everyone got along very well in the Registrar's Office. At that time there were no job descriptions and everyone pitched in at whatever

"Ladies of McGill." *Back Row*: Virginia Cameron, Registrar's Office, Dorothy McMurray, Principal's Office, Mrs O'Murtagh, Comptroller's Office, Isobel Oswald, Dean's Office, Arts and Science, Laura Robertson, Graduate Faculty, Phyllis O'Neill, Dean's Office, Law Faculty. *Middle Row*: Gladys Murray, Warden's Office, RVC, Merle Peden, Dean's Office, Faculty of Medicine, Patricia Budden, Registrar's Office, Margery Paterson, Registrar's Office, Alison Groome, Registrar's Office, Dorothy Asch, Chief Accountant's Office, Betsy Holland, Cashier's Office, Linda Hendrie, Athletics Office. *Front Row*: Anne Liston, Switchboard, unidentified, Kathleen Oliver, Registrar's Office, Janet Simpson, Bursar's Office.

job was in desperate need of doing. Afterthe Fall Convocations, Virginia Cameron used to give wonderful buffet dinners for us in her apartment on Sherbrooke Street West at the top of many flights of stairs. Mr Matthews would come and show his beautiful slides of his trips to the West Indies and Virginia's own slides of her European excursions were remarkable.

In the forties, it was very difficult for a non-academic woman to become a member of the Faculty Club, but I asked Mr Matthews to nominate me. It seemed to take months, but I was eventually admitted. Ladies were not permitted to enter the main lounge or to go above the second floor where bedrooms and the billiards room were located. Ordering one's meal by number was in itself a feat and this system was, fortunately, discontinued fairly soon.

Before Mr Matthews left, I approached him for permission to take time off to continue studies towards my BA degree while continuing to work. I was probably among the very few to try this at my own expense, as in those days there were no benefits or encouragement provided by a human resources department for a procedure which has now become very routine. Mr Matthews did not take to this suggestion too well, saying that he thought I had enough education at present, but he eventually gave in and with the help of Dr Cecil Solin, then assistant dean of the Faculty of Arts and Science, my application was accepted. I managed to find lectures which were given over the lunch hour or early afternoon and so completed two courses per year. These included fine arts, English, classics, and Italian, and I was privileged to have legendary teachers such as Professor Harold Files and Professor Hugh McLennan of the English department and Professor Paul McCullagh of classics. Although the oldest member in the class, I was treated exactly the same as the younger students, but I think I appreciated the teaching a great deal more.

In 1958 I was fortunate to receive a summer scholarship from the Italian government to study at the University for Foreigners in Perugia. This was a six-week course and meant struggling up the hill from my *pensione* to the university for classes every morning, then a break with everyone taking a three-hour siesta, then more classes at 4 p.m. We were taken on bus trips to surrounding hill towns and went on our own by train to Florence. It was very hot in July and August, which made it difficult to study, but it was a rewarding experience and a marvellous opportunity for me to learn about Italian art and architecture as well as the language. I will always be grateful to Professor Antonio d'Andrea and Professor Pamela Stewart of the Italian department for their help in giving me such a chance.

I graduated in the spring of 1962. It was fine weather and Convocation was held outside on the campus. I floated up the steps of the platform to whisper my name to Dean Kenneth Hare. At that point, I couldn't even remember my name (no name cards then), but, fortunately, he knew me and all went well. It was a very proud moment for me and well worth the nights of studying and trying to make the wheels go round in my head again. A special note of congratulation from Dr James is among my mementos. Little did I know that I would experience an even prouder moment in June 1987 when I received an honorary Master of Arts degree from McGill following my retirement.

By 1966 the administrative offices had once again outgrown the confines of Dawson Hall and were moved to new quarters in the totally renovated biological building. Planning the new offices was intense and the prospect of new furniture and carpeted floors was eagerly anticipated. The building was renamed the F. Cyril James Administration Building, for Dr James, who had retired in 1962. The new premises were a great improvement, but we missed the daily traffic of students, staff, and the public passing through to the Arts Building. I had

Convocation, June 11, 1987. Hugh Hallward, chairman of the Board of Governors, Gerard Pelletier, Hon. LL D, Margery Paterson, Hon. MA, David Johnston, principal and vice-chancellor.

achieved the title of assistant registrar in 1965 and now rejoiced in a glass-walled office where I could keep an eye on the general information counter and help out when necessary. With the untimely death of Virginia Cameron in 1967 I soon found it impossible to cope with extra duties as well as the Scholarships Committee, but it was with genuine regret that I surrendered my responsibilities there to take on new ones. I became associate registrar in 1970.

The sixties was a period of student protest and the building was in danger of student occupation from time to time. It sometimes became difficult to enter and exit the building and the lunchroom was occupied. One had to run a gauntlet of students in the corridors to get to the washroom and kitchen, but no physical violence occurred. One member of our staff, a dignified older lady, once sprayed the lunchroom occupiers with Lysol disinfectant in retaliation, but that was as far as it got. Profound admiration and respect for Principal Roche Robertson, senior administrators, and physical plant staff was shown by all for their staunch protection of university staff and property.

In 1973, it was decided to create a new department, the Secretariat, which would combine the operations of the secretary of the Board of Governors and the secretary of Senate. Colin McDougall relinquished his post as registrar and became secretary-general of the university. His departure was received with regret, but we were pleased with the appointment of assistant registrar Jean Paul Schuller as registrar. Completely bilingual, young, and skilled in computer technology, he was ideal for the job. I worked with him happily until I retired in 1986.

The principals I have known began with Dr Cyril James, outwardly austere and shy, but inwardly warm-hearted and kind, Dr Roche Robertson, who brought fresh life into the university and gave me a raise in salary, the late Dr Robert Bell, who always seemed one of us with his charming wife, Jeanne, and Professor David Johnston, whose energy, wit, and understanding are well known. The chancellor always presided at Convocation and my favourite was Conrad Harrington who, along with his wife, Joan, was a superstar in our Convocation cast of luminaries.

I could not begin to mention the names of all the good friends I made at McGill, both academic and non-academic, and on retirement I missed the daily contacts greatly. To work in a congenial atmosphere and enjoy work is a privilege which I have had at McGill. I continue to keep in contact with the university by serving on the Graduates' Society MATCH (McGill Alumni Too Can Help) Committee, helping proofread the Convocation programs, helping out at the book fair, and attending meetings of the Women Associates of McGill. I can still say proudly that McGill is my life.

A Journey to the Glass Ceiling

What interest can there be in how I "made" it at McGill at a time when women were scarce in academe and especially scarce in the higher reaches of middle management? Was it my upbringing, my character, luck, being the right person in the right place at the right time, my skills, my expertise, or a combination of many things? We will only know by examining the past in some detail – I hope you enjoy the journey with me.

My early life was much like that of any other young woman in Westmount. The only difference was that I was painfully shy and therefore did not make close and lasting friendships. I had acquaintances with whom I went to ballet, French lessons, birthday parties, and so forth but did not share really intimate conversations. I had two brothers but no sister. As a result I read a lot – in fact anything I could lay my hands on. With my intellectual parents, that meant a wide variety of novels, political treatises, philosophical works, newspapers, and magazines. By the time I reached high school I found I was better read than most of my teachers. There began my lack of respect for authority for authority's sake.

One day, our English teacher was absent but had left an assignment for the class to complete – to write a one-paragraph précis of a short story. As those who have read any minutes I have written would know, I have a natural talent for keeping things short and to the point. Therefore I completed the task quickly and then went back to reading the novel I always carried with me. The substitute teacher, a math teacher in the school, noticed me reading and asked why I wasn't completing the task. I explained that I had finished and was therefore reading. Somehow my response angered him; he asked to see my work, which I showed him; he told me it was messy and to redo it; I refused; he asked my name, which I gave him; on hearing it,

Sheila

he said "Another Sheldon!" and left the room. I discovered that my older brother had had this same teacher for math and had questioned his authority constantly. And my younger brother that morning had told the same teacher that it wasn't any of his business what length his hair was. Obviously something in our family training had taught us to stand up for what we considered important.

And on to university – not a happy or stellar time of my life. I started at McGill, got lost in the crowd, did not know how to study, and had difficulty making friends. While at McGill, in an effort to become more involved, I joined a sorority. In many ways it was the best thing I did. It provided me with my closest friends and it forced me for the first time to show leadership. However, my academic career was going nowhere, so I transferred to Bishop's. Things improved, but transferring to a small university in third year causes you to be always an outsider. Not a new role but one I would dearly have loved to drop. My degree was a BA with a major in political science; some would claim a necessary pre-requisite for succeeding in a university environment.

I graduated and started job hunting. Along with fifty or so others, I wrote a special exam at Northern Telecom for an entry-level management position. Ten passed, I was the only woman and the only one not to receive a job offer. I was too naïve to understand why. I finally got a job as a secretary to the court runner in a law firm. I couldn't type but said I could. I found I hated being a secretary – I had more brains than my male boss, who constantly arrived with a hangover – so I saved my money, quit, and went to Europe for six months, once again by myself.

When I returned in September 1971, I went to a sorority alumnae meeting. One of the alumnae worked for McGill in the personnel department. She told me they were looking for a statistical clerk in the planning office and that I should apply. I did and I got the job. Why? One, I bent the truth. When asked if I had ever done a statistics course, I replied in the affirmative without explaining that I had failed the course. Second, I think the head of the Office of Research for Planning and Development, Ed Desrosiers, was amused that my dad was executive assistant to the rector of Concordia University and that I would be working on some of the same "dossiers" from the McGill standpoint.

And so my career at McGill began – ignominiously. The second day, I wore a pant suit, one I had worn many times at the conservative law firm where I had previously worked. I was called into Mr Desrosiers's office and told that on the fifth floor of the James administration building, women did not wear pants to work. I responded that I thought that what was good enough for the law firm was good enough for McGill. A week later word was passed around that pant *suits* were acceptable attire for women on the fifth floor, if the jacket was at least hip length.

When I had started at McGill, my dad had said that one thing I had to do was join the Faculty Club. Ed Desrosiers agreed, took me over to join, and left me with the assistant manager, Mrs Campbell. Mrs Campbell was not amused. She sat me down, asked whether it was true I was merely a "C" (clerical worker), and then told me young ladies like myself did not join the Faculty Club because we made members uncomfortable. Since my dad was expecting me to invite him to the club, I simply told Mrs Campbell that I had been informed that I qualified for membership and that I therefore intended to join. She said she would take my application but she didn't expect that I would be accepted as a member. Well, she was wrong and it was at the McGill Faculty Club where I met most of the faculty who later became my close colleagues and friends.

Initially, the only other woman on the fifth floor who was not a secretary was Jan Morgan, assistant to the vice-principal academic. She was several years my senior. So I forged my own way. Because of my upbringing, I felt more at home with the faculty than the secretaries or other junior administrative staff. I therefore used to spend my lunch hours in the Faculty Club. I would ask to sit at one of the large tables in the ballroom and the gentlemen faculty would be too polite to say no. I would introduce myself and then sit and listen to their conversations on academic subjects, or more often, university politics.

In my job it became apparent that I was better at writing than doing statistics, and therefore I was asked to become the secretary of the Planning Commission, a Senate committee. Also a year after my arrival, the Planning Office hired two systems analysts to work on the analytical side of the office's mandate. Suddenly I was doing something I was good at and had two colleagues of my age and interests. Things were definitely looking up. Through the Planning Commission and its controversial reports to Senate I managed to meet a wide variety of faculty, including many of the same people I had met at lunch in the Faculty Club. I also started to attend Senate in the gallery. The assistant to the vice-principal academic, Marie-Ange Fyfe, and I would sit through numerous debates and tea breaks, the only people in the gallery. I believe attending these meetings gave me a unique opportunity to understand the university, and I think that more administrative and support staff should be encouraged to attend Senate regularly to observe the academic and political underpinnings of McGill.

When Senate set up a committee chaired by Tony Deutsch to draft tenure regulations, he requested that I act as secretary to the committee. My second career at McGill was launched. Through this drafting process, I met Peter Laing, the long-serving university solicitor and senior partner of a prestigious law firm. One member of the ad hoc committee (a forthright member of the Law faculty who was my age) and I took our first draft down to Peter to review. He tried to intimidate the two of us and lost. He became my friend and supporter from that time forward. Senate approved our regulations in 1976 and I became known as a drafter as well as a minute writer. Archie Malloch says this event was the catalyst to my future at McGill. I had commenced the long and difficult road of becoming trusted by the faculty – someone who understood their concerns and could translate that into procedures and regulations that were clear, fair, and flexible.

The year 1976/77 was a turning point for me at McGill. Ed Desrosiers went to Ontario, and Edward Stansbury became vice-principal planning. I began to consider whether it was time for me to move on as well and to find gainful employment outside McGill. I had expanded the position of planning assistant as much as I could and the last year or so had been difficult. Relationships in Planning at the senior level were strained and I often found myself as the ham in the sandwich.

This was not a role I relished but good training for my future positions at McGill. I will always remember Dale Thomson, then vice-principal planning, telling me that I was too smart to waste my life being someone's assistant. It is a conversation I frequently thought about when I was deciding whether to take the next step in my career. I can honestly say that Dale, although he probably doesn't even remember our discussion, was crucial to my ambitions. While I was thinking of my options, the associate secretary of Senate, Glenn Higginbotham, decided to leave McGill on completion of his law degrees. Colin McDougall, the secretary-general and an old family friend, approached me one day and asked me to apply for Higginbotham's position. He said Vice-Principal Yaffe had recommended me and that he thought I would enjoy the challenge. In February, 1977, Dr Yaffe came into my office, gave me a big hug, and said, "Congratulations – You are too good to lose." And so I became associate secretary of Senate. I remember well my first convocation in that capacity. In the Green Room with all the dignitaries, the marshall shouted, "The associate secretary of Senate – where is *he*?" I didn't know how to respond but Bob Bell did it for me. The usually soft-spoken Dr Bell yelled back, "The associate secretary is here and *she* will line up in a minute." My introduction to the problem of being a woman in management in the seventies was certainly loud.

It was during this time in my life that I started to shed my paralysing shyness. It was a gradual process and not accomplished by conscious decision. I just found that events and people didn't intimidate me the way they used to. Also I had ideas and thoughts that I wanted to put across. And the confidence in, and appreciation of, my work that was instilled in me by the senior administration certainly had an effect on my self-esteem.

Here I was in a new position, responsible suddenly for Senate, tenure regulations, retirement regulations, and immigration procedures for new faculty members. I cannot stand chaos or not knowing what is going to happen next, so I started designing systems to deal with each of my new duties in an orderly fashion. I gained credibility in the way I dealt with issues and became part of the real core of academic life. One of the frustrating parts of this job was that all the regulations were on bits of paper hidden in files, and I could never be sure I had the most recent version to work with. I therefore suggested consolidation to Vice-Principals Pedersen and Yaffe. They told me to go for it, and the *Handbook for Academic Staff* was born. As editor of the *Handbook*, I became its chief interpreter and the walking encyclopedia on university regulations. I think the favourite expression of deans and chairs was: "Ask Sheila." At the beginning I found this trust flattering, but it eventually became my "bête noire."

Senate at this time was where the action was. It included many of the major movers and thinkers of McGill and was an intellectual and political forum not to be missed. It was at Senate that Dr Sam Freedman, then dean of medicine, suggested that "blue ribbon" committees be established to review the programs in the university. That presentation made me realize that Dr Freedman's horizons extended beyond the Faculty of Medicine. After his appointment as vice-principal academic, I was not surprised to find Senate considering a proposal for cyclical reviews of academic programs.

Dr Robert Bell announced his retirement and the search for a new principal was started. Colin McDougall asked for my help in organizing the committee and establishing a system for its work. It was exhilarating. The results of the search are well known, and David Johnston was appointed principal of McGill. For me personally, the experience had several rewards. I met and worked with the chancellor and several members of the Board of Governors for the first time. When Colin McDougall had a stroke and was out of commission for a while, I learned that I could effectively operate on my own. It was then that I started to realize that I could head an office efficiently and well, even if my style was different from the traditional management mode. My positions at McGill had always emphasized the usual female traits of helpfulness and co-operation, yet my ability to assume authority for my decisions began to develop. I found that instead of simply providing the background for someone else to make the decision, I started making the decision and implementing it. No one objected. This was the beginning of my taking authority without being given it. Men seem to do this naturally in whatever position they hold. But women wait, sometimes endlessly, expecting someone to give them authority.

After David Johnston's appointment, my responsibilities increased. I worked well with him and became more involved in the university's administration. A joint Board of Governors/McGill Association of University Teachers/Administration Committee to draft new appeal and grievance procedures was formed. I was secretary and chief drafter of these procedures, and after their approval I became responsible for their implementation. Thus my career as an unofficial counsel to both the administration and MAUT grievance advisors began. No wonder the yoke of being the university encyclopedia grew heavier and heavier.

Around 1980, I decided that I would like to study law. My predecessor had done it, and I didn't see why I couldn't follow in his footsteps. To show the faculty that I was able to study and work at the same time, I took a property course and received a mark of B. However, the Faculty of Law turned down my application, saying I had not the academic credentials to succeed and that what I planned to do (work part-time and in the summer) was geared to failure, despite the fact that Glenn Higginbotham had done just that and that Raynald Mercille was admitted that year to the law faculty with the same plan. To prove I was capable, I enrolled in the MBA program part-time but took my courses during the day. After five three-credit courses, I had maintained a B+ average. Time to reapply to law, but in the meantime I had met Peter Collyer. I put off my ambition to study law to become a wife and stepmother and then a mother. Later I decided it would not further my career to obtain the degree. I was doing fine without it.

One of the amusing incidents in my career at McGill occurred when a senior member of the Faculty of Law dropped into my office a couple of years later to say that if I ever wanted to reapply, the Faculty would now be happy to have me as a student. I wonder what qualities or qualifications had suddenly become apparent that would allow them to change their minds?

In the early eighties, there was a shuffling of senior administrative positions. Although I became secretary of Senate (and later also secretary of the Board of Governors), I saw that men were preferred and my awareness of the roadblocks encountered by women grew. For example, my name was changed at this time. New letterhead had to be ordered and I received a telephone call during my vacation in August saying my name had been changed on this letterhead to reflect my marriage. The administration hoped I didn't object, since the letterhead was already printed. Contrary to my intentions, I found I was now Sheila Sheldon-Collyer. I started to become more and more frustrated by the fact that the opinions of women in the university, especially administrative women, were rarely sought and often ignored.

Also in the early eighties, David Johnston asked me to represent the administration on the committee organizing the celebration of the one-hundredth anniversary of the admission of women to McGill. For the first time since I had started at McGill, I was working with a group where I was not the only woman in the room. It was an empowering experience. My inherent feminism had found an outlet and I enjoyed it immensely. After the celebrations, the academic women formed the McGill Women's Networking Group (MWNG) to keep the lines of communication open. The membership was restricted to academic women. Every year I would write suggesting the group open its membership or change its name to reflect that it was restricted to academics. Finally, in 1988 the MWNG asked me to join their executive to help them expand their membership. My formal career as a feminist on campus began, and it culminated in my being president of the MWNG during the 1990–91 academic year.

Sheila Sheldon-Collyer, university secretary, witnessing the signature of Madame
Justice Rosalie Abella, LL D, University of Victoria
Photo: Don Pierce, U. Vic. Photographic Services

Life at McGill as a senior woman administrator was lonely and isolated. I did not have many colleagues with whom to chat or share experiences. Peggy Sheppard, director of admissions, Ann McCormick
in the dean of medicine's office, and Judith Barron Mee in the planning office were among the few. Luckily, in the mid-eighties, more
women started to move into senior positions. Honora Shaughnessy
became assistant to the principal and a close friend and confidant, as
did Mariela Johansen, Kate Williams, and Kyra Emo. Without these
women colleagues I would not have enjoyed my time at McGill as
much as I did. I finally had some co-workers to share my concerns
and plans and to consult as mentors.

I found that promotion required a struggle. I thought the combination of the positions of secretary of Senate and secretary of the Board of
Governors along with the added responsibilities I had assumed over
the years of secretary, co-ordinator, and drafter for various senior university committees deserved classification at the "E" or executive level.
If a male colleague had been offered the position, this would have been
taken care of by the senior administration. However, I found myself
having to justify my own reclassification. Without my inside knowledge of the university and its systems I would never have been able to
find the evidence to do so. Somehow I have always believed that pro-

motions are earned by meritorious service and not fought for over three months without any visible support from those who implemented the decision. It seemed that the "E" level classification was just another barrier for women staff members of the university.

This new position was interesting for about six to nine months while I reorganized. Then came the Statutory Committee to Nominate the Principal, the Ad Hoc Committee on Casual Staff, the Ad Hoc Committee on University Governance, and the Task Force on Priorities. For all these committees I carried out my usual tasks of secretary, co-ordinator, and report drafter. Even so, I felt stale – I could answer the continuous questions on immigration, tenure, promotions, and so forth in my sleep. I tried to delegate responsibility for these matters, but the deans and chairs insisted on speaking with me personally. The 1989–90 year brought everything into focus for me. During that year, the stress within McGill caused major internal rifts and the Joint Ad Hoc Committee on University Governance was established. Daily calls from members of the MAUT executive, Board members, Senate members, and others asking me to explain the positions of the other sides made me fractious. Everyone seemed to be speaking another language. That experience, together with my total boredom with the routine aspects of my job which I had carried out for thirteen years, made change a necessity for my sanity. I spoke seriously with the secretary-general and the principal about finding some new challenges and a new position at McGill. I suggested options but without success. I find it interesting that McGill is able to find new positions for men who either outgrow, get bored, or are no longer suited to their positions but is unable to do the same for women.

Thus it happened that one snowy cold day in February after meeting with David Johnston and not agreeing with him on an employment equity issue, I opened *University Affairs* to see an advertisement for the position of university secretary (registrar) at the University of Victoria. I called my husband, Peter, and then I applied. I didn't hear for months and assumed that my salary expectations and qualifications were not what they were looking for. Then at the end of May, Jim Currie from the University of Victoria called to say I was on the short list and asked my permission to contact my referees. Events then moved very quickly – I was interviewed on June 14th, offered the position on June 19th, and accepted it about a week later. It was time to move.

In my new position at the University of Victoria I have come to realize that I really like being in charge of my own department. The ability to control the budget, set priorities, and develop initiatives have all helped make my career exciting once more. Being a senior university administrator is stimulating and suits my psyche.

I look back now, a year later, with a certain nostalgia. For during my time at McGill, I matured and grew as a professional. It was a time and place that allowed innovation and personal expansion, yet a feeling of protection and caring was always there. The men for whom I worked allowed me to seek new horizons while being there to help me through the rough places. Particularly during my last ten years, credit has to be given to David Bourke, Sam Freedman, and David Johnston for having accepted my challenges to traditional roles. During twenty years I rose from planning clerk to senior administrator and held five different job titles. I gained a training in management, covering such diverse areas as human resources, finance and budgeting, and strategic planning. Despite McGill's failings, it did provide that type of opportunity for women in the seventies and eighties.

Split Infinitives

It was on a soft October day under a limpid Italian sky in the city of Florence that I first began to think about what it meant to be a woman. I was eleven, gap-toothed (a sign of luck, I was often told, but not a mark of beauty), with long, untidy hair and spectacles that kept sliding down my nose. Definitely not a candidate for adult male admiration, one would have thought. I was running along the Via Romana, late for school, pigtails, hat streamers, and bookbag bouncing over my shoulder, anxiously heading up towards the hillside avenue that would lead to my school, the Santissima Annunziata. Almost absent-mindedly, I noticed a group of young construction workers lounging by a scaffolding on the edge of the sidewalk. As I flew past, the young men began to smile and whistle. "*Bella ragazza*," they called out. "*Ciao, bella*." My astonishment at such attention nearly tripped me up. I recovered and ran on, pretending not to notice. Inside, however, I was secretly and deliciously flattered.

Nowadays such extravagant gallantry would make my own daughter, though far more deserving of admiration, acutely uncomfortable. She would feel diminished, she tells me, rather than appreciated and cherished. I understand her feelings. And yet, as I look back, it is hard not to feel a pang of regret, even nostalgia, for the thoughtless simplicity of it all.

Such an intense year that was – 1957 – full of revelations, vivid scenes, tastes, and smells that come instantly to mind some thirty-five years later. The dank currents of history filtering out onto the street from narrow passageways, the brusque intimacy of open urinals in public places, the poetry of cool sunshine on wrought iron, wisteria-covered balconies outside my bedroom, the satisfying counterpoint of apricot jam and cold sweet butter on crusty buns, the sophistication of baked fennel, red wine cut with water, and Bel Paese cheese. ...

So what was I doing at school in a palace in Florence, while the rest of my immediate family led a fairly conventional, middle-class English Canadian life at home in Montreal? It was all my grandparents' doing – or so I thought at the time. Later, of course, I understood the effort and sacrifice required of my parents. One day shortly after my eleventh birthday, my father's mother, Beatrix Lewis, the widow of an Anglican theologian and priest, unexpectedly proposed that I accompany her on her annual pilgrimage to Florence, where she lived in modest but genteel circumstances during the winter. The suggestion apparently found enthusiastic support in my mother's family, since my grandfather Wilder Penfield, a neurosurgeon who had trained in Germany, Spain, Britain, and the United States, had always encouraged his children to speak several languages at the earliest possible age. Any kind of travel would be highly educational for me, he thought. My parents agreed – they were both trilingual and had studied in Europe themselves – and the prospect of a year's separation from their oldest child seemed worth the financial and emotional cost.

Thus it came about that I was enrolled in Florence's renowned S.S. Annunziata. For ten months I followed the normal curriculum studied by all Italian children, taking oral and written exams in everything from geometry to poetry to geography. Solemnly decked in nineteenth-century costume, including Napoleonic cloak and wide-brimmed hat with streamers, I left my grandmother's pensione every morning throughout the first term to climb the hill for school. Eventually I became a boarder and took for granted the four-poster beds, frescoed parlours, and elegant fountains whose presence evoked the building's earlier vocation as a royal palace (the Poggio Imperiale). We were known as the Poggio girls.

Several years later, when I was back at school in Europe, this time with all my brothers and sisters in Grenoble, my sister Lyana and I were known as the Canadian girls – *les petites canadiennes*. Three months in a French high school and six months in a tiny Catholic convent surrounded by the Swiss Protestant canton of Vaud, on the outskirts of Geneva, taught me much about perception, about independence, about European history and culture, and about boys.

The good luck presaged by the gap in my front teeth has rarely forsaken me, though the space has narrowed, thanks to a zealous dentist. I was the oldest of six children and fifteen grandchildren, with comparatively few years between us, and I took my responsibilities seriously. Despite this mock maturity, my childhood bloomed through largely idyllic summers on the shores of Lake Memphremagog in the Eastern Townships, lapped in the warmth of sisters, brothers, cousins, aunts, uncles, parents, and grandparents. Those summers stretched on forever, punctuated by bonfires and sing-songs and by family prayers on

The six Lewis children and their parents, c. 1957

Sunday morning in my grandfather's living room. My mother, as I recall, provided the meals, clean laundry, bedtime stories, diving lessons, and – most important – the cocoa and oatmeal for dawn excursions to the neighbouring farm. She also argued a lot, forcing us to be precise, to say what we meant, to listen to our own voices. My father, on summer weekends, descended from the city, reeking of cigarette smoke, rumpled and tired and infinitely happy to be at the lake. His role was surely the more satisfying of the two: we welcomed him like a hero, applauding his impulsive purchases picked up at roadside stands – baskets of corn and raspberries and leafy lettuce.

My father was the one who encouraged us to be passionate, provoking us into bold declarations of opinion, urging us to react emotionally and instinctively, yet quick to rein us in when he disapproved. He expected us to share his values, especially his love of politics and literature, music, good food, and wine. His strong streak of sensuality led him to judge matters differently from my mother, whose work ethic and Presbyterian forebears (as well as the burden of raising six children while my father was away on business trips) coloured her views with a certain sardonic sternness. Underneath, however, she was ultimately the more tolerant and the more sceptical of the two of them.

From an affectionate, impulsive, sometimes mutinous relationship with my father I carried a certain recklessness into the arena of dating. For several years, I fell in and out of love all the time, enjoying the lustful embraces of teenage boys, savouring the power of refusal, the pleasure of indulgence, remaining a virgin long after many of my contemporaries, but delighting in the precipice. I had the reputation of being brainy but wild, a reputation I pretended to ignore though the hypocrisy caused me some grief. Sexual experience was reserved for males alone, a double standard which seemed cynical and demeaning to me even then, although there appeared to be little one could do about it – except conform.

Despite the fact that my mother had been a brilliant scholar and both my grandmothers attended college before the First World War, I did not grow up with specific career ambitions. As I began my twenties, relationships were all that mattered to me, and I rejected in advance the loneliness I anticipated would come from working for a distant goal. Indeed, although my mother tried her best to encourage her daughters to train for professional careers and although I did well at university, with honours in English and later a master's degree from the University of New Brunswick, my own sense of self-worth depended for many years on being able to bake my own bread, arrange wildflowers, grow vegetables, keep a clean house, and provide a comfortable, nurturing environment from which others could find what they needed. This is no doubt why I felt so foolishly wounded when my first husband rebuked me, after I had left the marriage, for having failed to clean the crumbs out from under the toaster! In retrospect I wonder that I could have been so vulnerable.

Through the prism of maturity I now look upon my first marriage, at the age of twenty-two, with wry amusement and occasional bewilderment. I could not be casual about my self-imposed role as nurturer: I would stay up all night working on my thesis because I insisted on spending the day cooking, cleaning, and caring for friends who dropped by all the time. I didn't even want my young husband to help with the dishes, because somehow I felt he was encroaching on my jurisdiction. This compulsiveness about what I subconsciously regarded as "womanly work" and which at the time gave me satisfaction and self-esteem has fortunately mellowed over the years, though my family still teases me about my reluctance to relax when there are domestic chores to be done.

It is difficult to shed old habits of mind. While the energy and excitement that come from challenging stereotypes have been rewards in themselves, the effort at times requires a consciousness and a conscientiousness that can be daunting. Thus I can readily recall incidents and anecdotes which, in retrospect, reveal the fine mesh of restriction, restrictions I still sometimes fail to question. When I was pregnant with my first child, for example, I remember my grandfather speculating about future careers for the baby. "If the baby is a girl, she will be a poet," he declared, "and when you have a son, he will be a neurosurgeon." Clearly he believed, and I tacitly concurred, that the sensitive, intuitive perspective of the poet was most naturally twinned with the female psyche, while the life of action and achievement in a public context should be the inevitable destiny of the male.

Another anecdote about my family suggests a carefree spirit I wish I had inherited. My great-grandmother, Mary Cordelia Kermott, received a visit from her daughter Helen some years after Helen's marriage to Wilder Penfield. Helen prided herself on her skills as household manager – in fact, her competence freed my grandfather to concentrate on his career – and her own mother's sloppy domesticity seemed irresponsible. One day Helen drew her mother's attention to the dirty windows in her house. "In a little while those panes of glass will be so dirty you won't be able to see a thing outside and what will you do then?" she asked rhetorically. Back came her mother's saucy reply: "Well, I suppose I shall simply call for the carriage and go for a ride." Such a sense of opportunities is a gift that I, her great-granddaughter, would dearly love to cultivate.

The relationship with McGill began long before I was born. In 1928 my grandfather Wilder Penfield accepted an invitation to join the Faculty of Medicine and moved his family from New York to Montreal. A few years later he founded the Montreal Neurological Institute and began an illustrious career that spanned many decades. The university, however, was never on my list of college choices – I wanted to study away from home and my grandfather's prominence cast a long shadow. It was not until I came back to Montreal in my mid-twenties and wandered into Richard Farley's office that McGill began to occupy real space in my life. Richard Farley was then director of libraries, and it was my great good fortune to be hired by him as his assistant in 1971. Before that, my chequered career had included stints as a teacher of English in Oxford, England, as a myopic cocktail waitress in Victoria, British Columbia (I was not allowed to wear my glasses), and as an Air Canada ground hostess and later an engineering company secretary in Calgary, Alberta. One of the most useful skills my mother ever encouraged in all her six children, boys as well as girls, was the ability to type. We had to practise every day, just as we did the piano, and later found our familiarity with both kinds of keyboard invaluable. Nevertheless, one of Richard Farley's most endearing traits was his own extraordinary proficiency on the typewriter: the speed with which he issued his own reports and memos allowed me to do what I found much more interesting in terms of writing and administration.

My first marriage to Sasha Bobak, the talented son of Canadian artists Molly and Bruno Bobak, was barely eight months old when I fell
suddenly in love with an auburn-haired Welshman from Cardiff,
Roger Williams. We met on the Lady Beaverbrook ice rink in Frederic-
ton, New Brunswick, registering for our master's degrees, and it was
indeed that astonishing phenomenon, love at first sight. The impact
of that encounter, terrifying and exhilarating as it was, has lasted almost two decades and shows no sign of diminishing. It took six years,
however, to sort everything out. When Roger and I finally did get
married, the ceremony at my grandfather's tholos high above the
lake and scented apple orchards provided a fairytale ending to a series of anguished partings. Indeed it was such a joyous event that ten
years later, in 1984, we had a special anniversary service at the same
spot with many of the same friends and family members – as well as
our children Hannah and Benjamin, who naturally insisted on being
very much part of the service.

Two months after my marriage to Roger, we were thrilled to discover
I was pregnant. We immediately made plans for me to give up my job
at McGill, which I did one week before Hannah was born. Thinking
back, I wonder whether I would have stayed on, had the university offered the same generous maternity benefits it now provides. It did not
occur to us at the time that we had an alternative, although Roger's
mother had worked as a district nurse in Wales throughout his entire
childhood and my own mother would never have discouraged me
from carrying on at McGill.

While the children were young, we lived in a small dark duplex in
the Montreal neighbourhood of Notre-Dame-de-Grace. From September to May I would devise strategies of distraction to keep us entertained: Ben still chuckles at the memory of our dancing to Raffi records
every afternoon, and he and Hannah both recall our "winter picnics"
on a blanket in the one sunny room at the front of the house. Since I
didn't drive, I also spent a lot of time on buses or dragging the two of
them through snowdrifts in a stroller. But I don't regret a moment of
it – for many reasons. Roger's flexible teaching schedule helped considerably. So did the knowledge that as soon as the lilacs bloomed in May
we could make plans to move to the lake, where we spent three months
working in the gardens, entertaining friends and family, playing in the
water, and chasing cows. Then too, given my own needs, I believe I am
a better parent because we had those years together. We learned from
one another and developed a certainty about our relationship as well as
an easy trust that grew out of that time in each other's company.

Cooking and cleaning and child-rearing were not my sole preoccu-
pations during this period. For four years I took courses in translation

The Williams family, 1979

at night, completing a diploma and then a certificate at McGill's Centre for Continuing Education, to add value to my master's degree. It was lonely working at home when the children were young: I missed the company of like-minded colleagues who could discuss the nuances of a French phrase or idiom. As the children grew older, I made a point of showing them first the original French text, when it arrived by courier at the door, and later the finished translation. The fact that Roger drove off to a real office every morning naturally lent much more credibility to his work. For this reason, when I eventually returned to a full-time job at McGill, I would hand out the children's weekly allowances with a flourish, to draw attention to my new role as a serious breadwinner.

Those ten years of working as a freelance translator and "growing up with the children" also included a very important three-year period as president of the Board of the Tudor Singers of Montreal at the very height of the choir's national and international success. This volunteer position as head of one of Canada's three professional mixed-voice choirs taught me how to budget, generate publicity, fundraise, and chair meetings. It was one of the strands which, together with my translation work, eventually drew me towards community relations as a career. I began to take courses at night again, this time in public relations, and started to cast around for a permanent position.

Shortly after we returned from sabbatical in Oxford when the children were six and eight, the Church of St Andrew and St Paul asked me to join the board of governors of a small girls' school as its representative. And that, indirectly, is how I came back to McGill, eventually ending up as director of university relations. Through the school board, I met Gordon Maclachlan, husband of one of the other governors and vice-principal of research at McGill. When he learned of my background and my studies in public relations, he urged me to send in my curriculum vitae. After an interview with David Bourke, the university's secretary-general, whom I had met and liked during my years in the library, I was hired.

Being a woman at McGill in a senior management position is sometimes frustrating, often fascinating. When I look at the thirty-five or so "executive-level positions," as they are classified, I note that most of the very few women included in this category are assigned what I would call sustaining roles: looking after public relations, student residences, human resources, employment equity. While I happen to think these are important positions, none of us is a member of the Principal's Advisory Group, where final decisions are made about the future of the university. This, in my opinion, is a loss for the institution. It is not that the senior men are overtly unsympathetic to women; it is rather that they do not think as women do. The product of their reflections, the decisions they make, are therefore sometimes skewed – less informed than if the group's deliberation were genuinely representative. Women reflect and react differently from men in certain situations – not necessarily more wisely, but differently. Whether this is due to gender or socialization, or both, I don't know, but it makes many of us impatient when men pretend that their way of thinking is inclusive. There are indeed some academics and administrators whose attitude is so utterly dismissive that I occasionally lose the courage to speak out unless there are other women around. Intimidation, though never explicit, is not entirely uncommon. By and large, however, I respect our differences, and it is impossible to imagine a job I would enjoy more. Moreover, there are definite signs that the climate is changing and that more and more women are being allowed to make a genuine contribution.

Working in communications in any institution has a subversive edge to it – one is always trying to break down barriers, open up passageways, push aside roadblocks. Sometimes I feel like a guerrilla fighter, lobbing grenades into traditional strongholds or fortresses of special interests. Ideally, a communicator should be a facilitator, contributing to an enlighted and effective decision, clarifying issues, encouraging people to talk to one another before the fortresses become impregnable. Ironically perhaps, the job has an almost maternal aspect to it, nurturing and creative, at its best, never an end in itself. A university with the ethos of McGill, intensely competitive, entrepreneurial, conscious of its traditions, delicately poised between cultures, takes pride in its complexity. Few issues can be reduced to an elegant simplicity that would make complete transparency possible or easy.

Ultimately, despite the long journey I've travelled since my early twenties and the affection I feel for McGill, it is still my personal relationships and the space to act within them that matter most. I like feminist Carolyn Heilbrun's definition of power as described in *Writing a Woman's Life:* "[power is] the ability to take one's place in whatever discourse is essential to action and the right to have one's part matter." This is the kind of power worth achieving, for everyone, as a working member of the McGill community, as a friend, a lover, a parent, a daughter, a sibling, a human being. "The right to have one's part matter" – now that's something to get passionate about!

La Bonne Étoile

I am a baby boomer. As part of the early cohort of that generation in Quebec, I have lived in two distinct eras demarcated by the Quiet Revolution. I have reaped, in the words of essayist François Ricard, the benefits of *"le bouleversement général de l'équilibre social, des mentalités, des modes de vie et des conditions mêmes de l'existence."*[1] ... Undoubtedly, I was born under a lucky star!

When I was a little girl, my home, my school, the parish church, and the streets in between those three points were my world, the extent of my horizon. The "adventures" in my life occurred mostly in the alley where all kids played. I was not allowed to go there, but I managed to escape regularly from our fenced-in yard where my mom used to try to keep me. I did not lack for siblings, but, since four years separated me from Lise and five years from Alain (Armand, Francine, and Christine were either older or younger), my two cousins, more my age, were my best pals. Jean and Normand were entertaining and resourceful, and our wild merriment bonded our friendship. The dark and scary sheds in the alley provided ideal shelter for our preferred childhood games of hide-and-seek, cowboys and Indians, and general warfare, which were full of suspense and perpetually reinvented.

In winter, we climbed the steel and iron fence at the corner of the street to toboggan on the grounds of the Montreal water works. In summer, we swam at the city pool. Being at the other end of town, we had to take the bus. This had a particular attraction for me because my father drove the 108 line from the Atwater Terminus to the Verdun Natatorium, picking me up at our street corner en route. How excited and proud I was when my dad was behind the wheel! As I grew up, my

---

1 François Ricard, *La génération lyrique: essai sur la vie et l'œuvre des premiers-nés du baby-boom* (Québec: Les éditions Boréal 1992), 49.

Bus driver's Christmas Party, December 1955. *1st row* from left to right: Alain, Lise, Ginette, Armand. *2nd row* from left to right: Mother, Santa, Father.

friends and I boarded the same bus to go in the other direction towards downtown. Popular outings included excursions to Mount-Royal and Parc Lafontaine, viewing films at the cinerama on Bleury Street, or visiting the recently built and "magnificent" Place Ville-Marie with its underground stores.

My parents, in the romantic setting of Crane's ammunition department, where they were both employed during the war, had met, fallen in love, and married. In 1941, they settled in Verdun, where my father's family had been established for over two decades. This southwest suburb of Montreal was then a blossoming new area full of hope and promise. My paternal grandfather had broken with family tradition and come to the metropolitan region after six generations in St-Michel-de-Bellechasse just south of Quebec City. My mom, a recent arrival to the city, had been raised in Rivière-au-Tonnerre, near Gilles Vigneault's Natashquan, on the distant north shore of the St Lawrence.

My family was Catholic, and from birth to age sixteen, my life was filled with religion. My parents, more zealous than anyone else on our block, participated in all the events the Church had to offer. As a family, we partook in the evening rituals of the months of Mary, of St Joseph, of the Rosary. We observed Ash Wednesday, did not eat any desserts or sweets during Lent; we visited seven churches on *jeudi saint* the Thursday before Easter and, on Good Friday, we prayed at the thirteen stations of the cross. We listened all year round to the nightly broadcast by Cardinal Léger of the *chapelet en famille*, attended Mass three times a week during the summer, and celebrated the *Fête-Dieu* along with the other parishioners by parading through the streets in early June. One summer my mom pledged my services to an obscure order of nuns who went begging from door to door. I had to wear hat and gloves, in the heat of the canicula, to accompany these religious ladies on their journey through the neighbourhood. Needless to say, I was mortified. Without doubt, in those early years, I accumulated a lifetime's worth of indulgences, enough to pave my way to heaven.

School was a problem. At six years old, I had had none of the fears that other children had starting grade 1. I did not cry on my first day and was proud of it. Yet, somehow, I did not take to school. The joy of learning was too closely influenced by the personality of the teacher. I remember a happy grade 3 and a terrific part of grade 5 (the latter teacher was transferred to another school, much to the chagrin of her pupils). But by high school I had switched off completely. The nuns of the *Congrégation Notre-Dame* did not stimulate my performance; quite the contrary, the atmosphere was stifling. Only educators headed for sainthood would have found any interest in the poor performer that I had become, emotional turbulence of adolescence having set in. My communications with family and school were virtually non-existent. Friendships and especially my bosom buddy, Suzanne, kept me going during those difficult years.

I grew up in a completely French milieu with no anglo in my immediate environment. At that time the two linguistic groups were neatly "*cloisonnés.*"[2] My father, who loved music, insisted that we sing along with him around the piano and during our Sunday afternoon drives. He had a vast repertoire of songs selected from French and American folklore, and we all memorized them. In 1954, we acquired a television set. My parents, both bilingual, controlled it. We children absorbed the second language by watching all the channels allowed us. At age thirteen, I considered myself bilingual. My first test came when a cousin my age, on my mother's side, with no French to speak of, arrived from Windsor, Ontario. Our conversation was arduous and most frustrating. To my great surprise, my clear understanding of English did not

    2 Jean-Claude Robert, "Montréal: L'Histoire," in *Montréal 1642–1992* (Montreal: Editions Hurtubise HMH Limitée 1992), 56.

manifest itself in smooth verbal ability but in awkward unintelligible gestures. It was only later, in the work place, that I learned to communicate, and, later still at the university, that I acquired facility in writing.

When I was in grade 10, my family moved to the South Shore. I began to neglect my Church obligations, including Mass, in favour of breakfast at the local restaurant on Sunday mornings. The secularization of Quebec public schools was underway. I enrolled in one of the first *polyvalentes*, *l'École régionale Gérard-Filion*, a product of the educational reform of the Quiet Revolution. I was but one of many students bussed in from the surrounding towns. In such circumstances, I was virtually anonymous and found it easy to evade regularly the "admittatur" system the school had invented to control student attendance. Instead I escaped to the *Cinéma Elysée*, the cafés of Clark Street, and the bars on the *rue de la Montagne*. As did much of the youth of my time, I became an ardent fan of the artistic manifestation of French expression. Literature, music, and cinema illuminated my life, soothed my emotions, and became my main occupation. I devoured the "forbidden" writings of the existentialists. I greatly admired Simone de Beauvoir and the path she retraced from her first recollections as a *jeune fille rangée* to maturity in *La force des choses*, a model of intellect and independence for the defiant and confused adolescent of the second sex that I was. I revelled in the stylistic realism of the cinema's *Nouvelle Vague* - a welcome relief from the Hollywood happy endings of the fifties. I developed a passion for the poetry in music of the *chansonniers* genre then flourishing in the *boîtes à chanson du Québec*.

Oddly enough, thanks to my school, I entered the workforce. One day, when I happened to be present, Bell Canada came to sing the praises of a career in their organization. Interviewed the next day, I was hired as a long-distance operator to commence work the following September. Meanwhile my family fell on hard times and went from crisis to crisis. My mom was working full time to raise the income for the large family to a subsistence level. My father, no longer a bus driver, had joined the *Commission des liqueurs* (the forerunner of the *Société des alcools*), but his failing health and the regular winter strikes were rendering the family impoverished. My older brother, Armand, had, some years before at the age of twelve, gone to join the *Communauté des frères du Sacré-Cœur*. My sister, Lise, a student, had been working to support the family, but she was to be married in the next year. Appropriately, I became an earning member of the family.

I took control of my life. I realized that I could perform well in a working environment. After eight months, I left Bell Canada to take a better job at Sun Life. Two years later I took time off to acquire business skills at O'Sullivan College, but I soon found that I had to work full-time in the evenings on the switchboard of the Berkeley Hotel to make ends meet.

From O'Sullivan, I went to work at Marine Industries. I took it as a matter of course that knowledge of English was required to join the Montreal labour market. This situation did not arouse in me feelings of inequity or injustice. But now, for the first time, I had the opportunity to work in a completely French milieu. The experience was exhilarating. More than any other, it awakened me to the Quebec dilemma. The former director of *Le Devoir*, Gérard Filion – after whom my high school was named – as president of Marine, had made French the working language of the head office and field operations. He transformed communications and procedures, and made available to Marine staff the terminology necessary to operate in daily business context. Filion understood that the dominant position of Anglo-American business had led to an unnecessary linguistic colonization, at least in a company totally owned by Quebec francophone interests.

I left Marine Industries for a better position in a non-profit educational organization, which offered business courses based on the case method developed at Harvard. It was a small organization with two full-time employees: the executive director, an enlightened and considerate boss, and me. I felt challenged in this climate of mixing education and business. At that time, at a suggestion by a close friend who was already a student there, I enrolled at Sir George Williams. Sir George was particularly attractive because it gave a mature student, like me, direct access to a university education. The thought of taking courses in English did not faze me in the least. I soon discovered, however, that speaking and understanding a language are one thing, but writing it is quite another.

The next few years were thrilling. I studied at my own pace; I had a chance to savour the courses I took each year. I liked everything. I began with French literature and linguistics, went on to Shakespeare and Chaucer, and then to Spanish. Even the dreaded science course, from Copernicus to modern day physics, allowed me to do research on the inspiring discoveries of Marie Curie. Little by little my writing improved. Meanwhile, a good friend came to my rescue, editing my papers while tutoring me in grammar. University in the evening is the best hobby anyone can have. I developed wonderful and enduring friendships. The intellectual nourishment I received had its impact on my travel and leisure activities: be it strolling by the Pantheon in Paris *"Aux grands hommes, la patrie reconnaissante,"* be it attending a gripping performance of *Richard II* at Stratford-upon-Avon, be it learning Spanish by frequenting Spanish and Latin American cafés in Montreal.

Dilettantish as I was in my academic pursuits, I elected to do an honours degree in history. My essay focused on Cuba's economic policies from 1959 to 1964 in Fidel Castro's first five years of government. I was fascinated by this hero of the late sixties, an incarnation of the David and Goliath parable, who believed that the empowerment of the people leads to collective fulfilment. When I graduated from Sir George Williams (by then Concordia), I sent a copy of my essay to Fidel Castro. I was delighted with an acknowledgment by Celia Sanchez, a prominent revolutionary, that it was received and appreciated. This enthusiasm for social and economic history led me to undertake graduate studies on late nineteenth- and early-twentieth-century Quebec at the *Université du Québec à Montréal*.

Like every Montrealer, I was proud of Expo 67 and how it symbolized the transformation of Quebec. Yet I remember the visit of President Charles de Gaulle to Canada that year, for reasons beyond that of his famous phrase *"Vive le Québec libre!"* His visit directly affected my life. At this time of the great *rapprochement* between Quebec and France, mutual exchanges in all sectors of the economy were encouraged. Cultural and scientific collaboration among universities was generously funded. The great Walter Hitschfeld, then dean of graduate studies at McGill, hired me to handle the France-Quebec dossier. France's tremendous culture, good science, and gastronomic quality of life were an easy sell on the McGill campus. I enjoyed that role immensely, the contacts with government officials, with colleagues in the other Quebec universities, and with our French partners. Later I added to the portfolio the coordination of all grants for international exchanges for faculty and students.

For the first few years, I was more than a little surprised to find myself a member of the McGill community. The institution, not far from my place of birth, had previously seemed completely out of my reach. The intellectually and financially well endowed, who, for the most part, were of a different cultural background than mine, frequented that institution. Once inside McGill, however, I discovered a welcoming environment, culturally diverse, where one is given a remarkably wide room to manoeuvre and where one's accomplishments are appreciated. I found that I was quickly accepted and I grew in this atmosphere, which was both enriching and stimulating. It was ideal for me, whose responsibilities required me to work in both cultural milieux.

In the late seventies, following on the initiatives of Neil Croll, I was asked to conduct a study on the feasibility of enhancing McGill's relations with developing countries. My earlier interest in Latin America and development studies suited me for this new role. My report, ap-

McGill's first director of Government Relations.

proved by the Senate, proposed the creation of an international office to look after the special needs of inter-university cooperation. McGill International was born, and I became a founding member of it under the dynamic leadership of Neil Croll. The great events of the world directly affected our office. McGill International was the first point of contact, whether for students at the end of the Cultural Revolution participating in the reopening of China, delegations from oil rich nations looking for educational opportunities, or groups from Asia, Africa, South America, or the Caribbean with proposals for institutional cooperation. With them came new views and new issues that contributed to the internationalizing of intellectual debate at the university. Issues such as the role of women, and of women in development, began to surface on the McGill and Macdonald campuses. My own horizons expanded through working visits to North Africa, Latin America, and southeast Asia. I realized that the mutual transfer of knowledge can heighten a genuine understanding of the world and can assist in overcoming disparities.

While maintaining a compelling curiosity for the world, I left McGill International to concentrate on more "provincial" matters. In 1991, in the wake of a cyclical review report recommendation, I suggested to Principal David Johnston that I look after relations between the university and governments, primarily the Quebec government. He agreed with this proposal and after a trial period of four months decided to create a position for that purpose. Government relations is not new to university administrations and has been growing in importance on both sides of the Canadian border. Tangible benefits accrue to the university through enhanced interactions and open communications with elected representatives and government officials. As a consequence, the assignment is not devoid of challenges. Although interdependent, governments and universities remain culturally worlds apart. Moreover, within Quebec this interdependence is embedded in the ongoing political reality.

McGill has not only transformed my professional life but has also had a major impact upon my private life. The popularity of the France-Quebec dossier contributed in no small way to igniting a passionate romance. One of my promotional memos for international exchanges, sent regularly to all faculty members, landed on a geophysicist's desk. His application for a France-Quebec mission to *l'Observatoire de Paris* having been approved, he invited me to meet him there. Spring in Paris worked its magic, we were soon engaged to be married. We chose San Francisco as the place to be wed and we did so just before Christmas. The first five years of the relationship were idyllic, a blissful extended honeymoon.

Although my husband and I thought we did not want children, the time came when we realized that we both had been deceiving ourselves: we longed to have a family. So Anders came and we fell head over heels for him. Annelise arrived two years later and captivated us. I felt a close bond to her and was able to dedicate myself to her care while Daddy looked after the now unruly two-year-old. For the first time in our life together, my husband and I found fault with each other. It is strange to see how two different upbringings get in the way when the time comes to look after, and to transmit customs to, the next generation. The bantering pertaining to one partner's background – first-generation western Canadian of Anglo-Danish roots versus *Québécoise de souche* of French descent – can be colourful and, in retrospect, quite amusing. Eventually, not long after Annelise's arrival, overwhelmed by the task at hand, we rallied our forces and assumed more rationally, and serenely, our parenting role.

At home in front of the Christmas tree, December 1992. From left to right: Anders, Annelise, Ginette

The greatest satisfaction of all is to see one's children grow up and develop their individual personalities. Anders is a sport-oriented twelve-year-old with a lot of presence, political opinions, and views on the matters of the world. Artistic and aloof, Annelise is an assertive ten-year-old whose determination knows no obstacles. The children are both very affectionate and seem reasonably happy with themselves. Orienting them through childhood and adolescence is, in essence, how I view my role as a parent. The development of their self and the cultivation of their special interests are essential. With proper nourishment, I hope they will blossom morally and spiritually.

When I was growing up, relations between parents and children were quite different. The Church, the school, the home imposed a uniformity of thought and values. Parents represented the authority to which children had to conform. Nonetheless, I learnt from my father honesty, tolerance, and fair play, while my mother instilled in me strength of character and a keen sense of responsibility, personal assets which I value. Today, barriers have fallen between parents and children; the two generations enjoy a closer rapport. More democratic, our children's upbringing provides them with a plethora of views and choices. But I wonder if they will acquire, as well, the character-building traits and the sense of community values that they will need to face up to their future.

Children today are made aware very early of a wide range of lifestyles. Consequently, Anders and Annelise have not been marked negatively by the legal ending of a fifteen-year marriage between their parents, as it took place in harmony with the mutual consent of both parties. An affectionate relationship endures between their father and me, which perpetuates the family bond. The children visit their father regularly, thus benefiting from his care and attention. Nor has their father's change of gender had a discernible impact on their development, although one might expect reactions further on as they reach puberty and in turn experience the turmoil of adolescence. Crossing the gender barrier would have been unthinkable in the Quebec of the fifties and is a bold move even in today's space age, one that challenges humankind. The children are learning first hand how complicated the world is and how accepting one must be of differences.

As for me, my husband's yearning to change gender left me perplexed and evoked in me a variety of emotions. These included not just shock and dismay but also a mild satisfaction from the fact that my condition as a female was being coveted, some annoyance at this "new" woman's assertive views on femininity and feminism, and a certain amusement from my former male partner's aspiration to become my girl friend. The irony and humour of the circumstance did not escape either of us. Had it not been for my children and for the fact that my husband and I shared the same working environment, I might have regarded the situation differently.

Other events helped to put my husband's transsexuality in perspective. I successfully came through a life-threatening surgical operation, so that improving my health became my main preoccupation. My husband's transformation paled in comparison to my anxiety over not being able to see my children through to adulthood. A romantic long-distance relationship blossoming at that time brought me the comfort and the serenity to move forward. The ultimate discovery for me was the sheer satisfaction one derives from being a *chef de famille*. Creating one's own nest and tending to it without interference and counter-planning is most rewarding.

A practising feminist, I have known since reaching maturity that I was born at the right time, at the right place. I have experienced sexual fullfilment, the freedom to have, to be, and to evolve. I have great admiration for the women of previous generations, many of them portrayed in *A Fair Shake* (the first collection of autobiographical essays by McGill women), who challenged adversity and were able to make their mark in the world. Like others, I owe an immense debt of gratitude to the visionaries who sought equality when its mere concept was met by ire and ridicule by the majority. Although society needs to redress the persistent inequities against women, I believe that the women and men of my generation will be the last ones requiring the feminist label. I am confident that in the twenty-first century this cause will have long ceased to be. My daughter and my son, and those of their generation, will have other high ideals to pursue.

There has been profound change in Quebec during the first four decades of my life, especially with respect to the passing from a clerical to a secular society. The tight hold which the Church had on our daily lives has relaxed. The major religious infrastructure fell apart like a house of cards. The rituals, the ceremonies, the obligations, the code of conduct vanished. Technological breakthroughs, however impressive they have been, cannot match the social permutations experienced by the children of my generation. We have lived in two distinct eras: the knowledge of the first helped us appreciate the immense advantages of the second. As François Ricard muses in his insightful essay on the subject, my generation is the lyrical generation, the lightness of the world generation, the epitome of modernity. I concur with him that the women and men of my generation were born under *la bonne étoile*.[3]

Although in coming to McGill I have not ventured far in geographical terms from the fenced-in enclosure that delineated my life as a child, it was the transformation of Quebec society that made my journey possible. During our youth, according to the poet Gilles Vigneault, we prepare a suitcase from which we replenish ourselves throughout life's journey.[4] My suitcase may differ from those of the polyglot McGill community, but it has served me well as a member of a generation challenged by ever-expanding horizons.

3 Ricard, *La génération lyrique*, 117, 193, and 63.
4 Gilles Vigneault in *Une enfance à Natashquan* by Michel Moreau (Montréal: Les Films 39, 1992).

Life: Parts I–IV

PART I: MY FATHER SAYS.

Age fifteen.
I am angry.
Furious.
Shaking.
My father says
Don't *look* at me that way
Don't use that tone of voice with me.
Now, tell me what's wrong.

Forget it, Dad.

My father takes this as an insult
Sends me to my room until I can be civil.
To him.
Always with the threat that I'm not too old
to turn over his knee.
He never does, of course.
The threat is enough keep me quiet.
Civil.

So now
I am angry. Furious. Shaking.
Silently.

Age sixteen. The dinner table.
A joke, and we laugh.
My father says

Christ, where in god's name did you get that laugh?
(as if I found it in a ditch somewhere;
like a dirty wet mitten or a muddy hairbrush)
it's not real is it?
(no Dad. It's plastic. Amazing how life-like they make them
these days, eh?)
don't be fake for Chrissake!
(ok, Dad. I'll try to do better next time).
Next time arrives.
I try a new laugh.
And my father says the same thing.
So now I don't laugh so much.
And I never feel at ease when I do.

Last Christmas I went home angry.
Distressed.
Disillusioned.
With the man who assaulted six wimmin
two blocks from my home.
With the students who distributed sexist
hate literature.
And tried to tell us about "different degrees of sensitivity."
With the fear of a womyn friend
living terrorized daily by her ex.
With the RCMP, who arrested a womyn
for reporting that she had been raped.
With my university, when it
glossed over
December 6th.
Out of sight … right?

My father
(who calls himself a feminist)
said – I think you should take a break
from these women's groups,
(who are my break from the world)
they're upsetting you.

No Dad,
It's not the wimmin that are hurting me at all,
Yes, but I think you're getting a little obsessed, dear.
With all due respect of course.
Of course,

My father the would-be psychiatrist.

And I'm supposed to tell him I'm a dyke?

My father
(whose favourite line is:
That's just not good enough)
has taught me many things.
I hope he's not
waiting for the day
when I thank him
for all of them.

PART II: HE SAYS.

He
(who is not my father)
says nothing.

A party. I'm sixteen.
And drunk
He's nineteen.
And not.

Guess what happens next.

We go into a room.
To fool around,
I suppose.
I'm certainly too drunk for conversation,

I pass out.
When I wake up,
he's fucking me.
Hard.

It *hurts.*
My body won't lubricate after drinking.
(Scrape)
And I didn't want this.
I say
No! Stop. You're hurting me.
Crying, I fight him.

He says
Nothing.

And he does not stop fucking me.
Until he is done.

Six years later I can barely remember
his face.
But I will never
forget
the pain.

He, whose name I will not
immortalize in writing,
but who has immortalized himself
in me
(temporarily – for I too will die some day)
has taught me many things.

Fear.
Powerlessness.
Passivity.
That I can be taken
and left
bleeding.
Yes, bleeding.
From my vagina.

That my words and my pain
mean nothing.

That I can be invaded, penetrated
violated
against my will.

That I am a walking Statistic

And that I have to live with this thing
which I never asked for.

For the rest of my life.

He said

Nothing.
When I cried.

PART III: THE REPERCUSSIONS.

Shut up.

That's the bottom line.
The difference is that my father loves me.
Would never knowingly hurt me.
But the message is the same

Shut up.
Don't talk back.
Don't fight back
Don't get too angry.
Don't laugh too loud.

Just shut and tell me what's wrong.
Just shut up and do what you're told.
Just shut up and let me fuck you, bitch.
Just try not shutting up.
Just try it.
Bitch.

Be quiet.
Be passive.
Be obedient.
Be docile.
Take your medicine.
Learn your lesson.
And shut up.

Now.

That's the bottom line.
And I, the good student,
I have learned it so well

PART IV: SHE LOOKS.

Breaking out.
Breaking through.

Coming out.
Seeing through
my barriers.

don't touch me.
                    don't leave me alone.
          hold me.
                              listen to me.
tell me, I'll understand.
                    I'm too afraid.
                              I don't know how.
          try to understand.

She looks.
At me!
She sees
something.
Worthwhile?
(I hope)
It's hard to believe
she does.
Very perceptive since it's/I'm buried
under years of
                    passivity
inhibition
                              suspicion
          fear.
That I didn't even know were there
until I met her.

She is confused
(bored?)
A flicker of me.
Then a barrage of defences
                    don't touch me!
          hold me!
                              don't know me!!
          listen, please.

I have built them well
though I did not want them
and I don't know how to
let them down.

I'm struggling.
But it's like walking through
gelatin,
with soap in my eyes.

She is not patient
(my fears)
She might give up on me
(I'm trying)
I'm not who she thought
(I know who I am)
That hurts so much
(I need this).

But that's not the point.
(oh – that's right. That's not the point)
The point is
I might give up.
On me.
That's the point.

How do I undo the damage
burned in my childhood mind?
Children learn faster than adults
and it sticks.

How do I learn to speak
(not passive)
With my own voice
(or laugh)
When I've never been free?
Never will be, really.

How do I let go the pain?

How can I let her touch me?
Her. Anybody. Touch me.
(please)

How can I walk away
from rape.
Whole?

I can't give up on me.
Because I have to live with me.
And I want to be happy
with me.

I want to live with
what she sees
(flickering).
I know it's there
(under my skin).
Live it on the outside.
Where I can see it every day.

Worthwhile.
All the time.
To me.

But I'm tired of learning
from my mistakes.
And living with those
of the men in my life.

Notes by a Non-Radical Feminist

Who and what defines a feminist? Although I share the aspirations of women who want to have their ideas and their work taken seriously, I haven't joined a protest march or a sit-in. I argue that women should have the same options as men for education and advancement in whatever path they desire, unfettered by patriarchal rules and taboos, and free from the threat of violence. But I haven't experienced the traumas described by my radical sisters.

I respect a woman's right to choose the way in which she will contribute to society and I believe that she should receive compensation and opportunities that are equal to a man's. But I prefer to persuade men to change their basic concepts through calm, persistent, and rational dialogue rather than through violent upheaval and angry confrontation.

That is, I want to be part of the feminist club, but on my own terms – as a non-radical feminist. In fact, during my adult life, I have also been a "quiet revolutionist," engaged in a sort of fifth-column campaign to influence the thinking of males who resist changes that affect their own status and institutions.

For me the questioning of women's status started when I got to high school, in 1948. Until then, I had always accepted life as it came, and I was fortunate to have had a happy childhood in the small city of Halifax. In elementary school, girls and boys were treated equally, and, if anything, we girls had the upper edge because we generally got better marks. But in high school, suddenly the boys seemed to count for more than girls within the school hierarchy.

For example, as a member of the girls' basketball team, I was ready to uphold the honour of my school against all rivals, but I soon learned that girls' teams did not enjoy the same status as those of boys. Not

First day of school in Halifax

only did the boys warrant better practice times, status, and even press coverage, it was also considered quite correct to outfit their basketball team with professionally sewn satin uniforms and matching bomber jackets in blue and gold, the school colours, while members of the girls' team had to make do with navy tunics and simple white gym blouses.

Budding student leaders of both sexes also learned a not-so-subtle lesson concerning the relative status of males and females. Elections to posts on the students' council were always hotly contested, but the top job was restricted: only boys could run for president, girls could aspire to nothing above vice-president.

When I questioned these concepts, I was considered presumptuous and given short shrift. Now, forty years later, I wish I had been more persistent in arguing the unfairness of the system. Such "accepted norms" seem archaic today, but perhaps they have their modern counterparts in controversies about whether girls should be allowed to play on boys' sports teams.

As a non-radical feminist, perhaps I am also marginalized in some respect, not quite fitting the accepted mould. Back in the days before "gender parity" and "political correctness" became buzz-words on campus, I took an introductory sociology course at McGill that described a person who shared neither the characteristics nor the opportunities of members of the dominant culture around her/him as a "marginal man." That is, the person did not fit the mould considered appropriate by the dominant population.

I have often felt that I didn't fully belong to many of the groups in which I was involved – whether they were composed of friends from well-to-do Montreal families who all seemed to be interconnected, or anti-poverty community activists networking at an inner-city women's shelter. Even within my own profession, as an editor and non-practising physiotherapist, I was marginalized with respect to those whose increasing clinical skills and knowledge gradually eclipsed my own.

This marginalization wasn't a hindrance, however. In fact it gave me a certain freedom, allowing me to slip from one camp to another.

Perhaps the margins had been drawn much earlier. Even in childhood, my family was unlike those of most of my friends. Their fathers were establishment lawyers or businessmen who owned cars and belonged to service clubs; mine was an editorial writer for the local newspaper, sans car, sans club. Their mothers were active in bridge clubs, church groups, and other "ladies'" activities; mine was a university-educated woman who had toured the province in a university comedy revue with my father before they were married but then chose to stay home, looking after her family and reading the *New Yorker*, and refusing to get involved with women's auxiliaries.

My father had served with the Royal Canadian Naval Volunteer Reserves during the Second World War and later became commander of "Scotian," the naval reservist base in Halifax. When I was a teenager, my parents' social life centred on activities in the Scotian Wardroom. None of my friends' families had the same interests. We didn't fit the mould. Looking back, I think I was embarrassed that my family didn't measure up to what I perceived to be the norm.

Unlike my parents, however, I became a joiner, blithely entering into whatever activities were offered – Brownies, Girl Guides, figure skating, team sports, school newspapers and clubs. I enjoyed defining tasks and seeing them through, and, as a result, I gradually developed some experience as a leader. Even so, I was slightly marginalized because I was a little younger than my classmates, which meant that they were entitled to age-related privileges denied to me. Also, during the summer I was fourteen, just before entering high school, I suffered a bout of spinal meningitis that kept me from participating fully in any activities during that socially crucial first year.

The illness struck while my family and I were en route by train to visit my grandparents in Cape Breton. The headache and fever became so severe that I was hospitalized within a day of arrival. I don't remember much of the following week or so because I was quite out of touch with reality most of the time.

It must have been terrible for my mother, who sat by my bed day after day not knowing whether I would recover. For me, having been unconscious for most of the illness, the worst shock came after the hospitalization when we got back to Halifax and my family doctor told me I would have to give up all after-school activities and be in bed every night by nine o'clock for a whole year! For an active teenager just heading into high school with all its imagined joys and freedoms, that came as a sentence of doom.

Nevertheless, I was obliged to comply, at least in the beginning; eventually, I was allowed a little more leeway, but it was a difficult year. During the next two years I was able to resume my activities and gradually I got back into sports, clubs, and parties.

Overall, I enjoyed high school. Although our teachers demanded disciplined behaviour, many of them also gave a lot of their personal time to guide us through extracurricular activities, and we benefited from their experience and interest.

In my final year, I was chosen for the coveted Edith Cavell Memorial Prize. Even at the time I thought it slightly ironic that the award was to be presented to one who exhibited "general proficiencies and womanly qualities." I thought of myself as a girl. What on earth were those womanly qualities? Perhaps a clue to society's view of womanly qualities was the four key words that formed part of the ornate, engraved book-plates: Courage, Mercy, Fortitude, and Sacrifice. These words, of course, were a tribute to Nurse Cavell's heroism during the First World War, but they made a strong impression on me. Although I thought I could handle Mercy and Fortitude, I doubted my own Courage and I wasn't sure that I was ready to Sacrifice myself, and if so to what cause. But I had survived the sometimes hazardous journey through the early teen years.

My choice of physiotherapy rather than the standard arts fare marginalized me in a new way. When I enrolled as a sophomore at McGill in 1951, there were no degree-granting programs at any Canadian physiotherapy schools. Although I enjoyed the three-year course and my experience in residence, I envied my arts friends their courses in literature and philosophy, and there was always the nagging feeling that those years were going to be incomplete without the prized degree that awaited my friends in other faculties. At the time, I didn't realize that practising physiotherapists were already chafing under restrictions imposed by the medical profession and that, gradually, the pressure for more research by physiotherapists themselves would lead beyond a simple B Sc to advanced degrees and the development of a more credible body of knowledge for the profession.

Two years after graduation, I accepted an invitation to return to McGill to complete the credits necessary for a science degree. Through a happy coincidence, Dr Muriel Roscoe was looking for a resident assistant, and Helen Gault, acting director of the School of Physical and Occupational Therapy, was offering assistance to former students who returned to upgrade their qualifications.

This new McGill phase proved more challenging than I had expected. In addition to wrestling with biochemistry, physiology, and the rest of a full academic load during my first year back, I was a part-time instructor in clinical courses at the School of Physical Therapy. I was also "den mother" to eighteen undergraduate physical and occupational therapy students housed in MacLennan Hall, an off-campus residence. My responsibility was to oversee the general physical and moral well-being of the students, but, because several of them were older than I, we operated more on a collegial than a hierarchial basis. The group bonded well and I enjoyed the family-like atmosphere. In fact, I did occasionally assume a mother-like role as counsellor and nurturer, and it was there that I met my first challenge in comforting the bereaved, when I had to help a young Haitian student who was devastated on learning that her father had died suddenly in that far-off island.

In my second year, I continued my own studies while holding the post of resident assistant at the Royal Victoria College, and I worked off my fees by becoming an assistant demonstrator in the anatomy lab and teaching a credit course on remedial exercises to fourth-year physical education students.

Despite the hard work, my return to McGill was a marvellous experience. Not only was I far better motivated to study as a mature student, but I also learned an enormous amount about organization and dealing with people because of my dual roles as teacher and resident assistant. Being neither purely student nor proper faculty during those years, however, I was again marginalized. I didn't fit either mould.

Following my second graduation, now a proud recipient of the long-coveted degree, I headed off on the almost obligatory European tour undertaken by so many university graduates of the time. After several months of backpacking and hostelling with friends, I found a temporary position as a physiotherapist in a very old hospital located in "The City," in London, England.

Living in London brought new challenges. Within the first week, my English roommate was rushed to hospital with appendicitis and I was suddenly faced with managing alone for the first time in my life. Gradually, I mastered the mysterious British gas heaters, an unforgiving telephone system, and the rental habits of a rather eccentric landlady. The thick London smog of that era made commuting itself an adventure, although it lost some of its allure the evening I arrived home to find the interior of the flat completely filled with fog. Nevertheless, working with delightful (if sometimes incomprehensible) Cockney patients and enjoying London's many theatres, I managed to eke out a living until just before Christmas, when I returned to Canada – bursting with new-found knowledge and confidence.

The idea of marginalization didn't resurface for some time. Marriage and a move to Toronto were not unusual. Life held many opportunities, and I was active in my professional field as well as enjoying a variety of activities with diverse friends. I got back into painting, joined a study group with the Canadian Institute of International Affairs, and continued with sports – tennis, skiing, curling.

By the time my husband and I moved back to Montreal, however, we had two small children, and, when I started working part-time as editor of the Canadian Physiotherapy Association journal, I was beginning to slip out of the mould of most of my social group. That is, I was not available for the coffee parties, lunches, and daytime volunteer work that served as networking links for most of my married friends. Almost none of them had jobs outside the home. I was not very interested in cooking or dressmaking and, although I loved the socializing of a good dinner party, I was there for the conversation, not the recipes.

Although I didn't really think it was necessary to compete in the domestic arena, now and then a slight feeling of guilt would creep into my consciousness. Perhaps it came from reading the popular press of the day. I wondered whether I was slacking off in my home-front duties. No one, least of all my husband, was pressuring me to perform culinary miracles. He understood my need to have other interests outside the home and was always very supportive of my activities. Meetings, conferences in town and away, files and books piled up in various corners of the house: all of this he accepted with equanimity. But as he himself was very busy and his office far from home, he was less available than I for domestic activities.

In response to what I perceived to be society's expectations, therefore, I became a prototype of the supermom. After a pressure-filled day dealing with authors, advertisers, and production people, I would hurry home to drive children to and from their after-school programs and whip up dinner while checking my notes for an evening French class or a volunteer meeting.

As the editorial office grew in size and responsibility, I gradually moved to full-time status, supervising a staff of three in Montreal and reporting to the association's executive director in Toronto. It was a dynamic and exhilarating twenty years. Working with words is one of my favourite pastimes (I've never been friends with numbers). I loved the challenge of creating a bi-monthly publication: seeing ideas transformed into print, dealing with the demands of production, and enjoying the rush of energy during the final countdown to press time.

Because physiotherapy is a predominantly female profession, most of my co-workers and even the volunteer board members were women. They knew how to get things done and they worked well together. Perhaps that's how I developed my consensus style of management. I gained a lot of organizational experience by working with the editorial board and the association's board of directors, which stood me in good stead later when I became active on community boards.

Through my volunteer work, which increased considerably after I retired at the end of 1986, perhaps I was at last falling back into the mould. Some examples might serve to reflect the type of support that interested me in the areas of higher education, social service, and the church. In each case, however, I was always looking at the best way to promote the female role and consideration of women's issues, in the spirit of a non-radical feminist.

Although I had always been a financial supporter of my alma mater and even attended the occasional alumni event, it is only in the past ten years that I have become more personally involved with McGill's Alumnae Society (women-only branch) and the Graduates' Society (which, since 1954, includes all men and women alumni). I also served on the editorial (later advisory) board of the *McGill News* (the alumni quarterly) and even did a short stint as pro-tem editor of

Joan Cleather (Alumnae Society president) and Josie Katz (past president, 1988)

the magazine when it had no editor in 1990. At present I have been recycled back to the board as its chair.

Although the Graduates' Society Board of Directors remained a strictly male preserve during its first 150 years, it began to evolve slowly about twenty years ago with the addition of a few women. Since the seventies, many women have been nominated to positions on the board and its subcommittees, and I have watched them perform effectively, with grace and humour. During my time on the board, I continued lobbying gently but persistently to sensitize men to women's concerns so that when the time came for decision making, they would see beyond their male parameters.

As president of the Alumnae Society during the one hundredth anniversary celebrations of McGill's first women graduates, I was an active participant in planning the various events. We increased our women's scholarship program and instituted our first fellowship – to be awarded to "a graduate student in any faculty who is pursuing studies of benefit or significance to women." My proudest achievement was the creation of McGill's first annual women's public lecture. After several years of discussion, preparing briefs, and fundraising, we held the inaugural Muriel V. Roscoe Lecture in October 1989, with Ruth Hubbard, noted Harvard professor, as speaker. It was a resounding success. The lecture is now an established annual event organized jointly by the Alumnae Society and the McGill Centre for Research and Teaching on Women.

The activity that I enjoyed the most, however, was writing the history of the Alumnae Society. Delving into the archives, reading old letters, minutes, and reports of the many activities that had engaged McGill alumnae during one hundred years made me realize how far we had come and how different were the needs and responsibilities of modern graduates. It was a fascinating project. But in light of the problems we were experiencing in recruiting volunteers and running programs, I also came to realize that the Alumnae Society had served its purpose, that its time was over. Fewer of today's young career women have time for volunteer activities, and those who do confine themselves to one or two organizations. As far as McGill is concerned, the young alumnae are drawn to the activities of the all-inclusive Graduates' Society.

Convinced that, as alumnae, we should channel our energies through that larger body, with its much greater scope and influence, I recommended to the Alumnae Society board that we celebrate the one hundredth anniversary by showing there was no longer a need for a special branch to protect women's interests, and that we would do far better by amalgamating completely with the Graduates' Society. Despite much rigorous debate, I was unable to persuade a majority to agree, and the Alumnae Society endured to limp on into its next century still unable to muster solid volunteer support. Meanwhile, in the autumn of 1992, the Graduates' Society board nominated one of our sister alumnae as a true vice-president, one who is actually slated to move on to a term as president – the first woman who will hold that post.

Although I had been invited to take on a major volunteer task for one of the local hospital auxiliaries, which would have brought me inside the establishment mould, I found myself instead caught up in the work of a day shelter for homeless women. Founded in 1974, Chez Doris provides a safe refuge for women in difficulty: those who are poor, those who are victims of physical or psychological abuse, and those who are unable to cope with medical, social, or psychological crises in the chaos of their daily lives. Through direct aid (food, clothing, baths) and information and referral services for those in crisis (housing, family abuse, psychological stress, substance abuse, and suicidal tendencies), the shelter offers friendly and helpful support in a non-institutional setting.

A woman's shelter is not standard fare for most middle-class volunteers, but I have found it very rewarding. I have been impressed with the dedication and understanding of the staff who are on the front lines daily. As a member of the board of directors and more recently as president, I learned a great deal about the difficulties and the horrors faced by many women in our society. I am glad to be able to be part of the team that helps to ease the pressures on the women who come to Chez Doris. We recently marked the fifteenth anniversary of the shelter, celebrating the strength of women in community and grateful that, despite rough economic times, we are still able to attract enough funding to keep the house open for any woman in difficulty.

Even in the volunteerism related to church activities, I didn't quite fit the expected mould. Instead of joining the so-called women's activities (rummage sales, bake days, and so on), I took the social service route, representing our anglophone parish on a multi-ethnic, bilingual, ecumenical council formed to help improve the quality of life for citizens in an economically depressed neighbouring sector, whose population mix included French and English Quebecers and a raft of newly arrived immigrants and refugees. My next experience as co-chair of our parish refugee committee brought me into contact with a great many parishioners, and I later became the first woman elected to the post of warden of our (Anglican) parish church.

Although the women parishioners had long proved their effective organizational skills through successful fund-raising and other events, there seemed to be an invisible dividing line between "men's" and "women's" responsibilities. When I was elected people's warden, there was some suggestion that I should relinquish the post of chairman of the Finance Committee that had been traditionally part of the warden's role. I refused. I was determined to prove that women could handle the financial portfolio and, as it turned out, during my term (with the help of a good finance committee), we ran one of the most successful pledge campaigns in years. Since then, other women have taken leading roles on the parish council and diocesan committees as well as serving as lay ministrants. Yet some resistance remains. A piece I wrote for our parish newsletter last year, about the need to examine the lack of opportunities for women in a church based on a patriarchal tradition, brought denial responses from several male clergy, including one bishop.

Although I have had my share of embarrassment, disappointment, and grief, on balance I have been very fortunate. Family, friends, work, and leisure activities have enriched my life's journey enormously. For the most part I have, in the words of Joseph Campbell, "followed my own bliss." Although I don't know what's ahead, I start each day (well, most of them) with enthusiasm and curiosity.

And here I am, in my sixtieth year, and I'm still not quite in step with my peer group. In an ironic reversal of roles, I took early retirement at a time when a number of my friends, having finally launched their children, were completing academic courses or other forms of retraining and returning to the job market or succeeding to positions of great responsibility in volunteer organizations.

When I left the journal, I enrolled in computer courses and began planning for a quiet life of nature study and writing, in a rural retreat. So far, it's been elusive – that serenity. Perhaps it was an illusion; my husband and I still have many commitments in Montreal. But we do spend a lot of time at our retirement house on a scenic cove in Nova Scotia, where I am building a garden.

The idea of creating something that will not be mature until long after I have ceased to be has given me pause. This is the first time that I have really faced my own mortality and the fact that my days on earth have finite limits. New questions pop into my head: Will I ever be able to stand in the shade of this oak tree? Will my grandchildren ever walk on these paths? Who will come after me to enjoy the garden that I am creating now? I have a sense of being part of a large continuum, something grand and universal. In this activity at least, I fit the mould of many women, feminists or generalists, past or present.

Why (What) Am I (Doing) Here: A Cameroonian Woman?

We were chit-chatting in an Indian restaurant, after having supper with a white, female, guest speaker to the McGill Centre for Research and Teaching on Women, when I was asked during the conversation to contribute to this anthology. I had very mixed feelings about it. I said to myself, "What is a Cameroonian, African, Third World woman going to say in an anthology that is *white*?" I now remember as I sit down to write that I asked Ann whether there were any other women *like myself* contributing and she said, "No," but then after a few moments of thought said, "Well, there is one Native woman," adding that she hoped I would soon meet her. Ann was genuinely enthusiastic about my participating and I was delighted at the opportunity, though I still had this weird empty feeling about it. For a while I did not think about it, I did not want to think about it, until I received a letter from Margaret and Ann, part of which stated: "We hope that this new collection [of autobiographical essays by McGill women] will give expression to the voices of women from diverse academic, professional, and ethnic backgrounds." Those two words "ethnic backgrounds" did it for me. I asked myself, how often does a Cameroonian woman find herself (studying) at McGill, how often do African women come to McGill? I had a feeling that writing this autobiography would be more difficult for me than writing a term paper on Lacanian psychoanalysis or postmodern feminism. Born in the era of an independent Cameroon grappling with postcolonial issues; nurtured, raised, and moulded by a strong, visionary mother; shaped by a strict Catholic background – I find having to combine all that baggage with my McGill experience on a few pages intimidating.

I came to the comparative literature program in the fall term of 1988. I had travelled from Douala through Paris to Montreal – Mirabel airport, where I arrived on a cool, bright day in the month of Au-

Juliana

gust with my three kids tugging at my elbow. The walls and halls of McGill were mine to discover in the next two weeks. In the meantime, I had to get my kids and myself settled into our new home and environment.

My mother had ten children, seven boys and three girls. She died on August 15, 1984. She was forty-six. I am the second child and the first daughter. I am from Beba, a rural village in Menchum Division of the

North-West Province of the Republic of Cameroon. I was not born in Beba. I went there for the first time, as far as I can remember, when I was twelve. Before we went to live in Beba, we lived in many other places in the South-West and North-West provinces where my father worked either as an elementary school teacher or principal of a school. My father is educated, my mother was not, but education, both spiritual and intellectual, i.e. "Western," turned out to be what my mother wanted the most for her children. I have come to believe that she, more than anyone else, understood how important education was for anybody in a postcolonial Cameroon where things were rapidly changing and people increasingly defined by the number of "white man's degrees" they had. My father's schoolteacher salary was all used up to provide us with the best private school education, and my mother spent most her life in the farms growing the crops that fed ten hungry mouths. In their modesty, generosity, and selflessness, they give us all they have. We are their pride.

I grew up with very devout parents. We went to church for Mass, said our prayers before and after meals, said our prayers before going to bed. ... My elder brother and I (especially) benefited from my father's profession and position. At the time that I went to school, the method used to determine whether a child was the right age for school was very simple. You were asked to put your right hand over your right ear, over your head and touch your left ear. My poor little fingers never found their way to my left ear. But my father was the headmaster of the school at the time and so I found myself in class 1 in 1962 at the age of four with most of my classmates three or four years older than I was. The legal age for entry into primary school at the time was six/seven years. My elder brother (who had also gone to school at age four) once told me how he often gave me "bonbons" in order to pull me along with him to school. He had this gorgeous benevolent smile on his face when he said to me, "You never liked going to school, even though you knew your ABCs and could count to twenty. I had to entice you with sweets," and he guffawed as I rarely see him do. So I had my seven years of primary education, then went on to Our Lady of Lourdes Secondary School for the five years of my secondary education.

Lourdes was particularly interesting. For the first time, I was leaving home to live somewhere else, and that sounded different and exciting to me. Needless to say, it was an all-girls boarding school that was more than 90 per cent Catholic with a sprinkling of Presbyterians. Apart from the one or two African sisters, all our reverend sisters were from the British Isles, most of them Irish. I had my own share of no-nonsense school discipline and I used to think my mother was strict ... ! Mass every morning (very cold mornings because Lourdes is built on top of a hill); the first five periods, a break, then the other five periods; lunch break and siesta; afternoon studies; a break for sports or club activities; supper and evening studies. By the way, speaking *pidgin English* on school premises was anathema and entailed severe punishment. How else were we going to become *ladies*? Lights out at 10 p.m. (or was it 10:30 p.m.?), then you slept and prayed the monitor would forget to ring the bell at 5 a.m. or was it 5:30 a.m.? The beginning was not only strenuous but perplexing to me, but then I got used to the routine and might even look forward to going to church on Sundays. What I loved about Sunday Mass was the singing. I have always loved hearing the choir and people sing together in church, and that special communion in song still gives me the impetus to go to church. When I am away from home, i.e. Beba, going to church gives me that sense of togetherness that I get in Beba performing folktales with my parents, brothers, and sisters.

I graduated from Lourdes in 1974 after writing the London University General Certificate of Education, Ordinary Level, and proceeded to Bambili, where two years later I wrote the Advanced Level exams. That was my ticket to the University of Yaounde. Going to Yaounde was as much a shock to me as going to Lourdes had been. I had been raised in anglophone provinces all my life and here I was in Yaounde, the capital city of Cameroon, at eighteen, away from my family, surrounded by a predominantly francophone community in a university that was overwhelmingly francophone.[1] Luckily for me, I had taken French literature as one of my A Level subjects, so although my spoken French was wanting, I understood a lot of what was said around me. Furthermore, most of my anglophone classmates had registered in the English BA, and I was among the few who had registered for a bilingual degree known as "Licence ès Lettres Bilingues (anglais/français)." Not only, therefore, was I an anglophone minority in Yaounde, I was in an even more marginal position (language, gender, background) in my bilingual degree class. I made many francophone

1 Cameroon is made up of ten provinces, eight of which are "French-speaking" and two of which are "English-speaking." French and English are our official languages. The University of Yaounde has maintained this unique system of bilingualism in its classrooms. Anglophone professors teach their courses in English and francophone professors teach their courses in French. I, for example, am a perfectly bilingual Cameroonian (English and French), although like most Cameroonians I speak other languages. Because English, not French, was my second language, and the background of my education is Anglo-Saxon, I will, in the Cameroon context, be identified, first of all, as "anglophone," followed by my tribal/cultural origins, then the rest can follow in any order. For obvious reasons, the student and faculty population is a good francophone majority.

friends and my spoken French improved tremendously, which I must say was the best thing that happened to me in that class.

I not only learned how to speak French fluently but also met a medical school student. He is from a predominantly French-speaking family of ten children, with a francophone/Cameroonian mother and a Ghanian father but an educational background like mine. I found myself pregnant in my third year. I had just turned twenty. My pregnancy, that of an unwed, twenty-year-old Catholic girl, caused my family immeasurable pain and anguish. The child was loved but my *shameless behaviour* was bitterly condemned. During my pregnancy, I kept on remembering how my father always ended his letters to me when I was in secondary and high school: "Remember that what a man can do, a woman can also." I only understood my father's words much later than they were written because I grew up in a seemingly unusual home where my mother subverted almost every gender role I can think of. For example, my brothers cook, clean house, babysit – in short, do those things that are "gendered female." We are all very competitive, albeit supportive of each other. In fact, what I miss the most in Montreal is that loving interdependency that has made being born into this family of ten kids priceless. None of my brothers ever said to me, "You can't do this because you are a girl." Because of my upbringing, I was not restricted to specific gender roles until I was projected out of "home," and only then would I take seriously the fact that only men *can* do certain things and women other things. I knew then that I had to prove wrong all those Beba people who said it was foolish to give a girl so much education.

My daughter, Patricia (who is now a Lourdes student), was born in February; I celebrated my twenty-first birthday in April and received my BA in June. I earned myself a "Maîtrise" the following academic year, got a teaching job and registered for a *Doctorat de Troisième Cycle* which I had to do part-time because I had to juggle my school work with my job and my family that grew from three to five. Adeline was born in November 1982, and my son Abbenyi in January of the year my mom died. My husband treated hundreds of patients at the hospital, I taught hundreds of young people at the high school.

I have never really felt or thought that children can stand in the way of my education or career. I have survived dreadful moments, excruciatingly painful events, but, even in my deepest moments of distress, I remain optimistic about a way out. I am also blessed with a man who relentlessly pushes me on, who often makes me see the speck in my eye that I took for a log, who like my father has supported me in my academic philosophy "the sky is the limit, no matter what." Instead of perceiving my children as a stumbling block, I see them as the catapult

The family on the Montreal metro: Amos Sam-Abbenyi, Patricia Ekwe Abbenyi, Adeline Tito Abbenyi, and Abbenyi Wa Abbenyi

that drives me to greater heights. They have been my greatest strength. I have lived the poorest and the most enriching moments of my life with these three children. The combination of going to school, working, and taking care of a family is just one of those things to deal with in life. I therefore arrived in Montreal with my three kids to meet their father (who had come to the University of Montreal the year before) and a whole new life ahead of us.

Living in Montreal meant getting used to a very different way of life. We had to settle into an apartment as opposed to the four-bedroom house with lawn and garage that we lived in in Limbe. We had to learn new eating habits, get used to eating different kinds of foods, as tropical foods are so much more expensive. How I miss the sweet aromas of spices and delicately delicious foods that drift from neighbouring houses, blending and invading one's nostrils! It took me a long time to know what was good for us and what was not. We had to learn how to dress for four seasons instead of two, worrying about the kids, about mittens, gloves, scarves, wet boots, always dreading the advent of winter and spring because of my son's asthma. I have longed for our two seasons ever so often. Not only are they more comfortable for me, there is no marked change in the dress code for either the rainy or dry season. We had to learn to say "purse" instead of "handbag"; "wallet" instead of "purse"; "pants" instead of "trousers"; "underwear" instead of "pants"! We had to develop new strategies for survival. Abbenyi (my husband) and I shared the chores: the cooking, taking the kids to or from school or ballet classes, doing the laundry, supervising homework. I used to come back from McGill with my school bag hung over my left shoulder, four litres of milk in my left hand and other groceries in my right hand. The kids would jump on me, kiss me, give me hugs, remark that I looked tired and needed some rest. Thirty minutes later, one and a half litres of milk are gone, I am being solicited to review assignments. I review their work, send them off to watch their cartoons, then remind myself of what to buy the next day: milk, fruits, plantains, okra, chicken.

Though armed with the knowledge that McGill is the bastion of Anglo-Saxon scholarship, when I walk through the gates and halls of McGill, nothing prepares me for the reality of its *whiteness*. This is one of the things that has haunted me the most about being and studying at McGill. I happened to be the only black student in all the eight courses that I took for credit. I audited other courses, one which included two black students (male/female). There were two black female students in a course that I TA'ed. It becomes very disturbing when you turn out to be the only black student in a course, and woe betide you if an issue on *blackness* comes up for discussion. People look at you from the tail of their eye; you are suddenly expected to respond, to say what it is, means, as if that were you, your life.

I have always wondered about how many "minority" or "Third World" students graduate yearly from McGill. I just have a gut feeling that tells me that McGill is unsympathetic to so-called "minority/ Third World" issues except those that fall squarely within its conservative Anglo-Saxon interests. If that were not the case, why do I not see "minority" students in the classrooms at McGill, or (let me dare to dream) why have I not been taught by a "minority" professor? Who are "deserving" faculty at McGill and what do they teach? Why do I have to get most of the primary material for my thesis, much of which comes from other Canadian universities, through inter-library loans? How/why is McGill, as I have been told and taught, and have read in newspapers, *the* Canadian university, when diversity here seems to be a far-fetched thought, when I feel so alienated? How many students *like myself* who graduate from McGill apply to teach at McGill? If they do not, investigating their reasons seems in order to me. I, personally, have mixed feelings about applying to teach at McGill. Whether they would hire me is a totally different issue. It seems to me that what I am worth intellectually is all that McGill needs/wants on paper, the rest of me ... well ... This is a very problematical issue for me. My wish: let us proceed with the *colouring* of McGill. Luckily, I cannot see all the raised eyebrows.

I often felt so isolated at McGill that I tended to duplicate what I felt at the university in my living. My family was my refuge. I did not make friends, neither did I seek them out. I was so isolated at McGill and so comfortable within my family that I never sought out friends. When I left my courses, I went home to talk, watch TV, argue about issues on the news with them so that I forgot about McGill until I sat down to study after the kids had gone to bed or the next day in class.

My husband completed his M Sc one year after we got here and had to go back home. His departure was a terrible blow to me. I was going to miss not only my lover and best friend, but also my major critic (we always read and criticize each other's work). I had to stay back here in Montreal with the kids and consequently constructed a whole new life around/with them. They became my sole advisers, confidants, and critics. I longed for and enjoyed the various things we did together, cherished our discussions while shopping, watching the news, cartoons, or sitcoms. Television changed the way we look at the world. The sheer hypocrisy embedded in First/Third World politics and played out in the media was enlightening to me. Watching the killings going on in Lebanon and on TV, my son would often say that if we did not go home, we would die in Canada; the girls would want to know why there were so many women in beer ads. The kids would comment on the fact that certain ads seemed to appear and disappear according to the seasons. We wondered why products like milk and toilet tissue were advertised at all, but once one walks down a supermarket aisle, one gets the message. We were disgusted by so much fast food on our screen, paradoxically in a society where people seem to have lost the simple ability to enjoy food. If someone walked by our door, hearing us arguing and laughing our heads off, they would have thought that there were a number of adults in there. But, it was just me and the kids. At such times McGill seemed far away. However, at the end of 1990 they also had to go home. Their father felt that having them with him would be less demanding on me and would give me more time for my own work. He has been taking care of them for the past two years. But when the kids left, my world seemed to have caved in on me. I had neither *friends* nor role models nor people I could relate to at McGill. I had never known such moments of intense loneliness.

Making friends at McGill or in Montreal in general has been difficult. At the beginning, I tried, because people wanted to know about my family, to learn about Africa. I would oblige. I was proud of Africa,

I loved speaking about Cameroon (especially after my travels to other African countries). I never really valued being a Cameroonian until I travelled to Kenya in 1986, hated what I saw, hated how the tourist industry had turned this beautiful country into a piece of meat. In tourist shops in Nairobi, I saw the faces of *white* owners everywhere. I resented feeling like an outsider on their beaches, my black body as conspicuous as Medusa's head in a maze of white bodies, in "my" own continent. I could not stand the singular deference to white tourists that still smacked of colonial privilege. That first experience with "other" Africa made me appreciate Cameroon better, our enormous linguistic and incredible cultural diversity among other things.

I therefore enjoyed talking to my friends and colleagues about Cameroon, about what I knew about Africa, but when I asked them to talk about Canada, about Canadian life, they shrugged it off with, "What's there to tell? Well, there's the constitutional crisis, there's the language thing here in Quebec, and that's about it. Actually, it's boring, nothing much to it. The stuff you see in the media every day. Could we talk some more about Beba, your village really sounds fascinating. ..." I soon realized that I was fast becoming to these people what Kenya, Nairobi, the giraffes, lions, the "jungle" were. I retreated into myself. I met black people who were more interested in "sisterhood" than my being African or Cameroonian. Although I value certain aspects of that"global"struggle, most never wanted to acknowledge my *difference* but spoke passionately of saving Africa, of saving the African woman from those patriarchal violent men who have made them into mules, mutilating their bodies for their selfish pleasure. I would look into those passionate eyes wondering whether they were speaking to me, wondering whether they realized they were speaking about me, that African woman, and why the hell did *they* of all people treat Africa like one nation? I grew weary of people, black or white, who only seemed to see me as exotic or victim. What was there to talk about? My eternal victimhood?

What I have loved the most about McGill has been the comparative literature program. The diverse backgrounds of the students in this program have been very encouraging. Unfortunately, the persistent power struggles by faculty who have disregarded the students and the *raison d'être* of this program have fuelled McGill's decision to close it down, and this will be a great loss, not only to McGill but to people like me. I was appalled by the obnoxious attitudes of some faculty members who openly opposed/devalued the work of other faculty members, thus creating not only an unhealthy and chilly climate but a pattern that filtered down and found itself duplicated within the student body. I knew I had to stay away from partisan bickering and remain focused on making the department let me do the kinds of research that I wanted, even if this research involved the "W" and "F" words. The interdisciplinary nature of this department provided me with a strong theoretical foundation and the possibility to engage in research that I enjoyed and found both original and stimulating. I wrote a term paper and one of my comprehensive exam projects using folktales that I had collected in Cameroon. I have treasured working with(in) feminist theory. What has been most rewarding for me has been the fact that not only have I read all these Western feminist theories, but I have also always sought to bring my own intervention, my own position to my feminist readings and thinking. Consequently, I have developed an interdisciplinary feminist dialogue/theory along the way, for the purposes of my own feminist research. Learning from these theories while simultaneously questioning them from my own standpoints, through my own identities, has made research at McGill particularly fulfilling.

I have worked hard at not letting the *whiteness* of McGill hurt my research and worked even harder at the racism prevalent in Montreal or North America as a whole. Back home in Cameroon, we identify two races (I think "identify" is the wrong word, given that we do not *identify* races, we just know there are two): there is "us" and the white people, a.k.a. Westerners, a.k.a. Europeans, a.k.a. the colonial masters. Then I came to North America and a whole new world opened up for me. There were the *real* white people like, say, George Bush, then the others – Hispanics (back home these people and many others are white to us, but here they are Hispanics), Latinos, and Amerasians – and then there are those other shades of the rainbow: people of colour, *visible* minorities (not to be confused with those real white people who also claim minority status), Native peoples, African-Americans, Afro-Americans, Blacks, niggers. My poor little head was spinning on its axis. Well, where was I? I lumped myself tentatively somewhere in between Hispanic and nigger (African, plain and simple, did not seem to be found anywhere). Silly me!

I have encountered racism in a number of ways here in Montreal, but, unfortunately, those that have stuck with me the most are incidents that happened at McGill. I found it easier to forgive the saleswoman who bluntly told me, simply because I had remarked that the beautiful purple coat I was admiring was expensive, that if I wanted a cheap coat, I should go to those stores where people like me shop. I bought that coat, not to prove the contrary to this woman, but because I love purple and look great in purple. Sometimes, I wished that coat had been another colour, but each time I wear it in the fall or spring, I think of that woman and other ignorant (sales) persons like herself.

I had a naïve view about the highest institutions of learning like McGill that compelled me to hope that racism would not show its ugly face in such an environment. After all, were these people not supposed to be the most educated, cultured, the most sought after? Racism can be encountered just about anywhere on campus, in the classroom, in the cafeteria, in the washroom (check out some of the graffiti!). I had classmates for whom my African-ness automatically implied an inability to cope academically at McGill. I had a professor who could not understand what an "uncivilized" woman/breeder of three children could be doing at McGill. My being female, African, and, worst of all, a mother told him all he wanted to know. I learned a hard lesson: racism has nothing to do with being educated and *everything to do with being educated*.

I have learned to manoeuvre and control my anger towards people who are blatantly racist. Sometimes I tell them off, negotiate dialogue, or just smile in their faces (incidentally, I have discovered that it makes some uncomfortable, for they just cannot figure out what is amusing), or I ignore/shut them out. A mother had difficulty stopping her daughter from playing with my "boubou" in the metro. This little girl was so fascinated by the splendour of the embroidery and intricate patterns on the African outfit I was wearing that she could not help but stick out a little finger and trace the patterns. I was completely taken by this little girl, wondering what was going through her mind. Her mother kept on whispering to her to stop doing what she was doing (Canadian racism can be so subtle!), and when the child would not, she quietly reminded her to remember "how these people are" and to "stop it right now." The little girl looked up at me and I asked her name. "Gena," she said, "what's yours?" "Juliana," I said. Her little finger went back to work. At the Peel metro station I told Gena I had to get off. "Why?" she asked. "Because I have to go to school," I replied. "To school? Will I see you again, Juliana?" "I hope so, and by the way, I have two girls and a boy that you might like to play with," I said. "Really?" "Yeah." The doors were closing in, I jumped out. Looking down as I was riding up the escalator, I saw Gena's eyes staring, her little finger pressed against the window. I will never know what she was thinking, but I shall maybe, one day, write my Montreal memories because of the Genas out there.

I have likened the struggle with racism to a race, like the ones I see on TV, on a ski slope. Replace the time-to-beat and medals to be won at the winning line with your life. Dealing with racism therefore depends on negotiating those curves and obstacles in such a way that you do not fall off the slope, breaking a leg or your neck and hurting someone else in the process of your fall. The target always has to be that prize waiting at the end of the course, and once one is *conscious* of that, one would negotiate those obstacles painfully, carefully, slowly. I have come to perceive and subvert my loneliness in the same way by learning to listen to silence, letting it speak to me. Solitude for me now is no longer that horrifying thing that it was at one point, especially when the kids left. I am never really alone. I always cherish walking into my apartment. That is because I have surrounded myself with all the people whom I love. They are on my walls, in my TV set, my VCR, my bathroom, my kitchen, my bedroom, my sofa, my books; like the spirits of my ancestors, they are simply in what/who I am, in me. They are with me on the bus, in the metro ... I have even learned to laugh with my eyes in the metro or the malls, when something I hear or see reminds me of them. Were I to laugh out loud, people would say, "This black woman is nuts," but they would not understand what is driving me crazy or making me ticklish all over. In my deepest moments of solitude, I sit in my sofa, sink deep inside, make myself comfortable, and pretend to watch TV. And suddenly memories will come cascading through me and all around me, an image on the screen, a look at a photo, a thought will spark something else, and the domino effect engulfs me. I wake up at midnight, maybe 1 a.m., 2 a.m., to the zipping noises of bullets and street-smart tough cops ... I turn off the TV, or turn off my radio and go to bed. When I wake up the following morning and look at the smooth fullness of my face, slowly two white lines running down my cheeks betray what went on in that sofa. I will gently wipe them off, and as I do so the smile on my face slowly broadens, reminiscent of how hysterically we make each other laugh or cry, hurt and heal, and I will break out into uncontrollable laughter, laughing at the world and most of all, at/with myself. Those Catholic sisters and my mother seemed to have done something right, after all.[2]

---

2 I am registered at McGill as Juliana Sam-Abbenyi; maiden names, Makuchi Nfah. I am now finishing my dissertation: "Gender in African Women's Writing: (Re)Constructing Identity, Sexuality, and Difference," a feminist study of selected works by sub-Saharan women writers.

Making a Place

"Write about what you know" was one of the main pieces of advice liberally sprinkled around when I was an editor for *Scrivener*, McGill's literary journal. That maxim, along with the timeless "show, don't tell," constituted our main, diplomatic criticism for the vast number of submissions we received. So as I write this I ask myself, what do *I* know? I know I am young. At least, I am just twenty-three and that seems young to me. I am still in school, I don't have a job, I haven't married, I don't have a child. I do know what it is to grow up in a prosperous Montreal suburb, to be a child of Scottish immigrants, to be an anglophone in Quebec, to attend a public school, to do an English BA at McGill, to have won a Rhodes Scholarship and now to be a graduate student at Oxford in England. I know what it is to work on a crisis telephone line and to listen to callers threaten suicide on the other end, I know what it is to read vast amounts of often painfully poor fiction for a literary journal, to have lived on a Scottish island, to have lived in a small Quebecois town, to have been a waitress, a bank teller, a library clerk, and to have travelled as a woman alone to foreign countries.

So, what do I know? I know that by traditional standards I have achieved a certain measure of success, for two years ago I was fortunate enough to win a Rhodes Scholarship which sent me to Oxford to pursue a master's degree in modern English literature. I hesitate to write about my scholarship for I have been taught to be appropriately modest and self-deprecating about any achievements. Although it has obviously become a part of my self-definition, I still can't believe it happened; an uncertain little voice continues to ask inside my head, "who ... me?". Like lightning, where the scholarship falls seems arbitrary, yet the impact is huge. I continue to be plagued by the feeling that somehow a mistake was made and that it is just a matter of time before I am unmasked and exposed as a fake. In fact, when I won I

Fiona in front of the Old Bodleian

was so convinced that there had been a mix-up that I called the secretary of the scholarship committee first thing on the Monday morning to ask if my name meant anything to her, just to double check!

Although I know this disbelief is often a typical reaction – many men I have talked to have admitted to the same insecurity – I do think it is particularly characteristic of women. Most of my female friends are extremely adept at attributing success to any other source except themselves – luck, a kind professor, lack of competition – and yet accepting any failure as their due.

Yet perhaps, considering the history of the Rhodes Scholarship, it is natural that I'm still disbelieving, for I am not exactly your historically stereotypical candidate. When Cecil Rhodes, the British diamond magnate and imperialist, left most of his large fortune for the establishment of the Rhodes Scholarship, he outlined in his will how the scholarship would be awarded to young men of the colonies who exhibited qualities of "success in manly outdoor sports," "manhood, truth, courage, devotion to duty"[1] and so on, along with their demonstration of literary and scholastic attainments. What these qualities connote in today's society is rapidly changing, and the Rhodes selection committees appear to obey the spirit, if not the letter, of the will. This is evidenced by my background, for my academic interest was feminist literary theory and my "sport" was helping to coordinate McGill Nightline, a telephone line run by students for the students of McGill. The element of "brutality," the fourth specification which Rhodes noted privately in his diary and unofficially desired every scholar to possess, seemed to have been lost, thankfully, somewhere in the shuffle.

Even though the Rhodes Scholarship was established at the very beginning of the century, women have only been eligible for it since 1976, when an order was passed by the UK government declaring the scholarships to be tenable by women, and supposedly "nullifying the effect of the words 'manly' and 'manhood' in the will."[2] I am proud to say that although the first women were only elected to Rhodes Scholarships in 1977, they have been quick to make their mark. Canada can hold its head particularly high, for, unlike most other countries where the scholarship is awarded, at least half of the annual eleven Canadian scholarships have been won by women in the last few years. It is important to recognize these facts because Cecil Rhodes, the founder of the scholarships, could be said to emblematize the imperialist, sexist, and racist attitudes and institutions of Western society, everything I perceive the feminist movements to be fighting *against*. For women now to be winning these scholarships and being able to use the opportunities offered to combat these systemic convictions is an important and valuable step. At least, that is my perception, and my aim.

So, I know that I am one of the lucky ones. And I consider it just that – luck. Although I am proud of the hard work I have done, and

1 *The Rhodes Trust and Rhodes House* (Oxford: Oxuniprint 1992), 3–4.
2 *The Rhodes Trust and Rhodes House*, 7.

the contributions I made to such organizations as McGill Nightline, which enabled me to win my scholarship, it was luck that put me in the position of privilege which gave me many opportunities, a good education, and a supportive background. I write this seemingly obvious fact because I hate what I call the "queen bee syndrome," the attitude of some successful women (successful in the traditional male definition, that is) who maintain that if they have made it, everyone can. I'm referring to the women who announce that they have succeeded without any help and who refuse to admit the existence of any sexual discrimination. I do not want to deny such women their individuality or detract from their, doubtless, long and hard work for their achievements, but it is important to recognize that it is in part through other women who are still struggling, and the women who have survived the struggle and paved the way before them, that they have reached their own heights. I am always conscious of what I *owe*, and believe all women should be offered support and encouragement and help, not as a generous gesture but as their due.

I know that one of the most positive ways to offer this support and encouragement is through being an active role model. I know I have depended on a large number of women as role models in my life. Where, or who, would I be if I didn't have the examples of my mother, who after moving to a new country, learning a new language, and raising three children for twelve years, went back to dental school at McGill and graduated top of her class? My sister, who persisted in medical school to become a doctor? My female professors at McGill, who demonstrated through their own lives what it is to survive as women in academia? My cousin, who lived for three years in Nepal teaching weaving? My own friends, who are currently struggling to make a place for themselves, attempting to achieve a balance between careers and relationships? The numerous literary role models, women who have offered their lives to me through writing and autobiographies that have sustained and encouraged me?

I also know that I am excited, and surprised, to be already having the opportunity to be a role model for other girls and women. One of my most rewarding memories springs from when a teacher from my high school called me up last year after I had won my scholarship and asked me to give a speech at a school assembly. Although my first nervous response was to mutter something about having to wash my hair that day (even though the invitation was for three months away), I decided to look upon it as a chance to talk to the students, especially the girls, in a way that I wished I had been talked to when I was in high school.

So – I prepared a speech and turned up on the arranged day. I had purposefully dressed down so as to seem more approachable: jeans, a

Fiona and her mother in front of Lady Margaret Hall, Oxford

waistcoat, my Doc Martens. I was met by the two students who were
going to introduce me, both dressed to the nines in three-inch heels,
skirts, nylons and perfectly applied make-up. They looked thirty and I
looked thirteen – I had forgotten what high school was like! It felt
strange to be back, and as I sat on the stage scanning the faces of the
girls I was reminded of all the old feelings – the insecurities, the lack of
self-confidence, the uncertainties – that seem inescapable at that age.
The girl who introduced me decided to read aloud my yearbook blurb
from my graduating year by way of an introduction. Talk about youthful words coming back to haunt you. The one saving grace was that it
was written in such "teenspeak" that it was incomprehensible to most,
but for me it demonstrated, in perhaps too powerful a fashion, how recently I had been sitting where they were sitting now. Then I gave my
speech. It was full of exhortations to "go for it," "you never know what

you can do until you try," "look at me, I never thought I would end up where I am," and so on. I specifically tried to encourage and inspire the girls, telling them how women are now succeeding in the traditionally male-only Rhodes Scholarship. I anticipated the reaction from the boys, some mild booing at being left out; the response from the girls was harder to gauge.

The sequel came only a week later. I was on a bus and noticed a young girl staring intently at me. Finally she said, "Hey, I know you. You gave a speech at my high school. I really liked what you said, you know, about girls being able to do it too. I cheered." Somehow I had managed to communicate something of what I had been trying to say.

If that is my immediate past, my immediate present is studying at Oxford, and more specifically knowing what it is to be a woman at Oxford in the early nineties. There is no question that there is a romantic aura to Oxford, a mystique that is hard to define but is tied up with its history, its beauty, and its traditions. But for me, as a woman, it is also emblematic of entrenched sexist and patriarchal institutions.

Being a woman at Oxford now is very different from being a woman at Oxford one hundred, fifty, even twenty years ago. It has changed considerably since Virginia Woolf described in *A Room of One's Own* being locked out of a mythical "Oxbridge" college library and denied access to the information contained within because she was a woman. The gold and silver she envisioned flowing into "Oxbridge" (although Woolf's point of reference was really Cambridge, the same observations can be made for Oxford) for hundreds of years to fund the foundations of the male-only colleges is now benefiting women as well as men.

The trailblazing for women currently studying at Oxford was done by the pioneering women back in the late nineteenth century. Thanks to their efforts, women need no longer *justify* their presence at Oxford, as their forerunners did. Although Virginia Woolf, who was herself denied a university education, wrote the following words to describe the debt she owed to the women writers who had preceded her, the words are also appropriate for the debt we owe the women who pried open the doors of formal education: for "the road was cut many years ago ... many famous women, and many more unknown and forgotten, have been before me, making the path smooth and regulating my steps."[3] Women are now well and truly established at Oxford: many brilliant women have studied here, continue to study here, and their presence and hard work have proved successes. My own college is

3 Virginia Woolf, "Professions for Women," *Collected Essays* (London: Hogarth Press 1966), 2:284.

Lady Margaret Hall, one of the first women's colleges to be established at Oxford in 1878. Although it began admitting men around 1975 and is now at least equally divided between the sexes, there continues to be the feeling that "great women have been here." I live my life surrounded by reminders of the debts I owe the women who have gone before me, reminded daily through their portraits in the halls, their names on the buildings, their generous bequests as alumnae, of their previous struggles and continued presence. Owing to their efforts, women continue to make their mark and establish their place, and most Oxford experiences are no longer restricted by sex barriers.

As a true child of the video generation, I seem to visualize and order my memories and experiences of Oxford as snapshots in a photograph album. This tendency is encouraged by people continually reminding me that these are supposed to be my "glory days," these are the years I will reminisce about with a slightly glazed, far-away look in my eye every time someone mentions "Oxford" or "England." Who knows, I might even begin sniffing nostalgically at cold, wet, rainy days! So I am consciously squirrelling away my experiences which supposedly are to sustain me in my later, greyer, years. Open the cover of my Oxford album and there is the first snapshot, walking through Port Meadow in the autumn for lunch at the Trout, among the peacocks by the weir. Snapshot two, dining by candlelight at high table in the wood-panelled hall of Magdalen College, with the heavy oil portraits of the founders of the college watching my every mouthful. Third snapshot, November now, a thick hoar-frost covering the gardens and buildings, rowing in an eight on the Isis with the water icing the blades. Turn the page and it's Christmas time, listening to evensong at New College sung by angelic boy sopranos. Suddenly it's spring and the photograph is of a punt on the Cherwell, going for a picnic at the Vicky Arms, then playing croquet on the perfectly manicured college lawns. It's summer and the picture is of the upper reading room of the Bodleian with the imposing façade of the Radcliffe Camera looming outside the window. Summer, and it's a survivors' picture of a college ball. These experiences are still wonderfully "Oxford," the Oxford familiar from fiction, and I am fortunate enough to include them in my lived experience.

But that is not the whole Oxford experience. Being a woman at Oxford has also meant for me having only male tutors, for there are few female dons. It's meant being excluded from the numerous men-only drinking societies, which are so entrenched that their presidents are often the masters of colleges. It's meant having the opportunity to study only one female author during my entire course in modern English literature, Virginia Woolf, the only woman to have been admitted to the syllabus. (Ironic, when her live presence was so emphatically excluded!) It's meant being greeted by a quizzical look by my tutors at mention of "feminist literary theory," followed by gentle discouragement and ultimate indifference. It's meant being called "darling girl" in tutorials while my male colleagues get called by their names. It's meant gnashing my teeth while the men's rowing team gets the better boat, the better blades, the better coaching, the only good coxen going; all this at a women's college that went co-ed less than twenty years ago. It's meant being outnumbered by the men at every social occasion, and fighting for my place in the conversations. This is also what it means to be a woman at Oxford today, encountering the more insidious aspects of the established sexism, making it all the more difficult to combat it.

Unfortunately, some women claim that this atmosphere divides women, making them feel threatened and promoting spiteful competition. Although I do not doubt this attitude, I am happy to say I have not had that experience; rather, I believe one of the few positive aspects to the low representation of women is an increased feeling of solidarity among the women at Oxford. I tend to treat other women as companions on a difficult journey, offering, and receiving in kind, support and encouragement as we pick our way along the often rough path of graduate work at Oxford.

So, I do know that what is hard as a woman at Oxford is to keep up the good fight. It is too easy to be quickly lulled into the encouraged conformity, and there are so many entrenched assumptions and traditions that it is difficult to oppose them. "Everything is done for good historical reason," a don informed me soon after my arrival. I did not realize what a young school, or young country for that matter, I came from until I started hitting my head against the weighty wall of almost eight hundred years of tradition. When you consider that women have only been establishing their tradition at Oxford for little over *one* hundred years, you can begin to get a sense of how far women still have to go. A powerful indication of this struggle is evidenced by the United Oxford and Cambridge Clubs, for alumni, where women continue to be entitled only to "lady associate" status. This reduced status means that women cannot walk on the main marble staircase, they are forbidden access to the library and to drinking in the members' bar, and they must use underground passages to gain access to rooms they are allowed to use.[4] It enrages me that my male friends and colleagues here are allowed full membership privileges, while I am not, based solely on

4 Leonard Stark, "Letter from Oxford: Exclusive? – The Social Challenge of Not Only Oxford," *American Oxonian* 80 (1993), 26.

the matter of our difference in sex. As this example clearly demonstrates, yes, women are accepted at Oxford ... only up to a point.

In the end I can offer no conclusions. In fact, writing an autobiographical essay when I feel so young and unremarkable seems somehow shameful: I should be a much older and wiser woman able to look back, reminisce, and laugh about my youthful ideals and follies. It feels funny not to be casting back to the past, but rather attempting to record moments of the present, and seeking to chart the future. I do not know where I am going next, or how I am going to make *my* place, but this is a beginning.

Rites of Passage

In Oaxaca, twelve days before my thirtieth birthday, I gave birth to my third son, Nicolá. Before the year was out my husband almost killed me by pointing a loaded gun in my direction and firing. He missed, his aim affected by his drunkenness. It took me another year and a half before I left him, taking only the boys and their clothes back to Montreal for a most uncertain future. At least it beat being dead or stark raving mad.

In Montreal, somewhere shortly before or after my fortieth birthday, I fell in love. This passion was so deep, so complete, and *so* unrequited that it totally transformed my life. It took me another year and a half to enter analysis in order to make sense out of my desolation. Although I hadn't been shot this time, the pain was excruciating as surely as if the misspent bullet of ten years earlier had sheared my body. Nothing in my upbringing had prepared me for being shot at at thirty or falling in love at forty!

Writing this autobiographical essay will exorcise these two major demons in my life.

From the moment I was thirteen or so I knew that I would have three children. What I didn't know then is that I would have three boys and their father would be a Mexican painter, an artist met while I was in Mexico as part of the first Canada-Mexico exchange for young specialists and technicians. Talk about cementing relationships between North American countries! This was not quite what I had envisaged in my early adolescence.

I was born in London, a by-product of my father's Nuffield Fellowship, which found him working at University College Hospital. My mother loves to regale people with details of my birth on a Saturday afternoon. She was out with my father doing her shopping when she

Marie-Francine, mother, and brothers, 1955

felt an urgent need to have me. They hailed one of London's famous black cabs. The driver had just thoroughly cleaned the inside and was not amused when he picked up this particular fare. Needless to say, my mother's waters broke in his impeccably clean back seat. When my soon-to-be parents arrived at Queen Charlotte Hospital, the admitting staff insisted on taking Mother to her room as per regulations. However, while riding the lift up, Mother quietly but forcefully indicated that she knew what was happening: "This is not my first but my second child. I'm having the baby here. There is no time for me to go to my room to undress."

And so it was that I came into the world without my mother being appropriately gowned for the occasion. This in no way should cast a shadow on my mother's irreproachable manners but rather on my impetuosity, a trait that has caused me more than once to wince and say "OOPS, perhaps I should have …" Yet the stage was set for an enduring love for England.

We returned to Montreal at the end of my father's fellowship. I never got over England and returned to study and to live there on two separate occasions. So it was quite out of character for me to find myself married to a Mexican painter, living in colonial Oaxaca when I had always imagined myself in green, lush England – civilized England. Somewhere along the way the decor for my life had been switched on me.

Being in the family way (don't you just love those euphemisms) is not a great reason for getting married, but it serves a purpose: saving the family name. I knew while standing at the altar that it was all a terrible mistake, except that having a child outside of marriage didn't seem like a viable alternative for this Westmount girl in 1974. The shame of it all! What will people say! Twelve years later my younger sister completed the deed for me by having her daughter out of wedlock. No one died then, nor did anyone bat an eyelid. There's nothing like good timing. In any event, Sebastián was born with his parents being duly married: his mother in Montreal ensconced in the bosom of her family and his father in Oaxaca. However, the old French aphorism *Qui prends mari, prends pays* (Who takes husband, takes country) became a reality (at least temporarily), and I moved to Mexico.

Oaxaca is a charming colonial town, surrounded by archaeological sites, blessed with a temperate climate, just ideal for tourists, but not for a white-skinned redhead. The problem was that, unbeknownst to me, I was a feminist in the land of the machos. What was more obvious to me was that being married, barefoot, and pregnant in the kitchen was not doing my mental health any good. I tried, oh God, I tried.

First we lived with my mother-in-law, who ran a *casa de huéspedes*, a boarding house for university students. The three of us had a small room to ourselves at the back of the house near the kitchen and the washing area. This wasn't London or Westmount. It wasn't even comparable to my very first apartment as a twenty-one-year-old in my last year at McGill: my very own one-and-a-half semi-basement on University Street. This was going to be the beginning to "they-lived-happily-ever-after." I was going to try to live a conventional life and put aside all the inner demons and visions which haunted my dreams and fantasies.

What memories! The most memorable of all was the night my father-in-law, Cuauhtémoc, got royally drunk a short time after our arrival. Like a lot of men in Mexico, my father-in-law had left his wife for greener, younger pastures. By the time he walked out, his wife, Doña Luvia, had worked herself to the bone tending his herds, making cheeses, raising five children, not counting the miscarriages, in the most inhospitable, fly-infested piece of land squeezed between Oaxaca, Chiapas, and Veracruz. He did, however, make occasional appearances.

I don't quite remember how it started; probably as it usually did. One drink to relax, and then another and another. And as always happens, you mustn't let the other man out-drink you. I had retired with Sebastián, who was eighteen months old, to our room for the night. My mother-in-law had also gone to hers, as had her lodgers. It was customary, if not *de rigueur*, that men drank together, heavily. Hey, this was macholand. Men only.

Around midnight, a loud commotion drew me to the front patio. Cuauhtémoc, in his drunken state, had decided to kill Luvia. We never found out why. It didn't really matter at the time. He was rushing around from room to room looking for her, revolver in hand. He stormed our room and woke the baby up in his mad search for her. Fearing for my mother-in-law's life and Sebastián's, I chased after this lunatic until I finally caught up with him in Luvia's bedroom. She had, very wisely, taken refuge in one of her lodger's quarters, instinctively knowing that he wouldn't disturb non-family. As I successfully wrestled the loaded gun from this very strong and very inebriated man, I thought to myself: "This can't possibly be happening to me. I'm a nice girl from Westmount. This has got to be a grade B movie." It had never occurred to me during the whole incident that he could have made minced meat out of me. A real babe in the woods!

Life in Oaxaca wasn't always such an adrenaline rush. It was very parochial, and until I enrolled Sebastián into the *jardin de niños* (kindergarten) I had no friends of my own. My social contacts were exclusively limited to my husband's family and friends. I was dying. I had no life. I actually left him for several months when I was pregnant with my second son, Vicente. I went home to Mother. After having consulted my father and my parish priest, this compliant and obedient daughter and a Catholic to boot returned to her husband after a five-month absence. I still had not legitimized my own existence.

Life was tough. The military were everywhere. There was a state of emergency in the capital where we lived. The rector of the university where my husband, Salvador, taught was attempting to democratize appointments. The rector was eventually ousted for his efforts. I, on the other hand, persisted in living the life of a dutiful wife. After having lived on the outskirts for six months, we moved into our own apartment in the city. This meant a certain amount of freedom. It meant that I wasn't so isolated any longer. I didn't have to wait around to be taken anywhere. Now I could walk to wherever I needed to go without waiting for my "saviour." (I always thought it ironic that my husband's name meant saviour!) But there wasn't anywhere to go except the usual rounds of the park, the market, the occasional visit to the doctor and my mother-in-law's.

Things started to brighten up when Sebastián began nursery school at three. He now had little friends to play with, and his mother, ever so slowly, became acquainted with his friends' mothers. Oaxaca was very insular. Even those from out-of-state found it hard to make friends. I managed to get a job teaching a French course at the local *Alliance française*. From there I went on to tutor students in English. Getting a work permit was out of the question. It required obtaining everyone's permission including your husband's, plus going back and forth between government ministries in Oaxaca and Mexico City. That's for the rich and for those with *palanca* (ability to pull strings). It was easier for Salvador to cash my cheques. I continued to lull myself into believing I was leading a conventional ordinary life. It was going to work itself out.

Well, it did not work itself out. Angst reared its ugly head as soon as I became pregnant with my third child. Deep down in the most fragile recesses of my being, a part of me that I didn't allow anyone to see and hardly acknowledged myself, I knew that a third child was a mistake. Yet when you are unsure of that small voice that represents your emerging self, being busy keeps you from questioning too deeply. Somehow you know that you aren't ready to deal with your own life. Best be doing what you were brought up to be and repress the questions. You're somebody's wife and somebody's mother. You're so occupied with others, you bury yourself in their needs; you couldn't possibly take time out to look around you to examine your own life. You merely drown yourself with what has to be done. It's so terribly acceptable. Nonetheless I had known instinctively that if I didn't have a third child soon after the second I would never have another. I kept thinking to myself, "How could any woman put herself through the grind after a lapse of time? Best get the breeding over with."

And so began a period of my life marked by constant domestic demands and simmering inner turmoil. First, while suffering several bouts of neuralgia and eczema, I hosted my parents in January and February. In March, Charlotte, my old Tunbridge Wells school chum, and her husband, David, came from London for ten days. She was sick most of the time she spent with us. Then, during a fortnight in May, Charles, my younger brother, came to recuperate from his nervous exhaustion with us. In June, Andrew, a friend and archaeologist from the days of the Canada-Mexico exchange program, dropped in for two nights while acting as a guide for the Art Gallery of Ontario and its blue-rinse crowd. By July, when my youngest sister, Marie-Hélène, finally arrived, I was spent both physically and mentally. Ostensibly MH (that's what I call her) came to acquaint herself with a sister twelve years older than herself and to give a helping hand during Vicente's operation for his cleft palate and Nicolá's birth. What she gave me was a reality check.

"Sebastián, will you please pick up your pyjamas," she said, hoping to tidy up the boys' room quickly.

"Picking up pyjamas is women's work," replied the budding macho. He was four years old. MH hit the roof. Joron women are not known for "withholding."

"What do you mean women's work?" she retorted. A cold wind blew in from the north, sweeping up in its path my unnamed emotions, returning them to me as resentment, rage, and untold questions about my life in Oaxaca. Her stay was marred by Salvador's drunkenness. I barely mentioned the fact that he was increasingly verbally abusive toward me or that he carried a gun on him. Real men carry guns to protect themselves in Mexico. I wasn't ready to face the music quite yet.

So I did not come to my senses while MH was with me, but I did come to with a bang in December 1979 while my other sister, Nicole, was visiting. Nicole was there to hear the shot that Salvador fired at me. I was not hit, but, at last, I began to ask myself, "Is this what I am meant to live? Must I put up with this any longer?" Even so, even with that awakening, and despite Nicole's desperate urgings that I leave immediately, I was still acculturated, too voiceless to act. I had bought into my mother-in-law's view of things. I had unwillingly slipped into accepting Mexican women's conventional lot.

Things deteriorated rapidly over the next year. Salvador continued to drink heavily and to threaten me with unnamed actions if I dared to leave him. I lived in fear of losing my sanity. I kept seeing nothingness hanging over me. It was this enormous white mass just begging to suck me into oblivion. One night in early 1981 I found myself in the kitchen holding a machete, saying to myself, "If he comes near me, I'll kill him." And in that instant some flicker of self-preservation took hold of me and I heard a small voice telling me that I didn't have to wait for him to kill me or, worse, for me to kill him. No indeed, I had not been brought up for this. I did not deserve this, nor did my three boys deserve to become orphans. I made up my mind to leave.

Leaving Salvador meant lying to him. I could not leave without the boys. His signature was needed on their passport. No signature, no children. I assured him that I was only going to Canada for a short holiday. And when we left, I took only the boys' clothes. I hated lying to him. I hated not being able to be straight with him. I was so scared he would kill me or take the children away. I had visions of snapping, of going mad. So until we were safely seated on the plane three months later, I lived on the edge of sanity.

I restrained myself from kissing the ground when I arrived at Dorval Airport, remarking inwardly to myself that John-Paul II almost had a monopoly on this kind of gesture.

Raising three boys on your own is never boring, it's a constant roller-coaster ride. I started off on welfare. This was not an easy step to take.

Westmount girls have pride. My aunt, a social worker, helped me get over that hurdle by seeing it as a return on my parents' investment into the system. I didn't last long on welfare as I swallowed more of my pride. I took one part-time secretarial job after another. Finally, eight months after my return from my Mexican adventures, I was offered a full-time position at Montreal's only tabloid newspaper. Life does play some weird tricks on snobbish people! At this point who cared? I had a real live paying job! A good upper-class upbringing didn't necessarily put bread on the table. I knew that for a fact.

We had our moments between then and early 1989. It never, but never, occurred to me that I was jinxed. So 1979 was a bad year, but hey, turning forty would be a cinch compared to turning thirty. No guns, no men to deal with, no having to start from scratch. I had a job, not a great one but it paid the bills. By then I was working for a consultant. I was finishing a certificate in human resources management and planning to enter a master's program in adult education. Things would unfold, positively. Wasn't I a survivor? Soon there would be light at the end of the tunnel. Soon my life would play itself out in a more orderly fashion. I was middle-aged and almost respectable!

Then, without warning, I fell in love. I was both swept up as in a whirlwind and struck dazed by a thunderbolt. Falling in love with this man totally transformed my life. Nothing has been the same since.

We met through work. Literally, "B" was the answer to my prayers. After one disastrous marriage, I certainly didn't wish to make the same mistake again, so I had drawn up a little private check-list of "must-not-be" and "must-be" for possible candidates! No more transcultural relationships, no more smokers, no more drinkers, no more artists. Once was enough. Next time, same background, same tastes and interests, and, most of all, he would be interested in all things spiritual. This was my clincher. I wasn't going to have another man in my life telling me religion and spirituality were the opium of the people. I was going to put the odds on my side. I wasn't going to be ruled by my emotions. I was going to develop a friendship first and foremost. Well, "B" checked high on my list and we became friends. All should have been fine. It was just that I fell in love and he didn't.

It took my breath away to be in his presence. I felt that I had found my "soul mate." Love's passion almost destroyed me. I was its prisoner for many months. One moment I felt connected to the universe, fused to everything beautiful and good, and the next moment awash with unnamed violent emotions, alone, adrift with my wretchedness. I had never experienced such highs and such lows. This passion took hold of me; it permeated my life. It became the backdrop against which I played out everything else. It was all-consuming.

I was crazy about this man. But I couldn't see it was all one way. All my friends knew, even my boys knew. Why is it that the most concerned invariably finds out last? Any sensible human being would have just walked away. Somehow I couldn't manage to do that. I kept thinking that our friendship was more important than anything else. I needed to keep it alive. "That's it," I said to myself, "I will contain my feelings." But for the next six months everything went wrong.

Early the next year I found myself without a job and the victim of transient asthma which remained undiagnosed for several months. I then developed a mysterious eye condition. "You couldn't possibly have this unless you've had tuberculosis," said the specialist, mystified. Well, I hadn't had tuberculosis and I still had this particular kind of keratitis. My alternatives seemed to be either losing my sight or taking long-term treatment with steroids that could induce cataracts. Crisis followed crisis. There was a car accident. One son broke his thumb, another was failing school, and another was acting out and becoming self-destructive to the point that I had to think of placing him in a home or sending him to his father. Yet I was possessed by life. I was taking on more challenges by deciding to write a master's thesis. Mercifully, as my mother says: *Il y a un Dieu pour les pas fins* (There's a God for the dimwitted). Finally, I came to my senses.

One evening at the closing dinner of a conference, "B" treated me badly. Actually, it was a minor lack of courtesy. He didn't dance with me but he did partner the other two women in our group. I wanted to die. I was totally crushed. I had been completely ignored. I didn't exist in his eyes. Reeling with pain yet drawing on a spark of self-preservation, I realized that dying for such an offence was really exaggerated. So part of the enchantment was broken and I determined to walk away from this relationship that meant more to me than anything in the world. It felt as though I was cutting off part of myself.

Distancing myself physically was already torture, distancing myself emotionally was impossible. He lived in me. I knew I had to do this but I was psychically emmeshed. In vain I kept repeating to myself: "He doesn't deserve you. You deserve better." But I kept being plagued by this longing. I cried and I cried. I cried for months on end. I was amazed at my capacity for tears. Everything and anything brought tears to my eyes. There's no doubt about it; I was living life intensely. Perhaps a little too intensely for those around me. A few friends stuck by me. Others just couldn't stand to see this survivor falling apart at the seams. "Why can't you will yourself out of this?" they said. I willed all right, but I was stuck like a car in a snowbank. I kept moving forward yet slipping back. What I needed was a shove.

Marie-Francine Joron, MA (McGill), 1993

At last I did something I had promised myself I would do six years earlier but had conveniently managed to avoid. In the spring of 1991 I entered analysis. An old Chinese proverb says, "When the student is ready, the master appears." In this case it was a mistress. (I know what the language does, it's quirky!) What the old proverb doesn't say but people who believe in synchronicity know is that nothing is ever wasted. By the time I decided to seek help, J.'s name had already been mentioned casually at a friend's house. J. is a Zurich-trained Jungian analyst. My initial conversation with J. brought to the surface something I knew from previous therapy sessions in 1984–85. To analyse and to understand my passion would require courage and a willingness to pay a great price, as it would inevitably lead to lifting the veil on several more profound mysteries. It became a matter of agreeing to go the distance.

J. could not see me right away; she would probably not have a free period for another year or so. She did, however, recommend someone who was training to become a Jungian analyst like herself. What has transpired in the meantime, I could not have anticipated in a million years. I wished to be a Jungian analyst. I had come to name that vocation that I had felt driving me, that had remained unnamed and unrecognized for so long. A year after my initial telephone conversation with J., I began seeing her weekly.

As soon as I started analysis in March 1991, all the years of wandering, of suffering, of questioning, of feeling that there exists no place in this world for exponents of the inner life were validated. Every moment lived had served a task. Every step, albeit in a roundabout way, had led me to where I needed to be: in contact with my true nature. I didn't feel like a fish out of water any longer. What a relief to find people who shared and understood my deep relentless desire for understanding! No more hearing, "You're so intense, can't you do something else beside questioning all the time?" or "Lighten up. Get a life."

Training to become a Jungian analyst entails many years of intensive work, and I have just begun the journey. But I see now that impossible loves as I had lived them at thirty and at forty did not necessarily have to be dead ends. They were purifying rites of passage, initiations into the deeper mysteries of my being. I have come to appreciate that the psyche always leads you to where you need to learn. It has led me to a space which gives purpose and meaning to my life. I have moved away from being a sufferer in someone else's life towards being a heroine in charge of writing my own destiny.

On Being Lucky

A close friend said to me in 1987: "Some people are just born lucky. You're one of them." It seemed a strange moment for such a remark. I was recovering from the second of two life-threatening illnesses in less than twelve months, and I had a daughter who weighed only two pounds in intensive neonatal care. She had been born fifteen weeks early when my appendix ruptured. I had no job and no prospects of one; the only immediate questions were whether the baby would survive, whether she would be blind or mentally handicapped, and whether I would succeed in looking after her. My Oxford doctorate in English literature, submitted in England a month before her birth, waited to be defended at some undetermined future date. I was not at all sure it would be accepted. My family lived far away and my husband had just started a demanding job he didn't particularly want, simply because our financial difficulties, after years of freelance writing, teaching, and graduate research, had become critical. I saw failure, both as an academic and as a mother, staring me in the face.

Yet since that time I have often reflected on my friend's comment. There are many kinds of luck – or kinds of privilege. Some I was born to; they included being white, English, and middle-class, and having devoted parents who nurtured five children (all born within seven years), giving us a basic strength of body and mind to survive the challenges of life. I also received a superb education, first in an English state primary school, then at a girls' high school and a women's college at Oxford. Other kinds of luck have come to me more unexpectedly. Several years after being told, in that moment of crisis, that I was lucky, I am. I have good health; a wonderful husband, Mark, and daughter, Kate; a stimulating career at McGill; supportive colleagues; many friends; and affectionate contacts with my far-flung family. I am also seven months pregnant, and appreciating McGill's and Quebec's

Head Girl, Prenton Primary School, 1967

generous maternity leave – won, I know, by the undaunted efforts of earlier women who insisted that combining motherhood and a career was possible. I'm not sure what luck really is, and I know that women often have a habit of assigning to luck what is also a matter of hard work, resilience, and survival instinct, but I do, even so, feel fortunate. I'm grateful to other women, past and present, whose courage and example allowed me to imagine succeeding, even at moments when everything seemed to be going wrong.

I'd like to recall three events that tell me what being lucky really means. These events all took place between my thirtieth and thirty-fourth birthdays, not so long ago, and marked, cumulatively, an enormous shift in my life and my perceptions. In each case the crisis was a direct result of being female, and forced me to explore that fact. I had always, subconsciously, wanted to be a man. As a child I preferred toy boats and cars to dolls and babies; as an adolescent I chose my father's world of the intellect rather than my mother's world of home-making. Yet these three crises, I believe, turned me into a woman who could at first accept and more recently even celebrate being born into the "second sex."

One day in November 1986 I was marking student papers in a claustrophobic, windowless office at McGill, where I had a sessional position. I began to feel dizzy and have severe abdominal pain. I could hardly stand and couldn't eat. A few hours later I found myself sitting in a gynaecologist's office staring out of his window at the grey November sky, high above Côte des Neiges (the wintry name seemed appropriate). The gynaecologist was telling me I had to have an emergency operation next day. I might have ovarian cancer; I certainly had severe endometriosis and could not live without this surgery. I saw my dissertation on Samuel Beckett's bilingualism slipping away from me into oblivion. The December deadline was, I had been told, the absolute limit, and I was not going to meet it now.

The work meant a lot to me. I had spent three years on it in Oxford, before emigrating to Canada. I had then tried to continue it while teaching wherever I could get work and completing an education diploma. I was still teaching all over Montreal for terrible pay, but had put the doctorate back at the centre of my life with a powerful sense of its significance. Contemporary intercultural studies were not then as fashionable as they are now, at least in Oxford's school of English, and neither was the French/English bilingualism of a major Irish writer – it upset too many apple-carts about national canons of literature and the nature of language. Yet coming to the bilingual environment of Montreal had confirmed my stubborn decision to insist on this interpretation of Beckett, concentrating on the idea of a "threshold" consciousness that would not sit comfortably within traditional academic disciplines and rational structures. Only later did I realize that dealing with bilingualism and biculturalism was a way of getting at my own experiences of living in two cultures. My father's family were staunchly Anglo-Saxon, while my mother's family were Welsh-speaking Celts. My own graduate studies in the male world of academe contrasted with the very different female influences of my home. Whatever my motivation, the idea of not finishing the doctorate after so much synthesizing effort appalled me.

As the specialist's voice droned on, authoritative and blunt, I also saw parenthood, something I had always intended "once the doctorate was finished," disappearing. My ovaries might have to be removed, and in any case endometriosis led to a high rate of infertility. I wondered about my marriage surviving all this. A wave of despair broke over me; I seemed to have done everything wrong. Yet that self-recrimination was, I realize now, something I had always struggled with, and perhaps at that moment I began to gain a degree of distance on it. Even as I castigated myself, a suspicion crept through that there might be other factors contributing to the mess I found myself in.

I was not a feminist at that time. I was just beginning to discover that there might be systemic problems affecting women's chances of success, and their mental and physical health, in the academic world I knew. I didn't realize that it was psychologically difficult for women to complete doctorates at ancient universities that had been designed for men. This was, and is, particularly true for women from traditional families like mine; my father was a university professor, while my mother (though very intelligent) had been obliged to leave school at sixteen to become a secretary. My two older brothers were high-achieving professionals, in agro-forestry research and medicine, while my two older sisters (again, equally talented) were both at home working more than full time as mothers and housewives. I had always loved learning, but never felt confident that it was my "right," in spite of the positive academic influences of my single-sex high school and college. I didn't know that my own fight to finish the doctorate, with a constant feeling of being fraudulent and inadequate, went with a learned sense of female inferiority going back to childhood.

Only later did I learn how the disease called endometriosis, still poorly understood by doctors, often hinders a woman's effort to have a career in a traditionally male field. In my own case, I felt sure that the stress, the denial of consciousness of my own body, the effort to mimic an alien voice and adapt to an inappropriate career path, had led to this inner tearing apart that the pain seemed to be – as if the male and female principles in me were at war. It took a long time to realize that my earlier reports of exceptionally long and painful periods had been misdiagnosed repeatedly, and that I had helped the doctors in this because of my lifelong training as a middle-class English girl to be "nice," and not to be a nuisance. I had made light of my unease, apologizing, almost, for the pain I felt, or ignoring it and living exclusively in my head. I was still obedient to doctors and other figures of authority, and had no independent or critical viewpoint on medicine's approach to "female concerns."

At the time, however, the dominant feeling was that all my efforts had come to nothing; I had failed and deserved to. I even thought, with a kind of gloomy relish, that if I died under surgery or of cancer afterwards, my husband would at least have a chance to marry someone else, have children, and find a life more serene than the one he had lived with this anguished (read "neurotic") graduate student for the last seven years.

In fact, to my amazement, the operation went well. Although the recuperation from it was painful and slow, I was overjoyed to find that I did not have cancer. The Oxford authorities generously delayed my deadline another six months – and I still had one and a half ovaries left. I could, perhaps, even conceive a child.

And so it happened. The "luck" came back into play. I took the necessary drugs, conceived, then finished my doctorate with a new sense of purpose. I submitted it in Oxford in July 1987, having revised the entire text five or six times. The final months before submission were intense, almost euphoric. Pregnancy, which I nurtured with good diet, exercise, and reading, gave me more strength and optimism than I had ever had (I never experienced nausea or weakness). I also wrote stories and poetry and joined a women writers' workshop. After submitting the thesis, when I was four and a half months pregnant, I returned to Canada in wonderfully good health and spirits. I looked forward to the other four and a half months, a time to think about another human life as well as about ideas. But once again the path of luck turned out to be much more wayward than expected.

I woke one day fifteen weeks before the baby's due date with (once again) strange abdominal pains. Deep in the following night my appendix ruptured, one of the most rare and unpredictable of medical emergencies during pregnancy. A skilful surgeon operated, hoping the pregnancy could be saved, but no: I went into twenty-seven hours of peculiar back-labour, lying terrified in a small, dark hospital room. Transfer to another hospital with an excellent neonatal unit happened in a sudden panic when the doctors realized the baby was about to be born. I gave birth, fully conscious and wrapped in blankets, while being rushed along a ground floor corridor on a wheeled bed. My appendix incision was not yet thirty hours old. Kate emerged on a busy Saturday morning next to the coffee shop and the bank machine, with at least forty people on hand (it must have been one of the more public births in Montreal's recent history). Conveniently we arrived at some opening elevator doors just as she made her appearance, so she could be whisked straight up to the neonatal unit and hooked to a mass of instruments from the moment the umbilical cord was cut. A brief moment of triumph followed; we were both alive and she was in good hands.

But two days later came a second experience of total despair, like that wintry day in 1986. Once again, I was gazing out of a hospital window, though this time with summer outside. I had just lived through the worst night of my life, worse, by far, than the birth itself. I had developed a fever, become almost delirious, and lain awake all night convinced that death was imminent; it was discovered later that I had salmonella poisoning, as well as the after-effects of appendicitis and birth. No one has ever attempted to explain where it came from. But the doctor who entered the room to speak some grim news was not concerned with me. This time, luckily, Mark was present; having had little sleep for sixty hours, he was in a state almost as hallucinatory as my own. The doctor brought a Polaroid photograph of our tiny daughter, who had been struggling for life in the intensive-care nursery since Saturday. He brought the photo because she was not expected to live more than an hour; all her systems had "crashed" three times. Mark and I clung to each other and wept. The August sunlight seemed a mockery, and so did my worries about my dissertation. Yet, strangely, Beckett turned into one of my greatest comforts. His stoical pessimism and concentration on illness and mortality, which have earned so much criticism, became in these conditions exactly my sense of reality. I grasped something about human suffering often obscured in privileged levels of society. The compassion of his writing was an enormous source of support.

With Mark still there I fell asleep – dimly hoping, in my exhaustion and pain, not to wake up.

Kate not only survived that day but also became one of the neonatal unit's great success stories. She is now a cheerful, healthy five-year-old who has just started kindergarten. Mark and I share her parenting, and, in spite of all the reports that suggest most men still don't do their share of domestic duties, he certainly does – if not more. I did defend my thesis successfully, after almost a year's delay, and am now planning to turn it into a book when time allows. I have presented or published several essays on Beckett in the interim, as well as material on the teaching of writing and the centre where I now work.

The thesis defence was memorable, and in retrospect, amusing. I had an eight-month-old baby (five months, corrected age) whom I carried down to Oxford's examination schools in my arms, wearing my regulation "sub fusc": black and white clothes with the MA gown and cap. Mark wheeled the heavy thesis in the pushchair by my side. We must have made an unusual sight for all the foreign tourists who still expect the typical Oxford student to be a solitary young man in tweeds. Mark and Kate went off to the park, while the thesis and I accompanied my two male examiners down corridor after corridor decorated with portraits of male worthies through the ages: kings, judges, scholars, and clergy. The defence was conducted aggressively and critically, without any indication that I would pass. Not only my self-re-

Ann, Mark, and Kate in 1989

spect but also my future career now depended on success; I had applied for, and, been offered, a tenure-track position at McGill, in the Writing Centre where I had worked as a sessional lecturer, on the condition that my doctorate was accepted. Instead of falling apart with nervousness, as I would once have done, I held my ground and became as aggressive as the examiners. After the crises of the last two years, no mere battle of words could scare me.

Once again, then, there was luck concealed in the eccentric circumstances of my passage into motherhood and academic life. I forget nothing of those weeks when my daughter hovered between life and death, the subsequent months as she fought for health, the weeks of my own recovery, first in hospital and then at home, initially so weak I couldn't walk. I haven't lost the insights of that time, about physical invasion, near mental collapse, the power of death when it hovers over you. I also learned the significance of articulating anger, panic, and loneliness, rather than bottling them up to fester inside, and of talking openly to other women about common experiences. This was something I had always shied away from in my earlier "male-defined" patterns of existence, which had valued a kind of lofty competitive reserve. (I am convinced that men, too, need this emotional release; I was struck by the support the fathers in the neonatal unit were able to give each other – if and when they opened up about their feelings.) I was given a new education by Kate's nurses, superb professionals who combined intuition and warmth with the expertise and decisive toughness necessary in any intensive care unit. In short, I entered, fully and for the first time, a successful, adult, female world.

It was a revelation. It gave me, belatedly, a true appreciation of my own mother's extraordinary strengths and talents. I finally learned not to expect men, those in authority especially, to have all the answers. Nothing could let me forget that the doctors were as taken by surprise by my three-day roller-coaster ride as I had been; and in the unit, the nurses were often more successful than many of the doctors in the delicate manipulation of needles and monitors for a critically ill infant. Ironically, at the same time, I began to know and feel more sympathy for patriarchy, seeing that the worlds in which men exercise power (medicine, academia, politics, the church, the law) were as vulnerable as I was in the face of death. The process of recovery also led me to many books about healing, creativity, and autonomy, especially in the context of post-Jungian psychology. My three months spent in the neonatal unit, interacting with the nurses, left me with an indelible impression of female consciousness as generous, "grounded," and whole in a way my earlier knowledge-systems, for all their intelligence and power, had not been. Once again, I had been lucky – and this time I realized that having been born female might be part of this good fortune.

The third experience of these transformative years is the hardest of all to describe. I have come to forget, now that I feel more secure about professional life and parenting, that in these years I was still struggling out of a sense of inner fearfulness that had been with me as long as I could remember. It is something many women have described, the tremendous negative conditioning female children receive about their abilities and status. In my first year full-time at McGill, exhausted by a demanding job and the care of a frail, asthmatic baby, as well as by the guilt that dual-role mothers feel, I could easily relapse into a state of fatalism and self-criticism I thought I had overcome.

There was also a disturbing state of inner division. As an adolescent and later I argued with myself and had to fight for my own beliefs. I found it hard to close doors against other people's needs, opinions, and feelings, and I often suffered from some trivial criticism or slight out of all proportion to the actual words. Some poems I had submitted to a student journal at Oxford in the late 1970s, for example, had earned only a sneering, contemptuous rejection. The male editor's reaction to my "female" writing, which he described as "rubbish," prevented me from showing any poetry to others for ten years. Later, a male tutor's criticism of my writing as being "too tentative, just not *masculine* enough," tied me in knots for months. At some deep level I had always felt wary of any risk, and feared walking alone at night or speaking out in lectures (which would make my heart beat so violently I would nearly pass out). I would also get acute headaches when I had to write or express my ideas in public, even though, inside my own head, in my private journal, and (oddly enough) in the exam room these ideas were strong and clear.

In 1989 I found out the source of these "symptoms" in a dramatic way. I know them now to be symptoms of something that was wrong because once the discovery was made they went away and have never returned. I was in bed with flu and reading Alice Miller's book *Thou Shalt Not Be Aware*. This book deals, in vivid and sympathetic detail, with the sexual abuse of children and its effects in later life. I fell asleep, woke, and as I woke suddenly regained an experience which had been hidden since early childhood.

I relived the event as a small child would see it. A man who was as big as a giant was standing over me in some rough ground near my house. (I believe, though proof is impossible now, that he was a neighbour, a bad-tempered man but also a respectable church-goer with a business, a wife, and four children). I was supposed to be with my older brothers and sisters, but as usual had been left behind because I couldn't run as fast as they could. The man lured me into a greenhouse, tried to rape me, and then ejaculated into my mouth. He also threatened to kill me if I told anyone. The memory returned crystal clear (if anything so dark in human behaviour can be called crystal). It would not be dislodged, dismissed, or silenced again after its twenty-nine-year concealment. Yet curiously there was a numbness where my feelings should be.

The emotional reaction occurred two days later when Mark was home, when I could at last allow the anger and pain to emerge. As I spoke the story an extraordinary thing happened. I felt the mental dividedness, that gap between inner consciousness and outer reality, disappear. A sense of wholeness followed, and I realized that this completed a kind of inner journey undertaken during the previous three years. For the first time since the day when I was three or four and had my world split into two, I did not feel threatened by patriarchal power. At such an early age my childhood mind had had to deal with an incomprehensible disparity between a man's public status and actual behaviour. The effort to accommodate such contradictions must have been enormous.

I believe now that the memory could only return – with the trigger of that particular book – at a time when I had finally reached a point of some security in my life. I had a career at last, Kate was doing well, Mark was also working full-time, and we had learned to survive as a couple, by communicating and learning parenthood together. The recovery of that memory of childhood assault, hideous though it was, became, once again, "lucky." It allowed me to begin to live, finally, with confidence and without fear.

As a child and teenager in the North of England, ignorant of my repressed memory, I had turned to reading and writing for comfort and protection. Words offered, perhaps, a way to explain. They called up other lives, other perspectives, and took me out of myself. I read obsessively from an early age, and was devouring adult literature by the age of eleven. I also at that age started a journal which I still keep today. These activities helped me to do well at school, to win a place at Oxford, to reach right up through a system in which (though I never felt I belonged) I always believed I would find an answer – even if I didn't know what the question was.

My voluntary emigration to Canada in 1983 must have come from a dim sense that this was a place to pursue the unknown question more freely, a place where I might more steadily look back, and forward. In my first visit to England after 1989 I realized that a shadow had lifted; my relationship with my native country had subtly changed. I could now assert myself against aggression, and deal with sexist assumptions with energy and humour. I could also walk into an Oxford library without that old uneasy feeling that the knowledge contained within it didn't, and couldn't, belong to me. More recently I have realized that my work as a writing teacher (a profession shaped by women) and my shift from literary criticism to a more holistic and democratic kind of writing context have a certain logic in terms of my earlier experiences. So does my current research on writing and gender.

The process of understanding our own pasts takes time, a long time, and may never really be finished. But regaining the memory of childhood assault has helped me in many ways. Above all, it has helped me to see other people as both individual and social beings, affected by personal experience and by the large social forces (such as the silencing of children, the objectifying of the female body, the constraining of women's intelligence *and* of men's emotional development) that surround us all. My childhood molester also emerged from a particular childhood and social context; he had no doubt learned that girls and women existed to be used and that his deviant sexuality and violence were excusable as long as they were hidden.

I have also become convinced of the necessity of honesty – whatever honesty we can command at a particular time – and of the crucial need for oppressed groups, whether they are women, children, or people affected by racist and sexual abuse, to gain a voice. The use of journals in the McGill writing course I teach confirms this. My respect for students mounts steadily as I read of their struggles to come to voice intellectually and emotionally in difficult times.

In a wonderful autobiography, *Lost in Translation*, Eva Hoffman wrote:

It is strange, in spite of all we know about such transactions, that the Looking Glass through which I step into the past releases me to go on into the present. Perhaps now I can get the different blocks of my story into the right proportions. As every writer knows, it's only when you come to a certain point in your manuscript that it becomes clear how the beginning should go, and what importance it has within the whole. And it's usually after revising from the middle that one can begin to go on with the rest.

I feel, at the age of thirty-six, that this is at last becoming possible. Having reached a certain point in the "manuscript" of my life, I can look back to the first half with fresh eyes and perhaps "revise from the middle" as I go on from here. None of the experiences I have mentioned had a pattern at the time, and none of them seemed fortunate as they were happening. But now a kind of shape emerges; and, false or true, it is one I can live with – until the next lucky surprise comes along.